# Sideways in Neverland

# Sideways in Neverland

◆

Life in the Santa Ynez Valley, California

*William Etling*

iUniverse, Inc.
New York  Lincoln  Shanghai

# Sideways in Neverland
## Life in the Santa Ynez Valley, California

Copyright © 2005 by William Etling

All rights reserved. No part of this book may be used or reproduced by any means, graphic, electronic, or mechanical, including photocopying, recording, taping or by any information storage retrieval system without the written permission of the publisher except in the case of brief quotations embodied in critical articles and reviews.

iUniverse books may be ordered through booksellers or by contacting:

iUniverse
2021 Pine Lake Road, Suite 100
Lincoln, NE 68512
www.iuniverse.com
1-800-Authors (1-800-288-4677)

Cover photo: The Cold Springs Arch Bridge is the gateway to the Santa Ynez Valley.
Photo by William Etling II

ISBN-13: 978-0-595-36190-8 (pbk)
ISBN-13: 978-0-595-81144-1 (cloth)
ISBN-13: 978-0-595-80637-9 (ebk)
ISBN-10: 0-595-36190-0 (pbk)
ISBN-10: 0-595-81144-2 (cloth)
ISBN-10: 0-595-80637-6 (ebk)

Printed in the United States of America

For Leah, William, and Debra

## Dover Beach

*The sea is calm tonight,*
*The tide is full, the moon lies fair*
*Upon the straits; on the French coast the light*
*Gleams and is gone; the cliffs of England stand,*
*Glimmering and vast, out in the tranquil bay.*
*Come to the window, sweet is the night air!*
*Only, from the long line of spray*
*Where the sea meets the moon-blanched land,*
*Listen! you hear the grating roar*
*Of pebbles which the waves draw back, and fling,*
*At their return, up the high strand,*
*Begin, and cease, and then again begin,*
*With tremulous cadence slow, and bring*
*The eternal note of sadness in.*
*Sophocles long ago*
*Heard it on the Aegean, and it brought*
*Into his mind the turbid ebb and flow*
*Of human misery...*

*Ah, love, let us be true*
*To one another! for the world, which seems*
*To lie before us like a land of dreams,*
*So various, so beautiful, so new,*
*Hath really neither joy, nor love, nor light,*
*Nor certitude, nor peace, nor help for pain;*
*And we are here as on a darkling plain*
*Swept with confused alarms of struggle and flight,*
*Where ignorant armies clash by night.*

        Matthew Arnold (1867)

# *Contents*

Introduction . . . . . . . . . . . . . . . . . . . . . . . . . . . . . . . . . . . . . . . . . . . . . . . . . 1
1. The Point Conception Coast . . . . . . . . . . . . . . . . . . . . . . . . . . . . . . . . 2
2. The Honorable Old West Lives On . . . . . . . . . . . . . . . . . . . . . . . . . . 5
3. Open House at Mike's—A Visit to Neverland . . . . . . . . . . . . . . . . . 8
4. Sideways In Neverland . . . . . . . . . . . . . . . . . . . . . . . . . . . . . . . . . . . 14
5. You Can't Go Home Again . . . . . . . . . . . . . . . . . . . . . . . . . . . . . . . . 17
6. Judgment Day For Michael Jackson . . . . . . . . . . . . . . . . . . . . . . . . 20
7. Sideways Insider Tells All . . . . . . . . . . . . . . . . . . . . . . . . . . . . . . . . 22
8. The Return of the King—Lance Armstrong's Last Ride . . . . . . . . 27
9. Rain . . . . . . . . . . . . . . . . . . . . . . . . . . . . . . . . . . . . . . . . . . . . . . . . . . 32
10. Wildflowers . . . . . . . . . . . . . . . . . . . . . . . . . . . . . . . . . . . . . . . . . . . 34
    2. Her Side Of the Mountain . . . . . . . . . . . . . . . . . . . . . . . . . . . . 36
11. Surf's Up . . . . . . . . . . . . . . . . . . . . . . . . . . . . . . . . . . . . . . . . . . . . . 39
    2. Surf & Turf . . . . . . . . . . . . . . . . . . . . . . . . . . . . . . . . . . . . . . . . 40
    3. Forgive Us Our Trespasses—Cowboys vs. J-Boyz . . . . . . . . . 42
    4. A Global Surfari . . . . . . . . . . . . . . . . . . . . . . . . . . . . . . . . . . . . 43
12. The Bachelor, Andrew Firestone . . . . . . . . . . . . . . . . . . . . . . . . . . 50
13. The Green Mile . . . . . . . . . . . . . . . . . . . . . . . . . . . . . . . . . . . . . . . 53
14. Danish Resistance Heroes . . . . . . . . . . . . . . . . . . . . . . . . . . . . . . . 55
15. Day in the Life of a Realtor . . . . . . . . . . . . . . . . . . . . . . . . . . . . . . 57
16. Of Gophers, Rural Peril & The Meaning of Life . . . . . . . . . . . . . . 60
17. Edward Borein . . . . . . . . . . . . . . . . . . . . . . . . . . . . . . . . . . . . . . . . 62
18. Do The Rancheros Visitadores Rule America? . . . . . . . . . . . . . . . 64
    2. Was Clarence Mattei Robbed? . . . . . . . . . . . . . . . . . . . . . . . . . 66
    3. The Past is Not Dead . . . . . . . . . . . . . . . . . . . . . . . . . . . . . . . . 68
19. President Reagan Looks Down On the Danes . . . . . . . . . . . . . . . 70

| | |
|---|---|
| 20. Saddlemaker To The Stars | 73 |
| 21. Living the Tuskegee Legacy | 75 |
|     2. A Roll Call of Honor, Written in Blood | 77 |
| 22. David Crosby, Noah Wyle, & Bo Derek Rip Community Plan | 79 |
|     2. Dude, Where's My Zoning? | 80 |
|     3. SYV Community Plan Rides Again | 82 |
|     4. All Quiet On The CP Front | 84 |
| 23. The Fuss About Fess Makes The Wall Street Journal | 87 |
|     2. Sugar, Cream, Casino? | 88 |
|     3. Tribe Dumping Davey? | 90 |
|     4. Boone-doggle: Fess Flops | 91 |
| 24. Reservations About Tribal Annexations | 93 |
| 25. Follow the Money—Politicians Hit The Casino Jackpot | 96 |
|     2. Fighting Annexation | 98 |
|     3. The Annexation Heard Across The Nation | 100 |
|     4. Gambling On Annexation | 102 |
| 26. Rural Ranchers Speak Out | 104 |
| 27. Land Trust Saves Endangered Species: Farmers & Ranchers | 107 |
|     2. Eric Gregersen | 109 |
| 28. West Pointer Katie Smyser | 111 |
| 29. Home, Home On the Range | 116 |
| 30. For Whom The Bale Tolls | 121 |
|     2. A Land of Dreams | 122 |
| 31. Mission Santa Inés | 133 |
|     2. Mending The Mission | 135 |
|     3. The Bells of Santa Ynez | 136 |
|     4. The Reluctant Pirate's Daily Grind | 138 |
| 32. Lost Art—Cave Paintings of the Chumash | 141 |
| 33. As San Andreas Said, It's Really Not My Fault | 143 |
| 34. Rancho De Los Olivos | 145 |
|     2. Phantom Hoofbeats At The Union Hotel | 147 |
| 35. Cowboy Up With Jake Copass | 149 |
|     2. Dutch Wilson | 150 |
| 36. Murder In De la Guerra Plaza | 153 |

37. Foxen Canyon Hosts Camp Jeep ............................. 155
38. The Longhorn Cafe. ............................................. 160
39. The Way We Were—Solvang Circa 1961. ................... 162
40. Ballard Pioneers ................................................. 167
    2. He Rode the PCRY ......................................... 169
41. Summertime, and the Living is Easy ......................... 171
42. Gathering Cattle ................................................. 175
43. It's Never Too Late To Honor Heroes ....................... 177
44. Something's Fishy: The Case of the Missing Mermaid .... 179
45. The Island of the Danish Bakers ............................. 182
46. The Happy Canyon Boys and the Secret of the Old Shaft. .. 184
47. The Danish Capital of America: Solvang. ................... 186
48. On the Viking Trail ............................................. 190
49. Danish for A Day ............................................... 192
    2. Dr. Danish Days ............................................. 193
50. Solvang Citizens ................................................. 196
    2. Renton Mitchell. ............................................. 197
    3. Peg Johnson. ................................................. 202
51. U.S.S. Yorktown Sailor Lauren Walter ...................... 205
    2. Naval Vet Runs Aground On DMV Reef ................. 206
52. Stem Cell Research Hits Home. .............................. 209
53. Americans Are Trailer Trash .................................. 211
54. Sculptor John Cody ............................................. 213
55. The Nature of Woman ......................................... 216
56. Rancho Days: The Vanishing Vaquero Legacy ............. 219
    2. Ailie Chamberlin's 99th Birthday. ........................ 220
    3. Rancho San Julian .......................................... 222
    4. Cattle Upon A Thousand Hills ............................ 223
57. The Vandenberg Air Force Base Odyssey .................. 225
58. Farewell to a Latter Day Dr. Livingstone—October, 2003 .. 228
59. On the Set of Seabiscuit With Tobey Maguire (January, 2003). ... 230
    2. Props That Eat. .............................................. 232
    3. A Drive-by Shouting ....................................... 234
60. It's A Small World, But It Has Big Tornados .............. 236

61. I Whacked Rudolph—Carnage on San Marcos Pass . . . . . . . . . . . . . . . . . . . . 239
62. If I Could Turn Back Time—An Orphan's Christmas. . . . . . . . . . . . . . . . . 241
    2. Oh, Holy Night—The Ghosts of Christmas Past . . . . . . . . . . . . . . . . . 242
63. The Best Gift Of All . . . . . . . . . . . . . . . . . . . . . . . . . . . . . . . . . . . . . . . . . . 245
64. A New Torah Scroll. . . . . . . . . . . . . . . . . . . . . . . . . . . . . . . . . . . . . . . . . . . 247
65. An Old Fashioned Christmas. . . . . . . . . . . . . . . . . . . . . . . . . . . . . . . . . . . 250
    2. Notes From Americanaville. . . . . . . . . . . . . . . . . . . . . . . . . . . . . . . . . . 252
66. Annual Review. . . . . . . . . . . . . . . . . . . . . . . . . . . . . . . . . . . . . . . . . . . . . . 259
67. Skiing the Santa Ynez Valley . . . . . . . . . . . . . . . . . . . . . . . . . . . . . . . . . . . 261
68. Eternal Vigilance—New Year's In Baghdad. . . . . . . . . . . . . . . . . . . . . . . . 263
69. Love & Spare Tires—Bringing It All Back Home . . . . . . . . . . . . . . . . . . . 265
70. Conclusion—Equal Opportunity Developer Bashers. . . . . . . . . . . . . . . . . 275
About the Author. . . . . . . . . . . . . . . . . . . . . . . . . . . . . . . . . . . . . . . . . . . . . . . . 279
Appendix: A Valley History . . . . . . . . . . . . . . . . . . . . . . . . . . . . . . . . . . . . . . . 281
Afterword . . . . . . . . . . . . . . . . . . . . . . . . . . . . . . . . . . . . . . . . . . . . . . . . . . . . . 286

# Introduction

Let's begin at the beginning.

As the name implies, that might be Point Conception, where the roiling winds and cold which send the morning fog up the Santa Ynez River are conceived in a maelstrom of froth and foam at the churning Pacific.

Or the day in 1966 when I first rode over San Marcos Pass, and felt the electric thrill of seeing the Santa Ynez Valley's rolling, sere golden hills dotted with majestic oaks, surrounding a sprawling inland sea, encompassed by stately mountains receding into the distance, all rolled out before me like a magic carpet.

Or it could have been the day *Santa Barbara News-Press* Managing Editor Jerry Roberts, formerly of the *San Francisco Chronicle,* recruited me to write a community column.

Ultimately, this story is about my neighbors in the tiny towns of Los Olivos, Santa Ynez, Solvang, Ballard, Los Alamos, and Buellton, about thirty miles north of Santa Barbara, California.

The men and women who pioneered this place, and those who surround me today, are truly astonishing in their variety and talents. Some have achieved international fame—or notoriety.

All the stories are true. Many first appeared in the *Santa Barbara News-Press,* between November of 2002 and July of 2005. Where possible, they're arranged to recreate a year of shifting seasons and annual events, and the lives intertwined within.

Together, they are a snapshot of a remarkable community at a moment in time. I am very grateful to be a part of it.

William Etling
Los Olivos, California

# 1. The Point Conception Coast

The Chumash Indians revere it as the door into eternity, the jumping-off place to the afterlife.

For mariners it is a place of fear, a tempestuous, treacherous, fearsome, white-capped corner. The great white shark haunts these waters, and has killed divers here. The surfers who brave the towering, icy-blue walls of glass, and the windsurfers who revel in the blasts of ripping wind, play in a watery valley of the shadow of death.

This is Point Conception; a mysterious, fog-shrouded, surf-torn promontory jutting into the Pacific, marking the northern entry to the Santa Barbara Channel. Atop the lonely, jagged black rocks that disappear into the wild roiling foam, framed by water and sky, haunted by the eerie cry of seagulls and the moan of the foghorn, shines the Point Conception Light, a bright beacon to mariners since 1856.

Hundreds of creaky, rotting wooden steps lead from the bluff down to the lighthouse. First built on the bluff, it had to be moved to the rocks below to get under the persistent fog. Inside is a cozy paneled living area, abandoned when automation replaced the lighthouse keeper with clockwork. The rich wood hues give way to the stark iron steps of a spiral staircase, leading to the light above.

The original lens, now retired, is a marvel. You can stand upright inside it, surrounded by hundreds of individually crafted prisms which throw sixteen piercing beams of light, like spokes from a wheel, miles into the darkness. Built in France in 1855, it is a twin to lights ringing the oceans of the world. Even the Great Lakes have versions of this Fresnel lens, whose welcome beams have saved countless sailors from death.

Offshore, the whales move in slow motion through the water, spouting white plumes high in the air. Dolphins pass in ethereal pods evidenced by sudden, shiny fins, slicing the water in graceful arcs.

This is a haunted land, marked by pieces of the past. Chinese laborers lived in makeshift camps here when they built the railroad up the coast, leaving coins, buttons, bits of opium pipes. Arrowheads and bowls are still found on the beach. Unknown fossils spill out of the crumbling sandstone that rings the pounding

Pacific's shore. Seals cavort on the desolate beaches, alongside the bleached bones of their friends.

A few miles north, the gaunt tower of Space Launch Complex Six stands like a specter in the fog. It was built to launch the space shuttle into orbit. The viewing area for the TV cameras, housing for the astronauts, and podium for President Reagan had all been mapped out, when the Challenger exploded.

A stone's throw away from this space-age skyscraper is Solstice Cave, a sacred Chumash site where shamans tracked the seasons, as a beam of sunlight pierced their painted cavern.

Juan Cabrillo was blown back toward home here on his expedition of 1543. Sebastian Vizcaino named it "Punta de la Limpia Concepcion," Point of the Immaculate Conception, in 1602.

At Honda Point, rusting iron appears from the waves at low tide. On September 8, 1923, in the worst peacetime naval disaster of all time, nine destroyers missed their turn and ran onto the rocks near here, killing 23 sailors. Only a miraculously calm ocean spared hundreds more from certain death in the dark, freezing water.

Cows crash through the tangled sagebrush in the rocky canyons of gnarled scrub oak. Huge rattlesnakes caution the unwary with their castanet vibrato in the thick underbrush. A lonely coyote trots warily over the sun-dried hills.

The tumbledown houses of former lighthouse keepers and coast guard families decay in the moving, salty mist, like a New England village lost in time.

At night, the stars gleam like insanely bright eyes from a knowing primeval darkness, onto the ghosts of the passing human parade.

And in the gathering fog, the light's bright beam peers into infinity.

*Afterword: The party's getting rough.

Bixby Ranch hastily turned me in to the Coast Guard for alleged trespassing and suspicion of theft of government property on the basis of my history column about Point Conception.

Looking on the bright side, at least somebody read it.

Bixby is a mega-corporation left over from gold rush days, when Lewellyn Bixby's extended family parleyed sheep and sugar into a real estate empire. They're still owners of huge chunks of the Golden State. 13,269 acres of their Jalama Ranch are on the block for $30 million.

"Your access was never authorized through this office," wrote a Nancy Drew kind of manager lady. "There was a theft of Government property from the lighthouse which triggered a federal investigation."

"This investigation is ongoing," the e-mail continued. "I have forwarded your article to the Coast Guard and our corporate office. Additionally, we would like to know how you accessed the Point Conception station."

Not even Nancy Drew's bumbling crooks were ever dumb enough to write up their transgressions for the local paper. I visited with a Bixby escort and obtained Coast Guard permission when I took photos of the lighthouse, which appeared rather publicly in *Santa Barbara Magazine.*

In the interest of heading off more unpleasantness, let's also state for the record that although I surely wrote about them, I did not actually ride with Cabrillo in 1543, I did not sail with Vizcaino in 1602, I am not Chumash, I did not build the railroad, and I did not steer the nine destroyers onto Honda Point.

# 2. The Honorable Old West Lives On

I came to the Santa Ynez Valley in 1966, at 13 years of age. I saw storybook villages and majestic ranches, all ringed by mountains, like a cowboy's Shangri-La.

Nostalgic desperados held quick draw contests at high noon on Saturdays, at the swap meet down by the Maverick Saloon. The Valley was like the West of legend, with Danish pastry.

I was delighted to be here from the first minute, even if some of my eighth grade classmates did seem destined for federal prisons.

It was, and still is, a small town with a sense of community. It's a place where your voice can be heard, with safe streets, good schools, clean air. Four decades later, my most telling observation is this: Most of the people here have enough money, moxie and imagination to live anywhere in the world, and they have chosen this place to spend their lives.

For example: Viola Tuckerman Schley Hansen, who was awarded the title of "Honorary Vaquera" by the SYV Historical Society. Only the second woman to ever earn the title, pioneer cattlewoman Vi Hansen has ranched in Happy Canyon since 1939.

She is a local legend for her selfless generosity, keen intelligence, her love for the equestrian community, her 20 years with Meals on Wheels, her fine family, and so much more. Vi was a founding member of the original Equestrian Association in the 1940s.

Like her late husband Sigvard Allerslev Hansen, Vi exemplifies the kind of West where you make a deal with a handshake, help those in need, and live each day with honor and integrity and a strong sense of adventure.

Sig Hansen was the Valley personified, a blend of Denmark and the old West. He left his home on the west coast of Denmark in 1929 at sixteen, driven by his Jack London-inspired dreams of the Wild West. He jumped ship in Galveston, Texas, and made his way to Montana. The only English he knew was "Do you have a job for me?"

He found work as a cook's helper on the chuck wagon on the Chappell Brothers CBC Ranch, a mammoth spread providing horses by the thousands for the

U.S. Army. The foreman, it turned out, was Danish, and had jumped ship himself in New York years before.

"Get him a horse and a bedroll," he declared.

"And from that moment on," Sig told me, "I was a cowboy."

And cowboy he did, all over the West, up to Alaska and down to Hollywood, where he rode as a stunt man in films. I hauled hay in the summertime with Sig Jr., and we frequently ate lunch at their ranch house, played poker with Sig Sr., swam, and soaked up some stories.

One day, as he beat my four aces with a royal flush, on the TV, Indians were madly chasing a stagecoach.

"Watch this Indian," Sig Sr. said, pointing to a wild, pony-tailed savage. "He'll lose his hair."

Sure enough, the rider hit the dirt on the edge of the screen. As he tumbled, his ponytails flopped off.

"That was me," Sig grinned.

His adventures led him to Costa Rica. At one time he had exclusive tuna fishing rights there.

"Starkist keeps calling," he explained, hanging up the phone at the ranch. He had invested in a timber operation in Costa Rica, too.

"A word of advice about logging," he confided. "Don't."

He was never afraid to speak out. Once, in a cantina far back in the Nicaraguan jungle, he overheard some guerillas boasting of an attack on unarmed villagers. To his companions' dismay, he made a point of telling the bad guys they were cowards.

"Cobardes!" he spat.

And then?

"My friends got me out of there," he nodded soberly.

Sig mentioned a night on a small boat with notoriously unstable dictator Anastasio Somoza.

"I woke up in the middle of the night, and we were speeding full tilt in the moonlight through the reefs offshore. He was wearing a pair of pistols. Every so often he would go to the bow, and fire off the fifty caliber machine gun. If we had hit some coral, that would have been it."

"Nothing I could do about it. I went back to sleep."

He met a kid on the streets of Costa Rica, Enrique van Browne, who impressed him so much that Sig paid his way through school. The young man served in Vietnam, and became a prominent attorney, influential in affairs of state.

Sig Jr. and I ran into Enrique when we were hauling hay on the ranch one day. The up-from-nothing Costa Rican looked us over, sweat soaked and dirty, covered with bits of straw.

"That's hard work," Enrique acknowledged, adding with a twinkle in his eye and a strategic pause, "for lights."

Sig wanted to help everyone; he had boundless optimism and energy. When I started my real estate business, he encouraged me and offered his assistance.

He was a superb rancher. Even quintessential Valley cowboy Jake Copass paid homage to Sig, writing a poem about him titled "Danish Cowboy."

And he had perspective.

"Twenty years?" he said to me, sitting on a stool at Arne's Solvang Restaurant. "It's the blink of an eye."

Sig once mentioned a Viking custom, when those legendary sailors were ready to leave this world for the next, of sailing past the horizon and burning their ship. That was what he wanted, he said.

My father-in-law, who had a 32' Grand Banks cabin cruiser, said "Remind me not to take Sig out in the boat."

We had lunch at Panino's in Los Olivos one sunny day in 1999, and Sig told me the story of how he came to America. A few days later, he was gone.

I was charmed by Sig's warm, outgoing personality. I was impressed by his adventures. I was flattered by the way he treated me like family, and I loved his lift-yourself-up-by-your-bootstraps life story. But what I most admired about him, and what I most cherish in Valley people, is the kindness, good-heartedness, and concern for others he exemplified.

In his 1935 poem *The Years*, Maynard Dixon wrote, "Ever more do I know that to win some happiness here, I must hold myself up, above petty disputes and distinctions, keeping some largeness of heart alike for those who trust me and those who distrust me."

"Largeness of heart" is what makes the Valley special. It is a spirit to cherish. Vi Hansen has it; Sig had it. All the great ones do.

In this is our hope for the future. In this fragile, evanescent soap bubble of a concept, reliant totally on good-will, rests our dreams.

## 3. Open House at Mike's—A Visit to Neverland

Last time I was here, a two-point buck appeared from a field of tall grass, bounded gracefully over three strands of barbed wire, bounced across the two lane blacktop, and arced smoothly into a newly plowed field.

Now the line of cars stretched for over a mile and a half along bucolic Figueroa Mountain Road. The battered flat red Chevy El Camino in front of me blew sooty smoke rigs in the crystal clear, summer like air of January. A lone man walked from car to car giving out t-shirts. They read: "1000% Innocent."

In a surprise move, Michael Jackson threw open the doors to his 2,676 acre Neverland Valley Ranch after his arraignment in Santa Maria. Hearing the news, crowds flocked to the mysterious Mecca of pop stardom, the secluded, incredible fantasy estate the embattled singer has created in the foothills of the rugged San Rafael mountains, five miles north of the tiny, two-block-long town of Los Olivos, population 1,000.

It was a glorious spring-like day, and the steep sage and pine-covered slopes reaching up to the mountains were bursting with new, neon green shoots from recent rains. The familiar triangle of local landmark Grass Mountain loomed above the ranch, gray-green streaks of serpentine rock at its base.

Frantic parents trying to get their kids at the nearby Family School drove in the wrong lane, and California Highway Patrolmen on motorcycles zoomed back and forth along the caravan of frantic fans. The El Camino's driver visited the roadside sagebrush as the line of cars slowly trundled toward the ornate but tiny gatehouse. A news chopper slowly hovered in circles above.

At the Neverland gate, the roadside was jammed with journalists from around the world jockeying for position. Film crews were set up, anchors prepped for the shoot. The camera van dishes were hoisted into the sky, while placid cattle munched grass in an adjacent field.

Across the street, along Alamo Pintado Creek, were the tidy brown cabins of Midland School, home to students from some of the wealthiest families in America.

Just inside the ranch, six lanes of cars were lined up in a field as the throng filled out agreements to allow Jackson to use THEIR image for free. He was videotaping the event for his own purposes. Cameras and cell phones were subject to confiscation.

"I just grabbed a camera at the top of the hill," a young female guard radioed to headquarters.

The asphalt drive with a serpentine-stone-studded curb led up an eighty-foot-high ridge and over a cattleguard by a "Neverland Valley—Welcome" sign, which features a little boy bending over to talk to a troll.

Beyond the ridge that gives total seclusion to the ranch, a paved parking lot at the base of the hill was too small for the hundreds of cars, eight busses, semi-trailer porta-potties, and two limos, one a stretched black Hummer. Many guests parked in lush grassy meadows under magnificent oak trees, where I hauled hay thirty years ago.

Jackson's thirty-seven developed acres of carnival and castle are in a staggeringly beautiful valley roughly a thousand feet wide, framed by the looming mountain range, studded with massive live oak trees, and landscaped to the square inch, with touches like miniature lights set in the sidewalks, which are cobblestone-patterned concrete.

Four Nation of Islam guys in distinctive skirty suit coats and bow ties, wielding metal detector wands, screened the excited, largely Latino and African-American crowd. Middle-aged white men like myself were as unusual as the three-foot-tall gentleman walking beside me as we approached the first of an extensive network of ponds and waterfalls, including four geysers shooting thirty feet in the air.

The shady path was complemented by arrays of freshly planted rings of colorful flowers around the trees, as at the entrance to Disneyland. Opera wafted on the air. Bronze statues of boys and girls dotted the gardens and falls, and an ornate gazebo offered a shady spot to enjoy the stunning tableau. Two trains carried visitors about. Five pink flamingos on an island in the stream coolly eyed onlookers. An ornate wrought iron fence lined the creek.

Across a arched stone bridge, a sprawling 14,000 square-foot, half-timbered, hip-roofed Tudor mansion, better suited to an English estate, was set among the live oaks, waterways, and walkways. A matching 2,200 square foot guest cottage was about a hundred feet away, on the shore of the lake.

Three shiny black Suburbans and a black Dodge Durango, all with heavily tinted windows, were parked out front. Hundreds of fans milled about, hoping for an appearance by Jackson, who was thought to be inside. Over a thousand guests were on the ranch. I've lived here thirty-eight years. I saw one person I knew.

More sharp dressed men shouted at anyone foolish enough to get too close to the guest house, but dozens of the throng trampled the landscaping to press their noses against the glass windows of the main house, shrieking.

"Is that Janet?!"

"I see Jermaine!"

Inside, the furnishings were regal. There was massive marble statuary, a suit of armor, sumptuous oak bookcases and parquetry floors, a serpentine sculpture of three hounds.

The recreation building, a few yards away, has thirty-five commercial video games, an ornate juke box, and a Slurpee dispenser. Screaming boys flew from game to game. The swimming pool and a sunken tennis court are next door.

On the hillside past the house is a replica of the Disneyland train station. Inside, a girl at a small concession stand was handing out Jujubes and ice cream. There were sixteen televisions in a wall-sized video game setup. Golden oak floors and trim gleamed. A richly decorated Christmas tree with hand-blown glass ornaments stood in the corner. A portrait of a very young Shirley Temple hung on the wall. Up a spiral staircase was a cozy lounge, with a fireplace.

Out back was a full-size, look-alike Disneyland steam train, christened *The Katherine,* after Michael's mother. The twenty-five ton locomotive and tender, twelve feet high and forty-five feet long, could cart a hundred visitors at a time on two open, oak-benched coaches. It's a three minute, half-mile ride to the theater and amusement park. The lonesome moan of the steam whistle can be heard for miles.

The path from the train to the amusement park crosses a swinging suspension bridge and passes a tree house complete with a colorful pirate figure. Unescorted preteen boys scampered everywhere.

*Peter Pan* was playing at the packed, 80-seat, 7,000 square-foot theatre. Popcorn and drinks were dished up gratis to the mobs at the concession stand in the entry. On the screen, Captain Hook had ten wide-eyed children bound and gagged, about to be fed to the crocodile.

Under white tents, 27 white-aproned, youthful servers dished up mounds of chicken, pasta, fruit, Caesar salad, turkey hotdogs and drinks, while Haagen-Dazs carts provided ice cream for dessert. Everything was free for the asking in this fantasyland. Guests ate at round tables on a vast lawn, under white umbrellas.

Nearby, amid the rides, two sound stages stood ready to rock. A band was taking a break. *Beat It* thumped loudly from hidden speakers.

The amusement park includes fourteen rides. Some are tame, little trains and teacups that go in short circles. A circus-like tent houses the bumper cars, where jubilant lads, faces flushed with excitement, rammed each other with enthusiasm.

A Ferris Wheel towers above this scene, challenged by *Sea Dragon*, a quasi-Viking ship around thirty feet long that swings in terrifying pendulum-like arcs, full of screaming quasi-Vikings. The full-sized carousel's colorful animals were custom carved for Jackson. *Wave Swinger*, a four-story tall, whirling swing set, spun dozens of riders in giddy oscillations high in the sky.

There are more challenging, full-sized puke-a-thons, like the *Spyder*, an octopus-armed spinning machine, and Michael's favorite, the *Zipper*, which has about a dozen enclosed cages that invert on a track as they swing and circle about madly some thirty feet in the air. Fans say Michael has ridden the *Zipper* for thirty-five minutes straight. It was closed.

Children and adults were going downhill fast on a massive multi-story slide built into the hillside. Three or four sliders abreast could careen down a shiny, steeply sloped series of dips and jumps.

The petting zoo village has a classic water tower and nine unique, Old-West-style cottages, that are home to birds, pigs, goats, alpacas and a miniature pony. Huge parrots and macaws were perched across the road. The 3,000 square foot snake barn houses cobras, rattlers, albino pythons and huge anacondas that could easily kill a man.

Gypsy the elephant has her own house, as do the orangutans. The bear, who looked depressed, hung out by the camel and four giraffes. I was there for two hours, but managed to miss the two-acre, paved go-cart track, Indian village, and the lions and tigers Jackson told Ed Bradley about on *Sixty Minutes*.

F. Scott Fitzgerald once told Ernest Hemingway "The rich are different from you and I."

Hemingway famously retorted, "Yeah—they have more money."

In this case, they're both right.

---

\* I hear that train a'comin': You usually hear it in the evening. It's a ghostly whistle out of the past; whining low and lonesome in the dusk, like the sound the Pacific Coast Railway steam engine to Los Olivos might have made in the 1880s.

Residents of the Santa Ynez foothills thought they had lost their minds when it first sounded in the twilight hour around 1994. Over the next hill someplace, somebody evidently had a railroad whistle so real you expected to see a train turn the corner any minute. The fact there actually was a whole train took a while to sink in.

Trainweb.org blew the whistle on the carefully guarded secret, revealing information gleaned from employees of Shop Services, a train restorer in Mt. Pleasant, Iowa. A 36" gauge Crown Metal Products locomotive, weighing some 25 tons, standing 12' 6" high and with a length of 45' for engine and tender, plus two coaches, had been restored and sent on massive lowboy trailers to the Neverland Ranch in Santa Ynez.

The engine was named *The Katherine*, after Jackson's mother, and the paint job on the tender alone cost $11,000. The new owner wanted the engine rebuilt so anyone would be able to run the 50-ton train with only 10 to 15 minutes instruction, and the staff of Shop Services were contractually obliged to tell no one, not even their spouses, who it was for or where it was going.

Upon arrival at the Figueroa Mountain Road ranch, some of the curves laid out for one of the world's only private railways were found to be too tight, and had to be redone. After some re-engineering, Engine #1, with the new owner's initials MJJ on its polished brass domes, and coaches originally built for Six Flags Great America amusement park, rebuilt with varnished, wood-slat benches, were on track, making a sentimental circuit through the oak forests and former hay fields.

*Overheard in "R" Country Store: "I've done nine interviews!"

The frenzy over the embattled megastar of Fort Neverland continues. Clear Channel Detroit, KGLA, and *Inside Edition* called for comment. I dodged them, but did talk to a radio station in Atlanta. I was interviewed by *USA Today*, *Forbes* magazine, and *The LA Times* (twice) and videoed by ABC, NBC and CBS. Correspondent Mike Taibbi of NBC News, and two of his co-workers, producer Matthew Carluccio and senior editorial pool writer Adam Gorfain, stopped in for a long chat.

Tom Stalsberg and Tom Martinsen, writing for *Dagbladets Helgemagasin*, trekked all the way from Tonsberg, Norway. They wrote something about me, but it was in Norwegian.

I asked Tom for a translation.

"Hi Bill," he wrote back. "Back home in the land of snow and lazy polar bears."

He translated:

In the valley of wine, we meet up with William Etling, real estate broker. On the wall, a battered, vintage Gibson Les Paul guitar.

In 1989, Michael Jackson bought his fort of fairytale for around 210 million Norwegian kroner.

"Are you reporters? So, you are interested in two things, wine and Neverland. Not interested in buying a ranch, then?"

# 4. Sideways In Neverland

Michael Jackson's life and career has always been like a streaking stock car, spectacularly fast and furious, blowing the doors off the competition. At his peak, it was no contest. No one else even came close to his incredible, international success.

In 2004 and early 2005, he was sliding sideways down the track at 200 miles an hour, spinning wildly and trailing smoke, with 2,000 journalists in hot pursuit.

Locals looked forward to the day tranquility would return, when reporters would no longer roam the streets of Los Olivos collaring citizens, cadging man-in-the-street interviews at "R" Country Store, the galleries and tasting rooms in this tiny town.

They asked "What kind of impact does Jackson have on the town?"

"Have you been out to the ranch?"

And "How do you feel about this media barrage?"

I'll tell you this: It's not the kind of press we wanted.

Then they asked you to go on TV.

There were two choices here, both bad, and they were not about the nose job. You were sure to be reviled by rabid fans if you objected to a middle aged man's fascination with other people's children, or scorned as an idiot by every responsible parent in the world if you didn't. Plan on hate mail, insults, death threats, lawsuits, bad things generally, either way, many in foreign languages.

Because I have an office in Los Olivos, I got off-the-wall inquiries from the media for comments. One self-titled "free lance journalist," evidently too embarrassed to admit he really worked for the *National Enquirer*, framed his theory this way: "I bet people there are really sick of the guy, aren't they?"

I freely admitted, there was no doubt that allegations of child molestation had hurt Jackson in this community. Where wouldn't such a charge resonate? Sodom and Gomorrah?

Michael Jackson last wandered down the street in Los Olivos in 2002, albeit in a surgeon's mask and with two hats, one on his head and one in his hand. He stopped in an antique shop; he bought a few things. No one bothered him, or his adult male companion. They seemed happy, having a little outing in the star's sometime home town.

The Santa Ynez Valley is a live and let live place. Celebrities like Bo Derek, Matt LeBlanc, Noah Wyle, Cheryl Ladd and John Forsythe go to local restaurants, shop at the grocery store and hardware, even send their kids to public school without any hubbub, with the possible exception of the Los Olivos elementary school kids' fuss over Robert Carradine's appearance in *Monte Walsh*.

We may love them, or the screen persona we think we know, but we leave them alone, mildly pleased generally that these talented people have chosen to live among us. The stars I have met who live here are giving, hard working people, largely unaffected by their strange brushes with fame's peril.

It's also a family place, where crowds of concerned parents attend school conferences, soccer fields are mobbed weekends, and the biggest arts event of the year is a youth talent show called "Applause." On a good day, this is America in the '50s, when the biggest school problems were gum under the desk and running in the halls.

And on a less good day, all these good people are faced with the moral dilemma of making choices and judgments about one of their unquestionably talented neighbors, a man whose personal generosity to thousands of children is tainted by suspicions that it's all just an elaborate come-on to abuse.

Parents were appalled, but few enough so to keep their kids from going on the school field trip to Neverland. They didn't see Jackson as a clear and present danger, more as an object lesson in how to really ruin a fabulous career. From a godlike stature, he plummeted with many to a place where he'd have to come up in the world to be riff-raff.

Most of my neighbors are honestly sorry that such incredible talent was spoiled for them by controversy that Jackson brought upon himself.

*Geraldo at large in Solvang: Geraldo Rivera had a late lunch at Manny's Mexican restaurant Sunday, Jan. 6, 2005, and signed a few autographs. In a tan sports coat and shades, with his arm around a pretty woman, he sauntered straight up the middle of Atterdag Road (stars don't use sidewalks), heading off to anchor his show live from outside the courthouse in Santa Maria.

His hour-long interview with Michael Jackson, the first Jackson has granted since he was indicted by a grand jury in April, aired the day before on FOX News Channel's *At Large With Geraldo Rivera*.

It was a rough night for live news. Geraldo announced an attack in Iraq, then had to retract it, as the Army denied the incident. The Italian Prime Minister's name was unpronounceable. The cutaway to "crowds" at a Boston Super Bowl party showed just two lonely people standing in the street.

Rivera interviewed some Jackson supporters standing in Santa Maria's cold, dark streets. Two had quit their jobs—in LA and Missouri—and moved to town for the duration.

As word of the show got around, a car began circling the block honking, its occupants screaming unintelligible messages. The clamor was clearly audible in the background as Rivera interviewed a Jackson spokesperson.

Geraldo said he believes Jackson is innocent, and will be acquitted.

# 5. You Can't Go Home Again

When novelist Thomas Wolfe wrote *You Can't Go Home Again*, he was talking about personal growth. For Michael Jackson, it was a deluge of dozens of deputies that changed his feelings for the old home place.

The embattled artist has announced he will never again permanently live in Fort Neverland, only visit from time to time, feeding the perpetual, popular rumor that the 2,676 acre carnival castle is for sale.

Full disclosure: I am a real estate broker close to Mr. Jackson, in the sense that I'm in Los Olivos, and he's five miles up the road. He walked past my office once.

Neverland Ranch is certainly not in our multiple listing service, and I doubt it ever will be. Properties like that don't need the mass market. There won't be any Sunday open houses.

So what's it worth? That's going to depend on who you talk to.

Take this into account: the broker who snags the listing will instantly become the highest profile Realtor in the world. You can imagine what that opportunity will do to the hyper-optimistic heart that beats in the average agent's chest. The realistic value will double, triple, quadruple, as brokers compete for instant celebrity.

If you want to be a real estate star, the advertising budget won't break the bank. The word is out. The problem will be screening the hordes of people without a dime who want to tour the Lost Boy's lair. Expensive estates can attract sick people.

An appraiser determines value by comparing and analyzing sales on the open market. Realtors do the same, but because we are not licensed appraisers, we don't call our study an appraisal. We call it a "comparative market analysis."

Few homes are directly comparable. We don't just add up the sales and divide to get an average price. Square footage, quality of construction, land area, views, neighbors, neighborhood, landscaping, amenities such as pools, tennis courts, barns, outbuildings, and guest houses, easements, access, and age are just a few of the considerations that must be weighed. Road noise, terrain, driveways, soils, water quality and quantity, environmental hazards, homeowner's association issues, zoning, market trends and a host of other issues come into play.

Clearly, any opinion of value is highly subjective, easily argued up or down. Until the surprise, "last hurrah" open house, I hadn't been on the property since I hauled hay there 30 years ago. It's changed a bit. But just for fun, let's run the numbers.

Eight thousand acres bordering Jackson's ranch sold in May of 2003 for a reported $8 million, or $1,000 per acre. It was not the caliber of Neverland. It was more remote, more rugged, with less oak forests, more steep, sage-covered hillsides. Access was from Foxen Canyon Road, not far from Fess Parker and Zaca Mesa wineries, along the gorgeous wine trail that meanders towards tiny Sisquoc and the courtroom in Santa Maria.

Let's be generous. If we suppose Jackson's land is worth more than what his neighbor got, say $10,000 an acre, his land alone is in the $27 million dollar range. Now we add what's built there, the buildings, roads, Ferris wheels and so on that make up the improvements. When Jackson bought in May of 1988 from Palm Springs—now Las Vegas—golf and mega-resort developer William Bone, he is said to have paid $14.6 million for the land and improvements.

Those of you who had trouble getting that patio cover approved will be amused to hear there was a 12,522 square foot home, 2,195 square foot guest house, 2,084 square foot "garage-office," 2,271 square foot "recreation building" and a pool on the property, plus several older homes and barns from its days as a working cattle ranch.

Jackson put in the 165 square foot guard house, barns, animal pens, 80 seat theatre, music stage, two trains, a train station, and numerous rides.

No buyer, not the fussiest, has ever asked me for a giraffe pen, snake barn, railway or amusement park. Appraisers call that kind of thing "misplaced improvements." Let's just add what the county assessor does, around $10 million. That brings our total for land and improvements to $37 million.

In addition, Jackson reportedly bought $12 million worth of personal property, such as custom furniture and African wall hangings. The fully stocked 640 square foot wine cellar held bottles valued at thousands of dollars each. Throw that in the pot, and the total is up to $49 million.

Now double, triple or quadruple that, as you strive to be the most optimistic—and most famous—listing broker in the world.

*Forbes* magazine's 2004 list of the ten most expensive homes publicly for sale in America in 2003 ranged from $38 to $75 million.

When it hits the market, Neverland will be among them. Call it a hunch.

*Only the lonely are on giraffe alert: The latest in a two-year-long wave of "Michael Jackson is broke" rumors got me out on Figueroa Mountain Road, looking for moving vans full of giraffes, elephants, bears and albino pythons.

But only lonely William Greenelsh of Santa Maria, and his friend Mr. Harris, contract camera operators sporting NBC caps, were at the Neverland gate. They were chasing the same story, to no avail.

Mr. Greenelsh swears all the gophers at Neverland pop out of their burrows simultaneously every day, at 11 am sharp. He photographed the phenomenon, sent it to headquarters in LA.

"They said I'd been out here too long," he laughed.

*If I ran the zoo: The birds and the beasts are there. The local vet who manages Michael's menagerie assures me that rumors of an animal exodus from Neverland are bogus.

"I told *Court TV* and *Fox News* that rumor wasn't true," he said. "They only seem to want to hear bad news."

*Fire on the mountain, cobras in the air: When a forest fire threatened to toast Jackson's ranch some years ago, the vet was told by the county fire department to evacuate Neverland's exotic zoo, or risk crispy critters.

They had barely begun on the 3,000 square foot reptile barn, full of cobras, rattlers, coral and other poisonous snakes, plus albino pythons, boa constrictors, and huge anacondas, when the vet got word that a snake wrangler had been bitten.

It was his worst nightmare.

"Imagine looking for anti-venin at midnight," he said, shaking his head. Fortunately, the attack snake was non-poisonous.

A wind shift spared the ranch.

# 6. Judgment Day For Michael Jackson

The Neverland gate is empty now. Not even one fan remains, hoping for a last glimpse.

Monday, June 13, 2005, was a bit surreal around here. On the grainy internet video, Michael Jackson's convoy of black SUVs approached the intersection of Figueroa Mountain Road and Hwy. 154. I looked up the street. Sure enough, they were turning the corner, off to Santa Maria and Judgment Day.

Two agents from Los Olivos Realty stepped out into the street and snapped a photo. A helicopter hovered. I waved at the pilot.

Inside "R" Country Store, a small group of shoppers had collected. As each new person walked in, saw the TV, and realized what was going on, they abandoned their errands, stopped in their tracks, riveted to the screen. It was like video flypaper.

A girl from Getty Images was taking pictures, wrangling a bit with the man behind the counter, who insisted she ask permission of those in the shot. She did. Some opted out.

When the verdict was read, there was dead silence; only a few smiles from the deli-counter girls. On-screen, a lady launched doves.

"What'd that cost us, five million?" wondered the veterinarian who manages Jackson's menagerie, shaking his head, on his way out the door.

Some of the seventy or so workers who keep up the grounds at Neverland Ranch come to this store for breakfast, lunch and dinner. Jackson has spent big money at local galleries. He's donated to the schools, hosted numerous field trips, picked up a few antiques, used local contractors to build his fantasyland.

Economically speaking, his win was their win, but no one was cheering about it. There was only a general sense of relief that the circus was over.

Meanwhile, back at the ranch, fans from around the world partied outside the ornate gates until twilight, when security guards suggested they go home. Michael Jackson did not appear.

As the Corner House coffee shop closed that evening, a Polish TV station wrapped up a final interview. Then, like all the other journalists who have made a pilgrimage to this quiet town since November of 2003, they packed their gear and their memories and rumbled down the road, on to the next debacle.

Jackson stayed behind his gates for two weeks, with nary a wave to the faithful, then jetted off to Bahrain for some R&R.

# 7. *Sideways* Insider Tells All

*Buellton gets sideways: A production company for a film called *Sideways* is currently camped out in Buellton, working on a comedy about a groom-to-be's last week of freedom with his wine-obsessed pal. The $12 million dollar film is directed by Stanford grad Alexander Payne, who did *About Schmidt* and *Election*. Get discovered: all shapes, sizes, races, ages and gender are sought for paid extra positions. Send a snap with pertinent statistics to John Jackson, Sideways Casting, 85 Industrial Way, Suite A, Buellton.

Here's a *Sideways* scene you'll never see on-screen. It's past midnight, and the Los Olivos Grange is filled with people, some sleeping on the tables, or nodding off in really uncomfortable metal folding chairs.

They're bundled up in heavy coats against the cold, or shivering, very quiet, a bit bleary. They've heard each other's life stories already during the long day. Now all they want is to get some sleep. But it's not over yet. They're still on call.

They're extras in the restaurant scene filming at the Los Olivos Café just down the alley, waiting for their turn to walk around in the background, sit at a table and pretend to eat, drive a car across the street, or, quite commonly, do absolutely nothing at all until the 1:30 am quitting time. It's a cross-section of society, young and old.

Occasionally a perky young girl with a clipboard and walkie-talkie runs in the back door and shouts "Bathroom walkers! Who hasn't done a cross?" and herds a few sleepy lambs over to the controlled chaos of the set.

Purple haired, pierced, Goth girls in black hover over the four stars playing Miles (Paul Giamatti), Jack (Thomas Hayden Church), Maya (Virginia Madsen) and Stephanie (Sandra Oh), touching up make-up. Director Alexander Payne, soundmen and camera guys prepare for yet another take, in a room strewn with cables, lighting equipment, and some mysterious individuals whose job apparently is to sit around.

The extras' day started at noon. They are paid minimum wage, plus overtime, and fed in a commissary set up in the vacant lot by Mattei's Tavern, next to some

RV's and a couple white semis full of film stuff: wardrobe, camera equipment, and the like.

Some are local. Others are from as far away as Paso Robles and Los Angeles, optimistic moths drawn to the gem-like flame of Hollywood. Few will ever catch a glimpse of so much as one of their body parts on the big screen.

After being bored to tears for days on the set of *Seabiscuit*, I swore I'd never fall for the siren's song again. Then my son called from the "Sideways" casting department where he was interning, and told me they needed some bodies. He'd signed the whole family on as "background."

My daughter Leah walks briskly through a Hitching Post scene. After a 12 hour day in which my wife never left her chair, she abruptly and quite cheerily ended her movie career. I stayed on for day two.

I'm a realtor. Mind-numbing boredom is my life. Maybe an actor needed a ranch.

The Los Olivos Café was draped in thick black fabric to keep out daylight. Behind the velvet curtain, I was a "bathroom walker," strolling by the stars' table, presumably looking for the facilities.

I was a technical advisor of sorts for about a quarter-second.

"Do they serve bread here?" a production assistant asked the mob. I assured him they did, and he ordered it placed on the tables.

The cafe was closed down, of course, rented to the production for three days for a rumored five-figure sum. Nevertheless, one clueless couple walked by the camera on tracks in the street, past the lights and caution tape, through all the people milling around, straight into the melee, and asked for a table for two.

I bathroom walked through the afternoon, moving up in the world as night fell. I was promoted to diner, pretending to pick at a scrumptious salad for hours in the freezing cold at a table on the patio outside the restaurant, while Miles and Jack shouted at each other—"Did you take your Xanax?" "I'm not drinking any merlot!"—over and over again.

Now I really was what the film industry contemptuously calls extras: "a prop that eats." Sort of.

"Just pretend to eat the food, people," scolded a production assistant.

Our "wine" was cranberry juice. I was paired up for the fake dinner with a tall, blond, 18 year old model from Pismo Beach, shivering in a thin summer dress. Her mother hovered anxiously nearby. On "Action!" we were to fake a cheery conversation, without making any sounds.

The girl risked pneumonia to be a speck in the background. My right arm made the scene, lowering a wine glass.

A woman sent to keep Sandra Oh's seat warm came back wide-eyed. The professional stand-in holding Jack's spot was a real-life rogue.

"That's a different breed of cat," she muttered enigmatically, shaking her head.

"Alexander Payne is married to Sandra Oh," explained one extra to another.

"I saw him kissing her, but I thought it was just one of those Hollywood things," she replied.

Other than those in the script, I saw no histrionics on the set. Director Payne is a soft-spoken man of infinite patience. He coddled his stars like a friendly psychologist, coaxing and crafting nuanced performances, gently encouraging, quietly coaching. There was no edge to his oversight, even as the tedious repetitions lasted long after midnight.

When Ms. Perky finally chirped "That's a wrap! Who's coming back tomorrow?!," I gratefully slipped out into the fog, my acting career over.

Oenophiles will spot Sanford tasting room manager Chris Burroughs playing "Chris at Sanford" with astonishing verisimilitude.

Local sign maker Atto Alexander was to be in a drunken dream sequence. Atto was rendered corpselike and filmed boating to Hades with Miles and Charon, the ferryman of the dead. Before the scene hit the cutting room floor, they rowed across Acheron, the river of woe, or maybe it was supposed to be Lethe, the river of forgetfulness, en route to eternal misery and damnation.

Eternal misery and damnation. That's an extra's life for you.

*Sideways* trivia: Virginia Madsen, who plays Maya, told interviewer Rebecca Murray "I knew it was in Santa Ynez, and I'd spent a lot of time there. So I wanted to make Maya like the Valley. I wanted her to represent the character of that geographical place, if that makes sense."

Paul Giamatti played a character named Pig Vomit in 1997's *Private Parts*. His dad was Bart Giamatti, onetime Yale University president and Major League Baseball commissioner.

Crabby Canadian critic Louis B. Hobson of the *Calgary Sun* says "*Sideways* is this year's *Lost in Translation*, an art film so in love with its own intellectual cleverness it doesn't even pretend to be mainstream."

Ann Geracimos at *The Washington Times* wrote "Product placement in filmdom never had it so good. Wine labels get so much screen time in *Sideways*, the romantic comedy set in and around the fertile vineyards of California's Santa Ynez Valley, that it's as though the drink is a separate character in the movie."

Then there's the enigmatic title. *The Milpitas Post* postulated "It's also about their approaches to seeking happiness—hence the title, which refers not only to how wine should be stored but also to the way Miles and Jack approach life and relationships."

Joe Baltake of *The Sacramento Bee* thinks "The film's sly, playful title, of course, refers to what happens when you imbibe too much."

Jeffrey Yohalim, writing in the *Yale Daily News*, says "...the title refers to the tipping of a wineglass to study color and individual particles in the aromatic liquid."

Bottles are stored on their sides. For race car guys, "getting sideways" is the prelude to a crash. Roguish Jack probably has his own definition.

Locals thought *Sideways* was harmless amusement, for the most part. They enjoyed picking out the shots filmed here, and looking for their friends in the background.

After three different guys dumped the spit bucket on themselves at Andrew Murray's tasting room alone, they are reassessing.

*Vintner's Festival: More than 60 county wineries will be pouring at the eagerly awaited annual Santa Barbara County Vintner's Festival, held the third weekend of May. Thousands attend the event, with standing orders for tickets from aficionados around the US.

"The first Vintner's Festival was at the Mission Santa Inés, in 1983. It was really tiny," said Diana Longoria, former Executive Director of the Vintner's Association.

"It was called the Santa Ynez Valley Vintner's Festival then, because there were no wineries in Santa Maria," according to Deborah Brown, the first Executive Director.

The annual festival, like the wine industry in the Valley, was in its infancy two decades ago. It has grown to be known nationally as an event to be savored.

Richard Longoria's small (4,000 case) local winery is a good example of how vintners here have earned a national reputation. The Washington Post's Michael Franz said of Longoria's Cabernet Franc, "Richard Longoria makes America's best in almost every vintage, with intense berry flavors braced by a touch of smoky oak."

Longoria topped Wine Country Living's list of 81 Pinot Noirs in 2003.

James Laube of The Wine Spectator, who awarded 98 points out of 100 to a Chardonnay Longoria made, said "This is as exciting a wine region as exists in the world today."

The Wine Advocate's Robert M. Parker, Jr., says the Valley would be one of his top picks for a vineyard outside of Napa.

"The Vintner's Festival is a great opportunity for wine lovers from all over to compare and contrast the intense varietals that derive from a combination of the County's spirited winemakers and the unique climate," said Tim Snider, SBCVA President.

Expect more than the winemaker's artistry. The vintners promise food prepared by some of the area's finest chefs as well.

"You get a glass, walk around and listen to music, and taste wine for three hours," said Diana Longoria. "Local restaurants serve hors d'oeuvres."

"There are special events at many wineries that weekend too, including open houses and winemaker dinners," continued Diana. "Lots of music, and winemakers breaking out old vintages."

Richard Longoria began learning his craft from wine legend Andre Tchelistcheff at the Buena Vista Winery in Sonoma in 1974.

He named his Fe Ciega (Blind Faith) vineyard partly with the Ginger Baker-Steve Winwood-Eric Clapton supergroup in mind, "and partly in honor of throwing caution to the wind."

"I like double meanings. With blind faith, I committed to plant and nurture a beautiful eight-acre site in the heart of the Santa Rita Hills in 1998," he said. The premier commercial pinot noir vintage was released in fall of 2001.

"Wine is part of your life. It expresses where you're coming from. I grew up in that generation, with *Cream* and so on," said Richard, a big fan of the blues.

Longoria's Blues Cuvee cabernet franc has an eye-catching label, featuring expressionistic paintings of blues musicians.

# 8. The Return of the King—Lance Armstrong's Last Ride

"You know, some guys go fishing, but we go to training camp," Lance Armstrong told reporters in Maryland, just before jetting here. "I love to get together with the guys and suffer."

And suffer they do. 2002 Giro d'Italia winner Paolo Savoldelli, 31, hit a rock, blew a tire, and crashed, breaking his collarbone in three places. Savoldelli had been favored for team leader if Armstrong made good his threat to sit out the 2005 Tour de France.

Six-time consecutive Tour de France champion Lance Armstrong returned to Solvang in January of 2005, along with a lot of old friends and a new sponsor. It's the third straight year he's trained here. A torrential week of rain came to a screeching halt in his honor, bowing to beautiful blue skies.

Armstrong's contract with the US Postal Pro Cycling Team ended in 2004, as the cyclists recorded their best season ever, winning 33 international events, including the Tour de France. His new sponsor is the *Discovery Channel*.

Lance arrived in town on a Monday. Mudslides at La Conchita delayed 27 more team members from 14 countries, who arrived a day later, for a ten day stay.

Almost as famous for his psychological warfare as his riding, Armstrong's first gambit in this year's head games was to announce that he may not even compete in the Tour de France.

"I'll definitely be in France this summer, I just might not be on a bike," Armstrong said. He'll decide in April.

"I think, roughly, the deal is that I will do a Tour, if not more," said the 33-year-old, explaining his contract with *The Discovery Channel*. "That could be in 2005 or 2006. But I'm fully committed to doing that.

"I've read some stuff where the organizers say, 'Well, maybe it's good if he sits out a year and lets somebody else win and then he comes back and then there's a rematch,'" Armstrong said. "That does sound like a good idea, but that's not going to be what makes the decision."

"Even if I do the Tour, there's always the possibility that someone else wins," Armstrong pointed out. "I'm fine with that. I've been fortunate enough to win six times, and that's something no one can take away."

Anybody counting Armstrong out will do well to remember his visit here in 2002, when he said, "From now on, as long as I race, I'll be racing to win the Tour de France."

Until his spill, Italian Paolo Savoldelli and Yaroslav Popovych, 25, from the Ukraine, were favored for team leader if Armstrong bowed out.

Early Wednesday morning at Solvang's Bulldog Café, where a large signed poster of Lance inscribed "To the Bulldog" graces the wall, cashier Courtney Bowman reported several riders had already stopped by for a jolt of joe. Café owner Barbara Meeks traded the team a birthday cake for the poster during last year's visit.

At a makeshift workshop in the parking lot behind the Royal Scandinavian Inn, team mechanic Vince Gee said "Cool area. Good training for the guys." Vince's lips were zipped about the bikes, but the cycling press reports that Trek has been busy in the wind tunnel, eking out yet another tiny aerodynamic edge.

The team was busy having official photos shot on the green of the Alisal River Course nearby, before taking off on a four hour ride, in two groups.

Discovery Channel riders are entered in over 50 events from January through the end of October, 2005. Armstrong may ride the revered Giro d'Italia in May or the Vuelta a España in August.

Their natty new blue and white jerseys include a familiar yellow band.

"When Discovery agreed that we could put the yellow (Livestrong) band on the sleeve, we were humbled. We're up to 28 or 30 million bands now," Armstrong told reporters. Sales of the Livestrong wristband fund cancer research and support groups.

The 2005 lineup includes Lance Armstrong, Jose Azevedo, Michael Barry, Manuel Beltran, Fumiyuki Beppu, Janez Brajkovic, Volodymyr Bileka, Michael Creed, Antonio Cruz, Tom Danielson, Stijn Devolder, Viatcheslav Ekimov, Roger Hammond, Ryder Hesjedal, George Hincapie, Leif Hoste, Benoit Joachim, Jason McCartney, Patrick McCarty, Gennady Mikhaylov, Benjamin Noval, Pavel Padrnos, Yaroslov Popovych, Hayden Roulston, Jose Luis Rubiera, Paolo Savoldelli, Jurgen Van Den Broeck, and Max Van Heeswijk.

Riders in years past have had ample praise for their stay here. Famed climber Roberto Heras of Spain, who finished second at the Tour of Spain and ninth in the Tour de France in 2002, said in January of 2003, "It's a nice place; the weather is good, training camp is very good; every day, hour for hour, it's 25 degrees (centigrade), it's perfect."

Steffen Kjaergaard of Tonsberg, Norway, two time Tour de France veteran, agreed.

"Beautiful, beautiful; it's very green, good nature, good roads, which is important; there's not too much traffic." Kjaergaard was right at home in Solvang.

"I go to Denmark a lot; my Dad is Danish. I feel the Danish culture when I get here, it's still a bit different than home, but I like it."

Michael Barry of Canada said, "I've trained down here a couple years before, and it's one of the best places in the country for riding. Great weather, nice countryside, friendly people."

Barry was run over by an event motorcycle in the 2002 Tour of Spain. Bloody, with torn uniform and two broken ribs, he got up and finished the stage.

2002 Tour de Murcia winner Victor Hugo Pena of Columbia remarked, "Yesterday, I said to Lance, this is the most beautiful place I have been in a training camp."

Kenny Labbe of Arlington Heights, Illinois, the only team member who was actually a Postal Service mail carrier, said "The training here has been fantastic. I can't even believe how little traffic there is. Some of the routes and loops we've been on, we haven't seen more than ten or fifteen cars per hour. It's been phenomenal."

And how does this compare to the Tour?

"I just race in the US. But I know that the two climbs we've done here, we've gone over Figueroa and Gibraltar. That's like an hour of climbing up each one, and I can't imagine a climb being much more difficult than either one of those," said Labbe.

An hour climb for him, maybe. I once rode the 42 mile loop from Solvang to the top of Figueroa and back. It took me nine hours. But then, Labbe was a former US National Record holder in the 12 hour time trial—252 miles.

Antonio Cruz of Long Beach, who won the US Olympic Trials road race in 2000, said "It's been great; the weather, the scenery, it's very picturesque."

Even class clown Dave Zabriskie from Salt Lake, who couldn't open his mouth without cracking everyone up, opined slyly, "It's quite nice!"

Since then, Damon Kluck, Kenny Labbe, Floyd Landis, Victor Hugo Pena Grisales, Daniel Rincon Quintana, and David Zabriskie moved on to other teams. Robbie Ventura retired.

Some fans came every day to the parking lot behind the Royal Scandinavian Inn in Solvang, many in cycling gear, all respectfully eyeing the electric blue Trek bicycles in the cordoned off mechanic's corral.

Some asked for autographs, or took pictures, as 27of the 28 Discovery Channel Pro Cycling team members from 15 countries trickled down to the compound, assembling for their daily training ride. Fans from six to sixty were among the thirty-some lingering there Wednesday morning, Jan 19, 2005, at 9:30 am.

"My wife and I are both cancer survivors," said Larry Oertel of Pismo Beach. "We're been riding for years. We went and saw the Tour de France last year. I think it's just great what he's been doing for cancer survivors; I'm very happy about that."

The parking lot pilgrimage has become an annual event for him.

"We were here last year, too. It's a chance to see the riders. It's a lot of fun," said Mr. Oertel.

Jennifer and Pam from Santa Barbara said "We do triathlons, and we watch the Tour, and find these guys really inspirational. We just kind of wanted to be a part of it."

David Walls of Santa Barbara was there in leather, waiting beside a huge, sleek, silver Aprilia motorcycle.

"I'm carrying a TV guy today," said Mr. Walls, the former chairman of a company that published bike industry bible *VeloNews*. "In 1997, I sold my interest, got a motorcycle, and started helping with bicycle races," he said. The videographer on the back of the big bike is shooting for Capital Sports and Entertainment of Austin, on behalf of Lance.

"I normally carry the still photographer. I was up here last week doing that," said Mr. Walls.

For Sammarye Lewis of Palo Alto, respect for Lance Armstrong became a profession. She's known in the cycling world as "Velogal," and publishes a daily blog about the team, plus dispatches for ThePaceline.com, the official Discovery Channel Pro Racing Team fan website.

"I started with a fan site for Lance. It's a tribute to courage," said Ms. Lewis, quoting Pericles on the subject. "I respect his courage and his integrity. I'm in the fifth year of the fan site, and then I write daily reports for *The Paceline*. For the Tour de France, I send in a report and a photo each day." Her fan site is lancearmstrongfanclub.com. "I love Solvang; the people are so friendly."

"It's really fun to come here," said Ms. Lewis. "I follow the team every day (in a silver Subaru Outback), helping any way I can. I just love going slowly through the countryside. Riders tell me the roads here, and the countryside, is very similar to Gerona, Spain, where some of the team live."

The cyclists are always just a moment away from a wipeout. Ms. Lewis reported that the riders spooked a horse, who in turn reared and spooked the riders, just before Paolo Salvodelli crashed and broke his collarbone in three places on Jan. 15. Horses are notoriously skittish of bicycles.

Velogal told me most locals were extremely considerate of the team, but she posted this cautionary tale.

"I always worry about the guys when folks behind us get impatient, and pass right into oncoming traffic. Some guy in a white van did that yesterday, and the oncoming car with two young guys decided to play chicken and swerved toward the van, instead of away—they barely missed each other, and right beside our guys. Both drivers were nuts, as far as I am concerned. In the grand scheme of things, what does 10 minutes mean in someone's life that they can't chill out and go slow once a year when we ride here?" Read more at velogal.blogspot.com.

The team set off without an appearance from the most famous athlete in the world.

"Lance has been staying in Santa Barbara," someone said as the riders disappeared. "He meets up with them outside of town."

Actually, he was up in room 344, but he did successfully evade most of the press and public.

Armstrong likes Valley motorists.

"It's been great; the roads are great; the other big difference is the people on the roads are much different, the drivers, the way they are, the patience is a little different, very supportive; you get your occasional salute (laughs) but it's been a great experience."

When the team left town, they hopped on their bikes, and pedaled off to Ojai, 67 miles away, for a weekend with their sponsors.

*Afterword: It was his last ride here, at least professionally. Armstrong won his seventh consecutive Tour de France, and retired from competition, in July of 2005.

# 9. Rain

It rained a symphony, and it rained a drowning. It rained all day and all night, and then it rained some more. It rained a mudslide, a nightmare, a heartache.

It rained on a canyon below Figueroa Mountain where the ground is sometimes covered with a living ladybug carpet. It rained on little lupine and poppies, struggling out of the steep slopes of Grass Mountain.

The raindrops fell on the just and the unjust. They fell on the hillsides and canyons of the back country, spooking the trout, who found their little pools spilling into bigger pools. The swollen streams slipped away downhill, foaming, wandering, becoming rivers.

Serpentine boulders pushed through time from the depths of the ocean to the top of the mountain knocked and thundered as they tumbled down steep streambeds. In the back country, Manzana Creek and Fish Creek and all the unnamed rivulets carving through the canyons gurgled off to join the Sisquoc and the Cuyama Rivers, and finally ride the Santa Maria River to the Pacific.

Nojoqui Falls swelled and soared, eerily blue in the shadows of the canyon. North of Refugio Pass, Quiota Creek ripped angrily across the road, aching to tear the asphalt apart.

Frothy cascades topped Gibraltar Dam, momentum for the Santa Ynez River's mad run. Sweetwater Creek and Santa Cruz Creek flowed directly into the lake. Cachuma grew inch by inch, finally sending a silver stream down the spillway, to search for the tempestuous sea.

It rained on wild horses in new homes. The four wild kitties in their tree house in the oak tree outside my garage heard the deluge from their toasty electric bed. Others, not so lucky, huddled in a hollow tree. The deer bedded down under the thick live oaks to wait it out. Feral pigs grunted ominously in the sagebrush. The buffalo herd in Ballard Canyon just shrugged it off.

In Santa Ynez, water in Zanja de Cota—"Cota's Ditch"—named after a mission era civil engineer, babbled in the shadow of the new casino and hotel.

Drops sluiced off the windmills and shining sidewalks in the Danish village, and wet the wine tasters in Los Olivos. Water filled the creek behind ghostly white Mattei's Tavern, just as it did in 1910 when chef Gin Lung Gin fished steelhead straight from the water for the dining table.

Ponds formed along the rich fields on Roblar Avenue, to be sliced to sheets by passing cars. Spray sailed from the cars spinning down the soggy concrete corridor of Highway 101.

It rained on grateful farmers, on glum retailers, on gamblers, a few tourists, out-of-work carpenters, and road crews. It rained on police directing traffic past the washouts, and crabby commuters driving longer, tedious, treacherous treks.

Figueroa Creek and Happy Canyon Creek fed Santa Agueda Creek, meeting the rolling river at the San Marcos Pass bridge. Lanky Alamo Pintado Creek drained the heart of the valley and gushed in just east of Solvang. Alisal Creek was close behind. Adobe Canyon Creek and Ballard Canyon Creek frothed in; Nojoqui Creek and Zaca Creek followed.

The milk chocolate tide left behind the bridges of Buellton and snaked in lazy esses down Santa Rosa Road, slopping like a spilled smoothie past the old dairy, and the Sanford Winery vineyards, and the ruins of the cloister, and the walnut orchards, and the rowed-out, fecund black soil, and the vegetable coolers. It coasted into Lompoc between the new Home Depot and River Park, past the new homes, the willows, the prison, and the rockets of Vandenberg, under the Southern Pacific trestle, to sand dollar strewn Surf Beach, and the churning ocean beyond.

Back home.

## 10. Wildflowers

The jackpot is just short of the Figueroa Mountain campground—a solid hillside of lupine, with a few poppies, and the odd jumbo pine cone, for accents.

Now's the time to take that scenic drive. The green tide has peaked. The mustard at Gaviota is so bright, it looks like the lemon-lime popsicle plant exploded. When the fog is just burning off the peaks, Gaviota gorge resembles lush, tropical Kauai, or mysterious Machu Picchu.

The motor nature excursion up Figueroa Mountain Road is more of an Easter egg hunt than an extravaganza. Clumps of bush lupine begin to appear just past Midland School. As you cross Alamo Pintado Creek and start up the mountain in a long green tunnel, the blue oak grove on the left is sprouting new foliage, and the sycamores in the waterway on the right are nearly phosphorescent.

Indian paintbrush appears at the first switchback. A few poppies seem to like the rocky serpentine soil on up the road, clinging to sheer cliffs of the sharp green rock. Across a yawning chasm, Grass Mountain is tinged a hazy blue from all the lupine on the steep slope.

Delicate shooting stars appear a little higher on the ridge, as sweeping vistas of the valley over the Sedgwick Reserve appear. It's a spectacular tableau.

You glimpse Lake Cachuma as you approach the meadows around the bend, the jumping off point for a steep trail down Birabent Canyon. Next up, just past Tunnell Road, is the solid slope of lupine, every square inch a riot of color. The sweet scent of the blossoms wafts in the wind. Bring lots of film.

Too bad the road to the fire lookout is closed. That's usually a floral fantasia. You can always hike it. If you stop at Figueroa campground, site 14 is the coveted secret spot, just a few steps from a stellar scenic vista.

Intrepid travelers will persevere on over the ridge, past the Davy Brown trailhead, and broad meadows full of tiny blossoms of all descriptions, plus more stunning vistas of the valley, Lake Cachuma, and the backcountry.

A spooky journey through the pine forest at the top of Ranger Peak leads to a steep descent towards the Davy Brown and Nira campgrounds. The Happy Canyon access road is still closed, due to slides.

Spiky yucca defy gravity on the hillsides. The tortured, twisted, striated, smeared veins of serpentine and shale streaking the cliffs are a geological cry of pain, mute witness to eons of nature's convulsions. Across the canyon is the rich red cinnabar ore deposit that sparked an 1874 mercury mining melee. That's still private property.

Rusted signs mark the trails that etch these canyons. The twisting torrents of Fish Creek beg to be explored. Near the bottom of a sage-covered gorge, along Sunset Valley Road, is the quiet enclave of Davy Brown campground, named after the onetime slaver, forty-niner, and bona fide mountain man, friend to John Muir. Davy lived in a cabin nearby.

"Here the pioneer hunter of Santa Ynez lives, and he presented us with his photograph, we being, as he said, the first lady who ever visited his camp," wrote a bold nineteenth century correspondent. "The pioneer hunter makes an uncommonly picturesque picture, arrayed in his hunting suit, with the deer's tail in his cap—an Indian sign that the wearer is on the warpath."

Babbling brooks foam across the road. Try not to run over any trout; fishing with a car is strictly prohibited. Picturesque patches of bright blossoms of all description appear, perched in the shale, hanging from cliffs, dotting the roadside, set off by the sparkling splashes of the tumbling current, and the stark, skeletal cottonwoods.

The road is paved all the way to Nira, the end of the line. Other than a few potholes, it's a pretty civilized excursion. Nira is the jumping off point for hikes up or down Manzana Creek, into the rugged back country.

Two wranglers and about thirty head of cattle were making their way slowly up the middle of the road towards Midland School as I headed home. Country etiquette: park while they pass.

Another day: The poppies make Grass Mountain look like it is on fire. On the way up Figueroa Mountain, a painter is at his easel, immortalizing the color across the canyon. Numerous cars have stopped at overlooks, to photograph the scene.

About sixteen miles out of Los Olivos, I have to park. A four-wheel-drive could make the next leg, but it's too much for the Volvo wagon. I ride for 1.3 miles on my mountain bike, to the end of what was once a road.

From there, I continue on a path just wide enough for foot traffic. About a quarter-mile down the trail, a long-abandoned Studebaker Hawk, riddled with bullet holes, is sliding down the canyon. It is hard to believe this was ever a road.

The trail to this Eden is heavily overgrown and almost indiscernible. My brother once surprised a bear here. It curled up in a ball, and rolled away down the hill. As I crawl on my hands and knees through the tangled manzanita, this is on my mind.

About a mile and a half from the trailhead, I see brush give way to blue sky. The view from the summit is majestic. Lake Cachuma glistens in the sun to the east. The Pacific is visible to the south, over the Coast Range, and to the west, past Lompoc.

Green foothills glow in the sun. Far across the canyon, I can see the painter's car.

Behind the mountain, in the back country, more jagged slopes rage fiery orange with wild poppies.

A charred frying pan from a Boy Scout camp kit is hanging on one of the many pines at the top of the face. An old campfire, circled by rocks, lies forsaken.

The flowers are phenomenal. The meadow is covered by ground lupine, bush lupine, tiny white blossoms, and acres of poppies. Warm air wafts their sweet perfume up the mountain. Honey bees as big as my thumb hover about.

A plane flies by, level with me. The pilot is startled to see me. He wags his wings, and swings around for a second look.

The slope is very steep. Huge cones from the pine groves on the face have rolled together in little piles, stopped by the flowers. If the slope was bare, they would roll for hundreds of yards.

From across the canyon, it had appeared the flowers were concentrated in several large areas. The truth is that every square inch of the face is covered with blossoms, but the areas where the lupines and poppies are mixed together have less saturated color than the poppies alone.

I shoot fifty pictures, one after another, with normal, wide angle, and telephoto lenses. I am so spellbound by this photographer's paradise, that I lose my camera case. It is somewhere in the depth of flowers, and although I carefully retrace my steps, I cannot find it.

Necessary losses.

## Part 2. Her Side of the Mountain

Everybody knows that poppies and lupine light up the San Rafael range like a neon sign in the spring. A discerning few, like Figueroa Mountain resident Cheryl Alter Morris, see a parade of blossoms year round.

"People think that once the poppies and lupine are over there's nothing out there. That's not true! There are flowers all year long," says Cheryl Alter Morris.

"As early as January, the milkmaids come up. They start at the bottom of the hill on the Midland school property. Once I see those, I start looking for others. As the air temperature warms up, they start moving up the hill. There are certain spots that I check."

Ms. Morris moved to the mountain with her parents in the early sixties from the San Joaquin valley to take over a cow-calf operation started by her grandparents, Johnny and Mildred Franzina. At one time the family ran 250 head on 40,000 leased acres ranging from Figueroa through Davy Brown to Sisquoc.

It was a family operation. Recalled Ms. Morris, "If they said 'be home to work cattle,' I was home to work cattle." It's a vanishing way of life. The Forest Service ended cattle leasing some years ago, and there's no longer private grazing in the forest.

She lives on a peaceful 80 acres set within the forest, which her grandparents purchased from the Tunnell family. Animal visitors include coyotes, bobcat, fox, squirrels, and the occasional bear. "We saw a young one a couple of years ago. They get in the garbage."

The road up the mountain was dirt then, sometimes blocked with snow and mudslides as she made her way to SY high. (Her mother, Dorothy Alter, is also a SY High grad.) "It was an interesting time, not knowing how you were going to get to school some days," said Cheryl. "When it was really wet, my dad drove us."

Their telephone was crank operated, working off the line going to the fire lookout. At first there was only a generator for electricity. "We just had butane, and kerosene lamps. It wasn't until I graduated from high school in 1966 that we had power." That changed when the Forest Service brought power to a well nearby.

Cheryl married and moved away, returning just over five years ago.

"That was the year we had sixty inches of rain, and the mountain was just alive with flowers. That piqued my interest."

She jumped into photography. "Neil Brundage at Village Frame and Photo helped bring me along. I like to catalog the wild flowers that come up every year. I take the Catway road, and go down into Davy Brown, check the hillside, look over the edge, and climb where I can climb and take pictures."

Rainfall and fire impact the cycles.

"From our house, I can see an open hillside toward Figueroa Mountain. The first year when I came back, we had all that rain and because of the fire there was a lot of brush that hadn't grown back up, and that little meadow was first yellow, then it turned pink. I walked down the Davy Brown trail, and the sides of the canyons were just covered in Chinese Houses. They were literally white—I've never seen it like that before. There were a lot of things that come up that year in such mass that hadn't before."

"Last year was an excellent year. Everybody commented that they'd never seen so many lupine on the hillside." Cheryl's advice: "When you go looking for wildflowers, look over the side of the road, not just along the side of the road. You'd be surprised how much you miss when you don't leave your car."

# 11. Surf's Up

Harsh winter is upon us. As I sit in the sun while the rest of the country struggles with their snow blowers, I think just one thing: Surf's up.

Not the least of the ways we're spoiled rotten here is the beach access. Until I was twelve I lived in Winston-Salem, North Carolina, a 300 mile drive from Cape Hatteras and the shifting sand dunes of the Outer Banks. It was a rare thing to go to the beach, an exotic adventure. We lived for days in a tent in the dunes, hiking to shipwrecks, eating gritty peanut butter and jelly sandwiches, chasing crabs in tide pools.

I still love the beach. If I had a tail, I'd wag it when I'm near the water.

One of the many happy surprises of my arrival here in 1966 was the Realtor's announcement that Refugio State Beach was just 12 miles away. You had to go straight up a rugged dirt road over the mountain to get that mileage, to be sure, but it was tantalizingly close nevertheless.

And what a beach! In 1972, I lived on St. Thomas in the Caribbean, surfing Hull Bay. In 1989, I was Planning Administrator for the island of Oahu for Hawaiian Tel. I surfed Sunset, Turtle Bay, Mokapu, Waikiki. Overall, I prefer Refugio.

Rincon has better surf, if you don't get a disease from the septic tanks seeping into the sea. But there are no palm trees. Refugio's line of swaying palms is the icing on this Southern California cake, framing a classic, idyllic, picture postcard crescent of sugary sand. Even Ansel Adams took pictures here.

Refugio surfers are mellow. Lots of longboards. You see entire families out. The protected cove straightens out mixed-up swells, cuts the wind, and makes it easier to get in and out of the lineup. And when you look back at the land from there, it's unspoiled California coastline, not much different from what the Chumash saw from their tomols. At Waikiki you see high-rise hotels. Here you can barbeque on raised grills, and dine at picnic tables on a lush lawn just feet from the sand.

El Capitan State Beach has a better point break, much like a miniature Rincon. The surfers are more competitive, and the rocks can be nasty, but it's still fabulous. Awe inspiring winter waves line up at Cap Point. Even the endless beach break is good for some fast tunnels.

The nature walk at El Cap Point is another joy, a mysterious trip into a lush, sun dappled grove of cottonwoods and jungle-like undergrowth along the bubbling creek that formed this spit of land.

An almost flat, staggeringly beautiful bikeway runs the few miles between the state parks, along the top of the beachside bluffs, with endless views to the Channel Islands and beyond.

Secret spots along the bike path known as The Cove and Hazards can break on the right swell. At low tide they're perfect for sunbathing, beachcombing, or a run with the dog, which you can't do on the state beaches. I found some cowries and a Stearn's tegula at Hazards, a shell named after the builder of Stearn's wharf.

Gaviota is great for a walk at low tide, with miles of pristine sand and sandstone. The ancient beach of millions of years ago is still there, as sandstone tilted on end, reaching for the sky, almost vertical to today's sand. Watch for fossils.

A pier here was one of the early SY Valley residents' links to the outside world, where goods and passengers came and went to San Francisco and Los Angeles. The tall trestle of the Southern Pacific tracks that made those days a forgotten memory looms above as you near the water.

Jalama County Park is a walk on the wild side, a place where you can feel like the only person on the planet when the wind whips the roiling waves to a frothy frenzy and the entire sweeping curve of the coastline stretches out vast and lonely before you. With no islands protecting the coast from the full fury of winter's blasts, this a place where only the strong survive. The mournful foghorn at the Point Conception lighthouse hauntingly echoes like a dying dinosaur through wisps of mist.

Jalama surfers brave fierce, cold waters, known for shark attacks. Sand dollars, heaps of tangled kelp, and, sadly, usually a seal or some other sea creatures are washed up on the beach. The blue whale whose skeleton is displayed at the Santa Barbara Museum of Natural History came ashore near here.

## Part 2. Surf & Turf

Some think surfers are small minded xenophobes, greeting outsiders with spears. Thankfully, that's rare. I've surfed for almost forty years now, and only once been hit intentionally. That was by an Australian at Kaiser's, just off the Hilton Hawaiian Village on the tip of Waikiki, who whacked me on the thigh with his fist as he paddled out.

I assumed it was intimidation, although maybe it's Aussie for "G'day, mate." He didn't stop to explain.

More cosmopolitan, broader-minded surfers all over the world, from Hull Bay on St. Thomas in the US Virgin Islands, to beaches all over the Hawaiian Islands, and particularly up and down the California coast, have been gracious enough to surf with me in peace. I even got some appreciative hoots at a break near Santa Monica, which frankly was the last thing I expected in the city.

Surf Nazis do exist, of course. Some are world famous. A judge in Ventura had to handle one repeat offender who acted badly in the water and vandalized property on shore. On Oahu, Makaha has a reputation for being fiercely local. The first day I arrived at Waikiki, I was advised not to surf the Ala Moana harbor mouth.

"You'll get hassled," confided a friendly local. Solution: go out 100 yards west, at Kaiser's, named after the aluminum baron who developed the place. I had no problems there, other than the odd Aussie, who of course was thousands of miles from home himself.

Overall, surfers get along pretty well. There's an etiquette in the water. You ignore it at your peril. It's ill advised to drop into a wave in front of someone who isn't falling off. He may run over you by accident. He may run over you on purpose. Or launch his board at you, a tactic known as "spearing."

Most surfers are pretty mellow. One briefly ended up in my arms when he took off in front of me on a crowded day at UCSB's Campus Point. We both thought it was hilarious. He promptly fell off, and left me gliding along with his board.

It is impossible to overstate the beauty of surfing. To be part of that sparkling mass of water moving through sunlight and space is ethereal, heightened by the reality that if you mess up, you're going to be chewed up and spit out by a massive mindless crushing machine. Surfers at world famous Maverick's compare it to being hit by a semi-truck. Champion surfer Mark Foo died there.

It's a cliché, but surfing can be truly "awesome." Surfing is like skiing an avalanche, with the whole mountain falling down around you. After a warm, sunny, perfect day at El Cap Point, with glassy sets lined up to the horizon, and dolphins leaping offshore, I heard a man say "This is better than sex!"

I have seen the ocean bottom below me as through a crystal clear window as I glided above. I have dropped into waves that scared me to death. Some I rode. Some rode me. I've been out until I shook with cold and couldn't feel my feet when I got to the beach. I have a bone spur on my rib from surfing. Caution: this sport is addictive.

With the sun behind me and an offshore wind blowing a storm of spray in my face, I once saw a perfect rain circle—a rainbow is a full circle if you are in the right spot, usually a plane—just feet from my face. A brighter, more colorful sight you cannot imagine.

Just looking at the coast from a board gently rocking on the water is glorious. All your senses are fully alive to the sparkle of the sunlight on the water, the tang of the salt, the sting of the cold water, the challenge.

In surfing, as in the rest of life, life-changing enlightenment comes when you realize that hatred, jealousy, greed and envy are self-defeating. They only hurt you. As the great writer Anne Lamott once said, "You may as well be drinking rat poison, and hoping the rat will die.'

## Part 3. Forgive Us Our Trespasses—Cowboys vs. J-Boyz

They're tough, hard-working, horse-riding, cattle-roping men with a capital "M" out on the rugged, sprawling, famously windy Cojo Ranch, near Point Conception, and they don't cotton to strangers. Before you cross them, reflect on this: forcibly removing critical body parts from crying animals is part of their job description.

They are not all humorless. Cowboy icon Dutch Wilson, who wrangled there in 1926, once joked there was a massive anchor chain tied to a tree that they used for a weather vane. When it was blown by the fierce ocean gales straight out from the trunk, Cojo cowboys went out to work anyway. If it was snapping links off, they might work in the bunkhouse.

"Fred H. Bixby bought the Cojo Ranch in 1913 and started cattle ranching with registered polled Herefords," reads the Cojo-Jalama Ranch history. "The ranch was expanded with the purchase of the neighboring Jalama Ranch in 1939. Together, the contiguous ranches encompass approximately 25,000 acres and remain today as working cattle ranches." The company owns huge ranches all over the state, a legacy of gold-rush-era entrepreneur Lewellyn Bixby's financial acumen.

Every few decades or so, when the dogies are all branded, fences are mended, the hay is in the barn, supper's over, boots are polished, and there's absolutely nothing else on earth for a concerned cowpoke to do, they get on the high wire and bark at the Sheriff's Department to come round up some lawless wave riders. Not all cowboys have Garth Brooks' public relations skills.

Really hardcore Jalama surfers sport "J-Boyz" tattoos. The offending outlaw surfers cross Cojo dirt when they park by the scenic Southern Pacific crossing and slide down a precipitous ravine to the break known as Tarantulas, thereby eliminating a half-hour walk from Jalama Beach Park.

Deputies must do their sworn duty. It's the law. There's little doubt the surfers are trespassing, even if they are miles from nowhere, on range no livestock will ever roam. Cows are too valuable to be allowed anywhere near the steep, eroded, sand-and-shale arroyo where the wave warriors tumble down to the beach.

Four Santa Barbara County sheriff's deputies from the rural crime unit answered the corporate call recently, and spent three hours on Saturday, July 23, writing 17 trespassing citations and ten parking tickets.

Imagine the joy on the thin blue line. A meth epidemic, bank robberies, gang violence, vast marijuana plantations in the national forest, and these macho public servants are assigned to ticket their friends at the beach.

I parked at the spot in question back in 1969, to go surfing. I parked there again last week, to take pictures of my son surfing. In between, about a million other surfers have parked there. It is one tempting, tasty shortcut.

I didn't get a ticket. Enforcement is sporadic, and the odds of snagging a citation are roughly the same as those of winning the lottery. Trespassing once costs $75. Twice, up to $1,000.

I have a lot of sympathy for the cowboys of the waves, and even some for the Cojo caballeros. The ranch has a valid concern. If someone falls off the cliff, they'll be named in the lawsuit. Also, if someone "openly, notoriously and hostilely" crosses your land for five years, they may try to acquire an easement.

Henry Kissinger once said, "Even the Hundred Year's War had to end sometime." Someday, an enlightened management at the Cojo Ranch will deed to the County Park the ratty sliver of land they've fruitlessly battled to keep generations of J-Boyz off, and kiss their liability goodbye, in exchange for a hefty tax write-off and huge "good guy" PR points.

The County will say they're broke, but the Surfrider Foundation will hold a fundraiser for a stairway and parking lot. And yet another seemingly endless range war will bite the dust.

## Part 4. A Global Surfari

Hull Bay, US Virgin Islands: Their rain soaked faces scanned the dying light of the sky. Warm breeze kissed the spray as it blew off the twisted lips of curling foam. The bay swept around them, falling from the mountains, cradling the waves, reaching for the small offshore islands with encircling arms.

When the face broke solid, white from end to end, the rushing foam reached the low white sands of the beach and flooded the tangled palms, rolling urchins and coral into the jungle before retreating to the jewel blue mass of sea.

Tom was carving left on a moving wall of wet light that dwarfed him, streaking semi-crouched on the board over the turning face. As Bill watched, directly in the path of the wave, not even the realization that this breaking wave was destined to thrash him could tame his savage joy at their salt water apotheosis. They were what they wanted to be, bold and free, at one with the unspeakable mystery of the planet. Tom, safe far left, turned and paddled back out.

Bill faced the whirling, pummeling mass. It was too big to fight. He thrust the board away and dove deep under the careening foam as it rolled upon him. He curled and spun, death gripped arms about legs, free-falling, weightless; the torrent spun him in dream circles, somewhere between the life above and the coral below.

Released, he broke for the sun.

Half a mile from shore, he began the long swim after his board, which had been swept around the bay by the maelstrom.

Another day: There was very little surf at all, only the inside break on the far left of the bay, splashing two-foot sunlit walls. For some time they thrashed about on the tiny rights; drop, slow turn, punch the lip and fall with the foam, turn and paddle and begin again. The small sets tended to shorebreak over the shallow coral reef, where the urchins on the bottom were stark black silhouettes against the coral and sand.

A left too far inside dropped him on the fire coral, which broke from its column-like moorings to drop him into beds of urchins. The chemical in the coral began to burn his skin; the water was too shallow to paddle away; the coral was too fragile to stand on. There was no way to the beach except through the urchin beds, and the swells came in waterless.

He made a desperate leap, crashing down on the coral; then another. A fortunate tidal push gave him freeboard; his board was upside down, fin in the air for extra clearance. Tom waited outside where he had been waved off, helpless.

With hands and feet spiked and burned, he paddled back out to catch some sunset rollers, and then start the long paddle home.

California: The green glow of a tube at Hazard's, rushing under the rising tide. So hard to explain a ray of light.

Standing at high tide on the promontory at the Cove, watching for the first rideable swell. Backwash recoils from the shale cliffs, sliding like all of California into the sea, a rock at a time.

He slid backside twice, ate a drop, carved right and got caught inside. He paddled around the break zone and back out. Limp white foam bubbles were disappearing all about, dome by tiny rainbowed dome, in crystal invisibilities of spray. A high sheer left; paddle, one! two! leap! with the surge as the swell walls and catches; drop, alive, alive, in the liquid explosions.

Lolling on the rocks like a seal, eating cashews and oranges for lunch.

A day at Jalama: 30-40 mile an hour Santa Ana winds, mild rainstorm, spray and chop.

A quarter-mile long rainbow flashed as the wave blew away. No one is out. Four to five foot chaos, sheer tumbling madness, hot winds and cold jagged water; salty eyes from the spray.

Magical reflections in the Devereau Point dunes: I am part of this ocean of wind blown sand. I dissolve and form again. The driven sand blows through me.

Surfing the Cove on a mystery swell. Well defined sets, four to five feet, pulsing through a calm sea. Fast walls. Best waves in a long time, a rising tide picking up in two semi-bowls, doable with suicide luck. Throwing ankles at the lip overhead and getting away with it; anti-gravity arms to the tumbling lip; outracing it.

Driving, leaping, flung over the inside breaking crest, he landed pirouetting backwards, submerged; awaiting the pull of the shock cord as the board was engulfed in a mean shorebreak. Occasional six wave sets, occasional long lulls. Making an unmakable one, the lip punched like a fist; salt water conflict sweeter than blood.

From the far left he threw the board high into the turning, critical wall where the energy catapult explodes. To describe the sensations of such a crystal life mesh seemed impossible. It was total mental and physical immersion into the now, like turning death threats into benedictions.

Life was obvious to him when he was in the water. Of course California surfers have untouchable spirits, he thought. They're too often slapped by an uncontrollable goddess ocean. They're addicted to the glory of human transubstantiation, man into water, turned into foam particles of crashing crystal force. They climb and soar with the living water, like bits of liquid sun beyond thought or explanation, a gestalt pair larger than the sum of sliding, free-falling, roaring salt life particles and a man released.

On a strange day it can be a moving wall, white as Kilimanjaro by the time you see it, so far outside there's no hope of beating past it. The only choice is to turn and run with it; or paddle straight into it, either right side up with your body pulled out over the nose of the board so you don't get flipped, or turned turtle, locking your legs around the board under water as the face pulls you up and slams you around inside a moving mass of foam.

You can kick a longboard up the face and fall back under the strangely quiet rumbling stomach of the wall as it passes overhead, roaring dully.

He was heading out to Morro Bay, with the yellow twin fin in the red Corvair wagon. Near the shore, an old man was digging for clams. They had the ocean to themselves. The surf fell in crumbling lines, foam walls jagged, incoherent, cold on the outside of the break line and warm by the power plant outlet.

Stark against the sky, Morro Rock jutted above the little cove that stretched off to meet the hazy horizon and become the endless coast of Northern California.

He was alone most days. Sometimes there were crowds, on the few smooth days. He surfed there throughout that winter. Sometimes he went farther north, between Morro Bay and Cayucos, sliding left and right with only the fish and an occasional fisherman on the old oil pier as silent partners.

Cars on Highway One passed, their noise hidden in the roar of the water. Vertical walls and shorebreak crashes.

Every cold grey day, on every wave, he tried to pump the power of the surf to Oakland, where Tom lay on his hospital bed, motionless, silent, alone.

The afternoon was gone. The sun was hidden behind a cloud. Darkness would soon force his retreat.

He was squinting into the sun, looking through the glare for the swell behind the swell, the bump that no one had glimpsed yet, just beyond what looks like the biggest wave of the set.

He had to paddle a half mile to get to a point where it was only a ten foot shorebreak instead of double-overhead. He somehow made it down the slide of a steep face into the white water, after backing away from the rolling lip of wave after wave that tried to throw him directly into a white maelstrom. The incoming waves were like two story buildings made of water. They loomed above him crazily.

He lost the board; the splitting cold water gave him an instant headache as he went under, paddling for the surface in the washing machine-like currents, searching for the bottom with his feet. He had been out for hours; his strength was already gone from paddling and fighting the cold. Freezing and exhausted, he felt the grim simple reality and helplessness of knowing that he couldn't win. There was no way his strength could match the limitless power of the sea. It had him in its grasp, and it could take him or deliver him up to live. The decision was not his to make.

As his strength flowed into the blackness, and he felt the undertow pulling him backwards out to sea, his numb foot struck the sand. He struggled against the hands of the rushing current, leaning clumsily into the rushing froth. Both feet held tight in the whirling, ripping sands.

He was free.

He staggered in the suddenly shallow water to the shore. The beach was very flat, and the foam seemed to slide forever in curious patterns of conflict.

He limped on deadened feet across the wide sand strand below the bluff and collapsed beside his board. The last bit of sun shone brightly as a cold wind swept over the deserted beach.

A gull sailed effortlessly by, never moving its wings.

Waikiki: Tiny fish jumped around me as I paddle out toward the break in the foaming reef. The Hilton catamaran is just coming into the channel. I hugged the buoy to avoid being run over. I knew they couldn't see me in the darkness of pre-dawn.

It was a long paddle to the waves. The stars faded and a rosy glow lit up the cotton candy clouds over Waikiki. The surf was rolling in with power, foam rushing down the faces on the offshore reef. The water was warmer than the air. The sun would change that soon enough.

There was already one other surfer out in the lifting darkness. He timed the sets with his marine watch. I had seen him before. He was there every morning, like me. He worked for Hawaiian Tel, like me, and had to get his waves before his shift.

Hawaiian waves have a power to them that is amazing. When they break, they re-form and push on all the way to the beach, rushing for a quarter-mile through deep water, pushing you like a machine to the end. I've never felt that power anywhere else. When it is big it can kill you without any effort.

The long board riders had an edge. Bruce the Hulk, a 300 pound Samoan, sat outside at Kaisers and nailed every set. He would pick up the wave on his battered, discolored long board way out there, and swoop with a Babar-like grace on the swell long before any white water showed, carving through the short boarders like a condor through sparrows. Nobody got in Bruce's way.

Down the line a half mile, at Fives, that happy girl did the same thing, catching them all outside. Everybody tried to cut her off because she seemed to welcome company, but she usually had more buoyancy from her huge board and simply ran away from them. Fives is where I decided to add two feet to my board.

When it was big it was like a football field stood on its long edge. The ocean rose up at an unbelievable angle and scared you to death. The warm water made it doable. It wasn't so bad to fight a million gallons of turbulence when it was as pleasant as a bathtub. And the thrill of cascading down one of those mountains was irresistibly addictive.

The North Shore was scarier. Sunset and Pipeline are where the photographers hang out, shooting for next month's *Surfer* or *Surfing* or *WaveRider* or the others. There the currents along the beach moved so quickly, you could drown three feet from shore. The waves were thicker, even more powerful. It was as if a freight train was being whipped sideways under water, the width and breadth of the wave above ponderous, huge, cascading over this underwater bulk, the drop so long that the g's hurt your knees in the bottom turn. I have never felt that weight anywhere but Sunset.

I didn't know there were outer reefs at Turtle Bay until I saw a cascading pile of foam like the white light of dawn on the horizon. As it descended on me, there was nothing to do but lessen the impact. I paddled with it and it hit me hard, a twelve-foot tall mass of churning foam and driving swell. It turned me head-over-toe twice, and spun me three times sideways. Then the sun broke out, and I realized I was in position on the reformed wave, headed toward shore at a good clip. I stood up and rode it in, and called it a day. I felt very lucky.

Off Fort DeRussy, the break is called Fives. It is a series of reefs, with no real focus. One fine day I caught it as it shaped up into endless thin walls of sheer spinning tubes.

"Magazine waves!" I marveled, as the crystal shoulder stretched endlessly before me. I was flying, stretching, speeding to make the wall and it just kept foaming before me, magical and endless. When the warm water splashed into roiling foam, I couldn't stop smiling. It was like stepping into a page of the prettiest picture of surf you ever saw. I rode for hours and staggered to shore, every grain of sand gleaming at me in this special blessed morning.

Later, I was pinned to the coral on the bottom at Kaiser's, under about six feet of water, on my back. I was there long enough to distinctly regard the moment and I thought "This isn't so great." I could see the bright sunshine, glowing blurry up above. I kicked off so hard I cut my foot on the coral, as the big hand let me up a bit.

There was such an abrupt drop to that spot, on some days it felt like stepping into a hole. You and the wave took a vertical trip together, then it would try to throw you as high in the air as you had fallen. After a particularly good crash, the locals would ask each other, "Did you get that elevator job?" with a laugh.

Rowing teams passed by, training. The Hilton catamaran, full of tourists, would scoot by heading for the channel, with a band playing *La Bamba*. Everyone waved. Some famous girl—I think it was Margo Godfrey Oberg—came out. A helicopter hovered over her, and wrecked the waves, trying for a picture.

At dusk the sunset lit the sky pink, and the glowing lights from the hotels and the town were so vivid. The lights onshore grew stronger as the waves became invisible, and the fast foam lit up with phosphorescence as I rushed into shore on a final wave of the day, speeding prone for about a quarter-mile, in the salty, humid hush of evening.

I am on that homebound wave in the darkness, forever.

## 12. *The Bachelor*, Andrew Firestone

I'm supposed to write about hot current topics. A friend suggested Andrew Firestone, *The Bachelor*.

He's rich! Well, his family is. And local! True. For real! unlike Joe Millionaire, who was a total fraud from the get-go. And he's being chased by twenty-five women on national TV!

The premise of this reality show, for those of you watching the war, instead of mindless fluff: 27 year old Andrew Firestone, "a real life millionaire" according to abcNEWS.com, dates 25 women, often at the same time, on camera, dumping a few luckless ones every so often until he winnows it down to "the one."

I don't believe he has to marry her, although the candidates seem to think so.

"This is a unique opportunity to meet a lot of beautiful women who come into this sincerely…without knowing my last name," University of San Diego grad Firestone told abcNEWS.com.

Andrew's parents established the Firestone Winery here in the early 1970's, where he works as sales manager. His stalwart Republican father, former two term Assemblyman Brooks Firestone, is the son of Leonard Firestone, Nixon's pick for Ambassador to Belgium in 1974. Andrew's mother, Catherine Boulton (Kate) Firestone, was a soloist with the British Royal Ballet. They met in London when Brooks was an executive with Firestone Tire and Rubber, founded by his grandfather Harvey.

I tuned in. I tried to watch it. In about five minutes, though, I was afflicted with acute nausea.

Hey, maybe vicarious dating is just not a guy thing. Girls certainly seem to like the show.

I overheard several at the dentist's office picking apart the candidates. They analyzed each moment of the program in excruciating detail.

"Why are they all white trash?" was one plaintive query.

"I don't know why he can't find a nice girl here. There's plenty of them around," sniffed another.

My own question: What would possess these beautiful, talented women to put up with all the varied humiliations imposed upon them on national television?

And not just by a handsome, well-educated heir, which I could sort of grudgingly understand, but by his friends as well, specifically an aiding and abetting couple who, in one particularly egregious invasion of privacy, quizzed the candidates on their sexual habits.

"Sex in the bedroom or sex on the beach?" and so on.

On your average date, that might be seen as an imposition. Speaking of average dates, one of Andrew's real life local pre-*Bachelor* dinner partners said their short time together was among the most boring evenings of her life. He has certainly ratcheted up the action quotient. Now he's into group mud baths at the Ojai Valley Inn. Live and learn.

Then again, these women don't seem to regard anything as an imposition. Apparently lack of self-respect was one of the qualifications for candidacy. They discuss their breast sizes, strip down to next to nothing for a coed massage, cat fight, and get drunk on camera, with no apparent remorse.

The extended Firestone family has something of a cross to bear with all the hubbub. It's fine for Andrew, who is certainly a desirable young guy in his own right. He gets a female feeding frenzy. The winery reaps incredible publicity worth millions. Older brother Adam, originally asked to star but slowed down by a wife and kids, put Andrew up to it, so we suppose he approves. Sisters Polly and Hayley are keeping a low profile.

His parents, meanwhile, suffer a raft of inane queries from the national media. Which is too bad, because in addition to being the single most prominent, wealthy, politically connected family in the Valley, Kate and Brooks Firestone are involved, generous, thoughtful, intelligent, articulate, accomplished, genuinely nice people with fingers in a lot of pies, who have better things to do.

I saw Andrew cut the crowd to three. Oh well. Most of them probably were banking less on a potential relationship than on a sure shot at reality TV stardom anyway. Their fifteen minutes of fame has arrived, and they're going for it. TV writer Joel Brown dismissed the episode in four words: "Sleaze Patrol rides again."

ABC seems determined to wring a few more mind numbing weeks out of this tripe. Eventually, those who can stomach it will discover the last girl to lose.

Groucho Marx once said "I wouldn't belong to any club that would have me as a member." Will the scion of a patrician line really marry someone who went on his TV show to find him?

Here's some reality: the show's been in the can for a while. Dead roses litter the landscape and a few tears may have been shed by all, but no nuptials have been scheduled yet at St. Mark's Episcopal, the Los Olivos church for which the Firestones donated the land.

*Afterword: It didn't last. The chosen one was last seen simultaneously dating 26 guys on a follow up show, *The Bachelorette.*

But Andrew Firestone's fling with fame created cult collectibles on eBay.

"You are bidding on a Firestone Vineyard wooden wine crate/rack. Yes, this is the one and only, Andrew Firestone, from *The Bachelor*, wooden wine crate. It has homely inscriptions on all sides of the box, overlooking a vineyard in one of the leading states in the U.S. in wine making."

Or, you could buy an empty bottle. "Andrew Firestone who was in *THE BACHELOR* and has his own vineyards in Santa Ynez Valley REAL HAND SIGNED BOTTLE OF SYRAH. Guaranteed authentic and comes with a COA from my company Hollywood Heroes. Bottle is empty because I DRANK IT AND LOVED IT. I met Andrew at Stew Leonards store in Farmingdale NY where he was autographing his bottles and taking pictures. Awesome guy and his wine is amazing. check, money order and paypal accepted. winner pays $9 shipping."

Enthusiasm, expressed in capital letters, and indifferent spelling and punctuation, are epidemic in the rush to market on-line.

## 13. The Green Mile

As the garbage man said, business is picking up.

Caltrans recently held California Cleanup Day. Statewide Coordinator Terri Porter urged all the Adopt-A-Highway volunteers in the state to do their duty simultaneously, and report their finds.

It was an impressive effort, resulting in the removal of mountains of crud from our roads. And it hit home with me, for I am an Adopt-A-Highway kind of guy.

After 9/11, I wanted to do something to help. I volunteered to pick up trash. It wasn't Ground Zero, but in a local way it seemed to be constructive.

A possible bonus was the advertising. 20,000 people in cars a day might see a dinky sign with my business' name on it, and only about 10,000 of those would feel compelled to throw something out the window on my two miles. Four miles, if you count both sides. I pick up from Hwy. 246 to the river. It's a pretty walk.

Unfortunately, there's a lot of what UCSB archaeologist Pandora Snethkamp once called "the detritus of a latter day civilization." Most of it is contraband, empty beer cans, vodka and gin bottles, stuff someone didn't want to talk to the nice officer about.

The full beer cans and unopened potato chips I attribute to a cooler blowing out of the boat. That would also account for the Styrofoam chunks. Shredded recaps are heavy, construction debris large. Lots of Marlboro packages. Apparently rugged Marlboro men like to trash the planet while catching cancer.

You would expect hubcaps. The coat, shirts, pants, etc., were a bit of a surprise. Evidently some people amuse themselves while traveling by disrobing and flinging their garments on public highways. I had no idea.

The memorable Day Of 100 Paper Plates And About A Million Napkins was depressing. It had an artsy flair though, sort of like picking up after a Christo exhibition. And what's with all the rubber gloves? Maybe I don't want to know.

Some littering is clearly accidental. Who in their right mind would throw a perfectly good *Bone Thugs 'N Harmony* CD out the window? The full tackle box, complete with a pack of smokes, ready for a day at the lake, is still, I suppose, a source of family spats.

"Where did you put my tackle box?"

"I didn't put it anywhere!"

Etcetera.

The casino trash I can understand. After you've lost all your money, who needs a valet parking ticket and coffee cups to remind you? Out they go. I feel your pain. Mostly in my back.

This must be the Bermuda Triangle of magnetic signs. I found three of them in the bushes. Good news for all of you missing signs! They weren't stolen, they just fell off! Unless some manic crisis comes over drivers here, inducing them to snatch their magnetic identities from their cars and fling them into the bushes. They probably abandon the car at the airport and fly to Fiji.

Other minutiae: I know who the top stockbroker of a local company was last month, because the brokerage's sales report, down to the penny, was stuck on a sagebrush.

I have seen a lot of homework.

"Honest, Teacher! Susie threw it out of the bus!" Sure enough. But who pitches their family photos out the window? There's a novel. And I have lost my love of *Easy-Ad* and *Auto Trader* after finding several thousand of them scattered from hell to breakfast.

I found 22 bags of this kind of cool stuff the first day. That took six hours. Now I can do it in under 3, averaging 11 bags a month. The biggest thing was a car hood. The heaviest thing was a five gallon can of solid cement. The saddest thing was the tightly curled talon of a hawk.

Caltrans' David Martinez instructed me not to pick up dead animals, firearms, or bodies. I call for backup.

Economically speaking, my demented Easter egg hunt has been a bust. No one has come into my office and announced "I'm here because you're a garbage man."

Some probably deliberately stay away, even though I always wear gloves and never get closer than three feet to the junk, thanks to a really marvelously effective little robot arm. It'll pick up anything!

My mother tried repeatedly to find my tiny sign, without success. It's okay, because I'm rewarded spiritually. I get paid in appreciative honks. I average about a honk an hour.

At least, I think they're appreciative. Maybe they just want me to see them throw out their clothes. I wave my shiny tool in salute, and walk on.

# 14. Danish Resistance Heroes

On September 19, 1944, with sabotage and underground activities on the rise, the German troops who had occupied Denmark since 1940 tried to arrest the entire Danish police force.

Twenty-six year old Patrolman Knud Dyby was bicycling to work in Copenhagen when he saw his fellow officers being forced into trucks by the Nazis. His decision was instantaneous.

The daring Mr. Dyby dashed to a building next door to the police station, into a civil patrol office where he was a part-time supervisor, and filled a sack with forms for passports, birth certificates, and identification cards. Too burdened to get back on the bike, he hailed a cab.

He was going underground.

Danish Resistance hero Knud Dyby spoke in Solvang at the Bethania Lutheran Church parish hall, accompanied by author Martha Loeffler, who wrote the book "Boats in the Night," which chronicles his exploits.

The Germans captured 1,900 police officers, about half the force, who were deported to concentration camps. Most of the rest of the officers joined the resistance, aiding a rescue effort that spirited nearly all 7,000 of Denmark's Jews to safety. Only 256 were arrested.

Amid many harrowing, narrow escapes, ex-patrolman Dyby personally rescued around 100, taking on an assumed name, and living in hiding behind a steel plated door. An avid sailor, he knew the best hiding places on the Danish coastline, and the patrol routines of the German navy.

One thousand, eight hundred and forty four refugees, including Allied airmen, saboteurs, Baltic refugees and others, were saved in 700 boat trips to Sweden by the Danish-Swedish refugee service. From September of 1944 until May 4, 1945, Mr. Dyby directed runs by five fishing skippers who crossed the sound hundreds of times with guns, mail, money and 12 fugitives at a time, in 21 foot long boats.

When Denmark's surviving Jews returned after the war, they found their homes and property had been protected by their neighbors.

"What hurt the victims the most was not the cruelty of the Nazis, but the silence of the bystanders," Mr. Dyby told an interviewer.

His courageous work was commended by President Dwight Eisenhower. Israel awarded him the title *Righteous Among the Nations* for his courage and bravery. His name is listed on the commemorative wall in the Avenue of the Righteous of the Nations at Yad Vashem in Jerusalem.

It's a story that resonates in this Danish village. Paul Hanberg of Solvang, who owned Solvang Shoe Store for many years, was part of two resistance operations in Denmark in 1944-1945.

Eighteen years old, he couriered packages of underground newspapers to drop-off points throughout Copenhagen, and was part of a shadowy group called P-4, headed up by a Danish Army officer, who were to rise against the Germans at the American signal.

The Danish army had been disbanded by the Germans in 1943. Mr. Hanberg's group drilled at secret locations in the forest.

When the printer he worked with was captured and sent to a concentration camp, Mr. Hanberg disappeared for two months, working in the opposite end of the country until the coast was clear. His friend returned after the war.

The BBC announced on the night of May 4, 1945, that the occupation would end the following day. Mr. Hanberg rendezvoused with over a hundred P-4 members, who took up arms and attacked a German barracks at a nearby school. They were driven off by rifle fire, but the Germans soon packed up and marched home.

# 15. Day in the Life of a Realtor

A brief history of time: the dinosaurs roamed the prehistoric world. They died and fell into swamps, where they turned into unleaded gasoline.

Realtors then evolved, to use up the gas.

Full disclosure: I am a Realtor. I am the owner/broker of Ranchland Real Estate, in Los Olivos, California.

I knew something was wrong with my job when my dog Loki refused to go to work with me. She crawled under the bed, put her paws over her eyes, and wouldn't budge.

As a 20 year veteran of the real estate wars, I assure you, this is a difficult profession. Ideally one has the patience of a saint, nerves of steel, the wisdom of Solomon, the luck of the Irish, wolf-like reflexes, rich friends AND a nice car.

Realtor aptitude test: Jump off the Empire State Building. If you yell "All right so far!" at each window you pass on the way down, you've got potential.

If the name wasn't taken, they'd call us waiters. We wait, endlessly, for people to call, show up, make up their minds, buy, sue us, etc.

The perfect Realtor would probably be a dropout from the French Foreign Legion, inured to chaos, death and disfigurement. A hopeless romantic, answering glorious bugle calls against impossible odds.

When someone walks through my door I don't know them from Adam. They could be escaped convicts looking for a getaway car. I have about ten seconds to convince total strangers that I am worthy of helping them spend vast sums of money.

Job two is to find out if they have vast sums of money. In a society where everyone is coy about their finances, this is not easy.

They sometimes turn homicidal when they find out a fixer starts at $700,000 in Los Olivos. One woman from Wisconsin turned bright red and advanced on me with her fists clenched in the air. I was saved by her husband, who grabbed her and dragged her bodily from the office. "Honey, it's not his fault," he assured her on the way out.

And it isn't. Sellers want top dollar for their homes, and buyers willing to pay make the market. The Realtor is just along for the ride. If I could make prices do what I want I would have retired long ago.

Brochures in the window help break the news. Some passersby laugh, some are outraged. If they're from Montecito they say "Gee, this isn't bad at all." The really sad part is that there is almost no way in the world for a young person to save enough money to buy a house. Unless you have help, you can't get into the game.

Once I begin to actually show property, it is good to know every price of every house on every street. It is even better to know the life history of every person, place and thing you pass and be able to amusingly pass it along.

Meanwhile, I'm fumbling through a bulky Multiple Listing Service book, juggling appointments on the cell phone because my carefully laid out schedule was blown up when they arrived an hour late, had seen the first three homes with another agent, and hated the next three so much they wouldn't get out of the car.

This while avoiding major traffic accidents, trying to remember their names, and wishing I'd bought gas and gone to the bathroom. Plus I'm getting calls from people who listed yesterday, demanding "Why haven't you sold it yet?"

And calls from people already in escrow, saying they've decided not to sell.

If they do buy something, we enter a dark tangled jungle of legalese, inspectors, contractors, and form after form until you can't believe there's a tree left standing.

In 1982 the basic purchase contract was one page, and half of that was spare blanks. Now it's ten pages of small print, and that's just the start of a river of disclosure forms designed to protect everyone from the nightmare of litigation that has consumed the industry.

We tackle sex offenders, mold, minerals, toxics, quakes, flood, fire, septic, termites, radon, title, financing, easements and endless ordinances, just for starters. In this haunted swamp, spooks jump out at all turns, until the sale either limps to the finish line or falls apart. Real estate is like a horror film: just when you think things couldn't get any worse, they do.

Most clients are a joy. Some become lifelong friends. And a few turn into mad dogs, consumed by greed. You never really know someone until you have done a deal with them.

Oh, well. To each his own, and may yours be a happy home.

\* Tracking prices by the screams: The swearometer is off the charts outside my office these days, as people look at the brochures in the window and scream bloody murder. One man yelled "Sick! Sick! Sick!" as he stomped off.

# 16. Of Gophers, Rural Peril & The Meaning of Life

This week in Solvang, O.J. Reichmann asks the age old question, "Why are there gophers?"

Why indeed. I have often pondered just this very thing, usually while staring in stunned disbelief at mounds of dirt as tall as the Pyramids, which appeared overnight to devastate a pristine greensward.

My cat Huckle thinks gophers are here for his amusement. After I say "Hucklecat, let's go out to eat" and pitch him out the door, he can sit for hours peering into a teeny tunnel.

Fortunately for Mr. Gopher, Huckle's Zen-like zeal hasn't helped his hunting. He's never caught anything but a toy mouse, unlike Cotton The Warrior, who would drape his trophies on the windshield of the car to ensure proper credit for his work.

But I digress. The public is invited to a free lecture by UCSB Professor and Mammologist O.J. Reichman titled, *Why Are There Gophers? The Role of Underground Herbivores in Natural Ecosystems.* Mark the calendar.

Dr. Reichman is Director of the National Center for Ecological Analysis and Synthesis in Santa Barbara, Professor in the Department of Ecology, Evolution, and Marine Biology at UCSB, and past president of the Society of Mammologists.

All ages are welcome. No gophers need apply.

Living in the country, we have many animal friends. A lecture on wild (okay! feral!) pigs would be nice. Pigologists tell me that feral pigs, as opposed to true wild pigs, are ex-cons, someone's pet or project ham now living a life on the lam.

A big black boar leads nightly raids on my lawn, accompanied by a gang of snooty porcine pals, giving a whole new dimension to boorish behavior. Fish and Game, clearly in the pig's pocket, won't return frenzied phone calls for help.

If you think Kendall-Jackson is hard on oak trees, you've never seen a pack of pigs roto-till acres of little seedlings to mush. Since we can't seem to get rid of them—and there are dozens of them rooting up the grass, tilling for acorns—perhaps we can understand and even learn to love them.

But I doubt it. Imagine a dark night on a twisty country road, winding ever deeper through the scary forest. Suddenly, about a zillion beady, disembodied eyes appear in your headlights, accompanied by a hideous chorus of mad grunting and the staccato clatter of scrambling cloven hooves on a small sea of belligerent bacon. Folks, it's a sight.

We could use a coyote seminar. It may help prepare me for the day those ghostly wraiths who haunt the foothills eat Huckle. Or me. Not too long ago, in broad daylight, a mangy looking coyote stalked my wife and I as we were out for a walk, waiting, I suppose, for us to weaken and drop in our tracks. "I don't have to outrun the coyote," she said. "I just have to outrun you."

One Christmas day, eight deer walked in single file through the back yard, looking for all the world as if Santa had given them the rest of the day off. Deer are truly lovely, gentle creatures. Outraged gardeners know them as voracious consumers of every flower known to man, even the ones advertised as deer-proof. Roses are their favorite. And Bambi can jump a seven foot fence.

A voyeuristic bobcat once peered into my bathroom window. He didn't seem afraid, boldly sauntering off after being busted.

Years ago, Cotton The Warrior saved my kids from a rattler who slithered onto the lawn where they were playing. He fearlessly attacked, jumping and hissing around the sizeable satanic serpent until the main body of troops could move in. That day we added "The Warrior" to his name.

Colonel Coats' donkeys Eeyore and Brighty used to like to play *The Fugitive* in my landscaping, munching and crunching around midnight. And three heifers who had decided not to grow up to be Big Macs after all once trooped through my yard, leaving tokens of their appreciation on their way to freedom.

By far the worst incursion, though, was on a day of resurrection. One sunny Easter afternoon, two horseback riders and their dogs came by on the road. After the riders passed, their dogs cornered Cotton The Warrior.

Cotton had walked out of the sagebrush and into our lives about twelve years before. He was the kids' best friend as they grew up. Unless you were a gopher, a kinder, wiser, gentler, more noble cat you could not imagine.

My son found him under the big oak tree. I'll never forget his tear-stained, stricken face.

"Cotton's dead!" he cried.

For an encore, the marauders loped off down the street and killed the neighbor's cat, too.

Life is a miracle. Enjoy it while you can.

## 17. Edward Borein

We're lucky to have numerous fine small museums here, including the Elverhoj, the SYV Historical Society Museum and Parks-Janeway Carriage House, Hans Christian Andersen Museum, Solvang Motorcycle Museum, and the Wildling Museum.

I can't say enough good things about the remarkable Elverhoj Museum in Solvang. Named after Denmark's most famous folk play, the name means "Elves on a Hill."

It's in an unlikely spot in a residential area of Solvang, formerly the home of internationally recognized Danish artist Viggo Brandt-Erichsen and his wife Martha Mott. Permanent exhibits include items from early Denmark, a child's room, early Solvang settlers and the "best room," a typical Danish parlor.

The show *Capturing the California Vaquero* was a spectacular presentation of one of the West's finest artists, Santa Barbara's own Edward Borein. Director Marilyn Cronk masterfully assembled etchings, drawings, illustrated book covers, printing plates, and watercolors; priceless items from private collections.

Born in 1872 in San Leandro, California, Borein dropped out of art school in San Francisco after just one month to become a cowboy. Among other ranches, Borein cowboyed on the 45,000 acre Rancho Jesus Y Lolita near Lompoc before it became Vandenberg Air Force Base. A fine La Purisima Mission etching may date from that period, when he would sketch in the saddle during the day, then revisit the drawings with India ink by the light of the campfire.

He also worked on the Hacienda Babicora in Mexico, a 500,000 acre ranch owned by the Hearst family, in an area immortalized in Cormac McCarthy's superb novel, *All the Pretty Horses*. There Borein helped drive 3,800 cattle to New Mexico. It was an era that was passing as he sketched.

He lived in Santa Barbara from 1921 until his death in 1945, and his El Paseo studio was legendary in the art world.

It was Borein who in 1929 came up with the idea of Los Rancheros Visitadores, the men's riding group whose annual pilgrimage draws the rich and powerful from across the nation to sleepy Santa Ynez for riding and revelry in remote rustic camps scattered about the Valley.

Borein, who counted among his friends Theodore Roosevelt, Charlie Russell, Will Rogers, Maynard Dixon, and countless other influential western figures, once told his friend Fred Warde, "I will leave only an accurate history of the West, nothing else but that. If anything isn't authentic or just right, I won't put it in any of my work."

The show included remarkable etchings and water colors loaned by Linda Paitch and Jim Grimm, Pat and Monty Roberts, Linda Kohn and Joseph Sherwood, Kenneth Shields, Richard and June Christensen, Roger and Christina Haley and sons Bret, Brad, and Bryan, and Maxine Michaelis.

*California Vaquero* was once part of the Katherine H. Haley collection. That legendary collector called it "probably one of the finest watercolors ever painted by Borein, because of the quality of the draftsmanship plus the beautiful action of the principal figures." It's particularly evocative, as is *Horse Bucking Rider*. *Overland Mail Stage* practically makes you seasick with its joltingly realistic portrayal of the flying team and stagecoach.

## 18. Do The Rancheros Visitadores Rule America?

The Learjet smoothly cruised to a stop on the taxiway at tiny Santa Ynez airport, after a short, searing touchdown on the streaked asphalt strip pilots know as Runway Two Six.

The door stair swung open with a pneumatic hiss. A lanky man in denim, boots and cowboy hat sauntered down the steps, and casually tossed his duffel and a rifle case on the ground.

A Ranchero had arrived.

Not all of the Rancheros Visitadores arriving this week have their own jet, but they all share membership in a group with an undeniably rich cachet. Ever since the all male riding group was born in 1930, brainchild of cowboy artist Edward Borein, it has been the domain of wealthy, powerful, connected men from all walks of life. The name means "visiting ranchers."

It's among the ultimate in exclusive networking opportunities, some say second only to the storied Bohemian Grove retreat held annually in the redwoods 65 miles north of San Francisco. Herbert Hoover called the Grove gathering "the greatest men's party on earth."

Prophetic professor G. William Dornhoff of UC Santa Cruz asked if Bohemians and Rancheros ruled America in his 1967 tome *Who Rules America?* His conclusion: They'd like to.

Sure enough, in 1981, Visitadore-Bohemian Ronald Reagan ascended to the Presidency of the US. For eight years, a Ranchero was in the number one saddle in the world.

Bohemian and Yale grad John J. Mitchell, a director emeritus of United Airlines and husband of Lolita Armour of the famed Chicago meat packing family, ran with Borein's inspiration, structuring a Bohemian Grove on horseback for 1930. Numerous carriages now in the SY Museum came from Mitchell, who used them on the annual rides.

The Mitchells owned the 12,000 acre Juan y Lolita ranch on Refugio Road on the Santa Ynez River, including a sprawling, 10,000 square foot hacienda later acquired in turn by Jimmy Stewart and Dean Martin.

The RVs start the annual week long outing at the Jackson Camp on Alisal Ranch, riding to the Mission Santa Inés Saturday for a blessing by a priest. Then, to the call "Ride, Rancheros, ride!," they hit the dusty trail towards Lake Cachuma, on horses aglitter with silver tack, over 700 strong.

Clark Gable, Walt Disney, Art Linkletter, Thomas Storke, Eisenhower's Assistant Secretary of Defense, Charles Finucane; Mercury, Gemini, and Apollo astronaut Wally Schirra, Reagan's Secretary of the Interior, William P. Clark; Marine Corps Commandant and member of the Joint Chiefs of Staff, Paul Kelley; and many, many more have enjoyed the ride, as members or guests.

Entry to the exclusive club, which emphasizes a common love of horsemanship and the outdoors, is by invitation only. There are different categories of belonging, and full membership may take years. Within the club are sub-camps with their own names, including Los Borrachos, Los Chingadores, Los Flojos, Los Bandidos, Los Tontos, Los Amigos, Los Piscadores, and Los Vigilantes. There are said to be over seventeen in all.

Safe in the closed camps along the riding route, some members delight in acting as outrageously as possible, but nobody's talking on the record. "Whiskeydore" stories are hard to verify. After all, who'd want some of the richest, most powerful men in America mad at you?

"You wouldn't believe what goes on in there," a wide-eyed videographer once hired to document the revels claimed. In 1997, a miffed wife talked of a breakfast served by topless waitresses. Photos of a rider who liked to wear a Nazi uniform slipped out in 1969.

In town, teenage waitresses have been reduced to tears by the vacationing cowboys. Others report generous tips. Hotel manager Hazel Sechler said of the Visitadores' 1958 visit, "I never was much afraid of anything after that."

A broken rider too inebriated to speak for himself was reportedly once sent to the local hospital with a diagnosis and prescription penned on his bare chest by a physician member.

On May 7, 1988, a Visitadore from San Francisco died at the Mollekroen bar in Solvang after being decked by a local welder in a midnight melee. The autopsy blamed an aneurysm.

Their meals are catered, and the entertainment is first class. "Minstrel of the Range" Don Edwards, "the best purveyor of cowboy music in America today," according to Bobby Weaver of the National Cowboy Hall of Fame, was one performer at 2004's party.

In 1955, co-founder J.J. Mitchell, ending 25 years as El Presidente, wrote "All the pledges and secret oaths in the universe cannot tie men, our kind of men, together like the mutual appreciation of a beautiful horse, the moon behind a cloud, a song around the campfire or a ride down the Santa Ynez Valley. These are experiences common on our ride, but unknown to most of our daily lives."

"Our organization, to all appearances, is the most informal imaginable. Yet there are men here who see one another once a year, yet feel a bond closer than between those they have known all their lives."

## Part 2. Was Clarence Mattei Robbed?

Part of the thrill of being an esteemed columnist: the mortar rounds that come in out of left field, shortly after the paper thwacks down in the driveway by the dawn's early light.

The Rancheros Visitadores have ridden off into the sunset for another year, but the dust evidently has yet to settle on who takes the credit/blame for their boys only horseback jaunt in the first place.

Retired U.S. Navy Lieutenant Commander James B. Canby IV thinks artist Clarence Mattei deserves some of the credit given to Edward Borein for the brainstorm that led to the raucous riders.

"For over 50 years, Clarence has taken a backseat to Ed Borein," Mr. Canby writes from his home in the Pacific Northwest.

"My mother gave me your article before I left Santa Barbara. She was somewhat surprised at the accolades provided specifically to Ed Borein. I packed my bags in my father's den, gazed at the four Boreins on the wall, and the special one of the Bell Mare that Borein did for my parents as a wedding gift.

"A generally accepted story may, in fact, be controversial. What you attribute to Mr. Borein was probably more evolutionary than revolutionary," claims Mr. Canby.

"I have to wonder whether Dr. Luton, Selden Spaulding, Harold Chase, William Walker and Edgar Park were in the party," he said. "Major Fleishmann would make sure he had a part. Reggie Fernald would have been fun.

"The official ride of 1930 does not appear too ambitious, sticking close to the river from Dwight Murphy's to the Alisal. I grew up listening to stories about these people. It is as if I knew them.

"Some 70 years ago, my mother rode her horse on regular occasions from San Roque down to Hendry's Beach for a swim. It was not unusual for a group of friends to go on a ride. Next to my mother's home on Ontare Road were the Dabneys. They had a cabin on the Manzana river. It was not uncommon for them to go on pack trips with friends into the back country. I have over on my desk, a black and white photo of my Grandmother Margaret Waterman, taken at

Davy Brown cabin about 1910, with Jessie Boyd and Donald Myrick, David Myrick's father.

"In my home, I have the Mattei print of my grandmother, Margaret Waterman, but I also have two pieces of turn of the century Los Olivos characters, done by Clarence, in pencil, at the age of 16," he continued.

"I think you miss the color and flavor of the community of the time. On this recent visit, my mother explained to me that clubs and fraternal organizations abounded when she grew up. Getting together with chums was more than just commonplace. My grandmother Rogers and Mrs. Borein were in a club together called P.E.O. No one has any idea what it means. My grandfather always believed it stood for "Phone Each Other."

"It was a very small, very tight community. My grandmother Margaret died at a very early age, having fallen on the steps leading to Clarence Mattei's studio where she had been attending a party. Clarence Mattei's studio was directly above Ed Borein's. They were chums. They had two things in common, love of the old west, and love of art.

"To declare Rancheros Visitadores as the brainchild of Ed Borein is liberal journalistic license indeed," concludes Mr. Canby.

Well, scholars? This is your chance to weigh in. I have no personal bias. It was Elmer Awl who told historian Walker Tompkins that Borein suggested an annual event while dining at Mattei's Tavern with Awl and Jack Mitchell after the 1930 ride, as told in Tompkins's 1974 *Mattei's Tavern*.

One thing's for sure: Clarence Mattei, whose father Felix founded the famed Los Olivos landmark, was an outstanding artist. Tompkins wrote "Clarence had the good fortune to catch the eye of Mrs. Herman Duryea of New York, whose husband used Mattei's Tavern as a base camp while on hunting expeditions. They sent Clarence to art school in San Francisco in 1901-02, where he won a scholarship to a New York academy which sent him to Paris for six years of study at the Julian Academy of Art."

"He ran a studio in New York from 1910 until moving to Santa Barbara in 1922, during which period he did charcoal portraits or oil paintings of some of America's most famous people," says Tompkin's book.

Clarence Mattei's most famous oil painting, entitled *Pinochle*, of his father and cohort Gustave Berg at the tavern's card table, once hung in the Metropolitan Museum of Art.

## Part 3. The Past is Not Dead

Nobel Prize winning novelist William Faulkner wrote "The past is never dead. It's not even past."

Born in the South, albeit to carpetbaggers, I've always had an affinity for Wild Bill and his tortured characters that probably sets my Union veteran ancestors to kicking their crypts. Long before I was an English major at UCSB, I found the twisted cypress swamps of his southern novels, draped everywhere with the swaying Spanish moss of human misery, irresistible.

That quote always resonated, but never more so than during the past week, as the murky waters of Rancheros Visitadore history swirled around what has to be the least important question of the century: Whose bright idea was the horseback boys' club, anyway?

Perhaps because there's so little at stake, readers have stormed the electronic barricades in a curiously passionate debate, unfortunately throwing off more heat than light, so far.

James B. Canby IV started the current ruckus, when he claimed that artist Clarence Mattei deserves equal billing with Edward Borein for thinking up the RVs.

"I don't think Clarence is the one," says Los Olivos historian Jim Norris. "It would more likely have been someone in the Los Alamos Society, which existed for twenty years before the Rancheros."

Mr. Norris brought me Harold Keeney Doulton's *I Remember*, which credits J. J. Mitchell for bringing to fruition an idea spawned by Borein, Elmer Awl and Sam Kramer. Doulton worked with the RVs for 31 years, retiring as assistant manager, and is a man of few words. "Nothing particularly unusual happened on the rides from 1949 through 1955," he wrote.

Edward A. Hartfeld forwarded a chapter from his 85,000 word work in progress, the *Dwight Murphy Memorial Project*. The first official ride traversed Murphy's Los Prietos ranch on May 9, 1930. "I have never seen anything authoritative that contradicts the notion that both Ed Borein and J.J. Mitchell jointly deserve credit for the idea," says Mr. Hartfeld.

The RV's own fiftieth anniversary history says the ride "began in a thought that occurred to J.J. Mitchell in the summer of 1929…under the giant redwood trees in the Bohemian Grove."

The rich riders, meanwhile, honored me by sending round a personal emissary straight out of the pages of Andy Adams' 1902 classic, *Log of a Cowboy*. The long, tall Marlboro man, whose local roots date back to Presidio days, delivered a message: the RVs are sick of publicity, be it good, bad or indifferent.

What is this, *The Sopranos*? I'll never even get close to matching his writing, but I can be just as contrary as Faulkner, who reportedly quit his postmaster job back in the days of cheap stamps because he didn't want to be at the beck and call of anybody with two cents. Some say "A stranger rides into town" is the only story line in all of literature. Five hundred cowboys riding into town is a never-ending novel. Bury me not on the lone prairie.

Mr. Canby also wondered what PEO stood for. "I was at a PEO meeting yesterday," said June Blakely. It's the Philanthropic and Educational Organization for Women, a sisterhood 250,000 strong. They've given girls $88 million in scholarships since their founding in 1869 at Iowa Wesleyan College.

Third generation Barbareno Shirley Rouse Roby writes "My mother, Stella Haverland Rouse, was born in Santa Barbara in 1908 and wrote a daily column for the *News-Press* called "In Old Santa Barbara" and a Sunday column called *Olden Days*. She gleaned her information using the old newspapers which were stored in the tower at the *News Press*, and later microfilm copies when those papers were no longer available. She ONLY published facts which she found in the papers and many times did extensive research to make sure that THOSE articles were accurate. If some old timer told her a story she made sure the facts jibed with the 'memories' before she published. If she could not verify, she did not publish.

"Unfortunately, it is because of people too lazy to do research, and swayed by the interesting stories of the old duffers, that history gets changed over the years," writes Ms. Roby.

"Facts and truth really don't have much to do with each other," mused William Faulkner.

# 19. President Reagan Looks Down On the Danes

Meanwhile, back at the ranch: Ronald Reagan relaxed at his 680 acre ranch here, "Rancho Del Cielo" (Ranch of the Sky). He bought it in 1974, when he was still Governor, and he loved it atop the Santa Ynez mountains, close to heaven, as the name implied.

Riding with Nancy, chopping wood, or just taking in the incredible views made him happy. The Danish village and the Santa Ynez Valley stretched out far below him; clouds drifted past the modest adobe cottage he had personally remodeled.

He was up at the ranch, in a jovial mood, the day he joked, "The bombing starts in five minutes." Blame it on too much fresh air.

His neighbors, overwhelmingly, were proud to have him nearby. They held an annual "Reagan Country Roundup," raising funds for the Republican Party. They winced when the press called it his "Santa Barbara" ranch. And they cried when he died in 2004.

My brother, Bert Etling, editor of *The Cambrian*, wrote for the *Santa Ynez Valley News* when Ronald Reagan came down the mountain from his Rancho Del Cielo here to add his vote to a landslide 1984 win.

"When Reagan handed in his absentee ballot in Solvang in 1984—he was in a Valley precinct, but it was one so small everyone automatically was issued an absentee ballot—I was a cub reporter assigned to a national news story," said Bert Etling.

"That Tuesday afternoon, I got into the same news-pen on the front lawn of the Veterans Memorial Building in Solvang as the national press, as we awaited the Reagan motorcade. Some curious fourth estaters inquired as to why the spelling for the Valley and the Mission across the street were different." (According to the Mission: "The Spanish for Agnes is Inés, hence the name of the church; the American Yankees anglicized the spelling of the Spanish pronunciation and named the town Santa Ynez.")

"Protesters hung off what was then the Security Pacific Bank sign across the street. Finally, the limo pulled up after the trek from the SYV Airport, where stalwart reporter Jill Pettley Schafer was staked out."

"A helicopter had taken the president and first lady from the old Tip-Top Ranch, renamed Rancho del Cielo when Reagan took over, to the Valley floor. In the seconds it took the president and first lady to stride the 40 or so steps into the hall, I snapped off about a dozen shots.

"After the party reemerged, flowed back into the vehicles and sped off, a pool reporter came out and told of how Reagan handed in his ballot and, in his usual charming manner, made small talk with the lady at the booth, who happened to be the senior poll volunteer on duty, a sweet white haired lady."

*The Valley News* reported on 11-8-84 that Barbara Thomsen, Helen Askler, Elaine Johanson, and Barbara Poulsen staffed polling place 219. Asked by the President what township he should write on the address line of the ballot, Askler replied "We want to claim you for Solvang."

"Good," the President said, "I want to be claimed by Solvang."

"The ladies were taken by the cordiality of the security men, but wondered about the rather haughty looking dog that was brought in early in the morning to sniff for explosives."

"Asked if the German Shepherd was friendly, a Secret Serviceman replied 'He loves people—but he hates bombs.'"

"He said, 'That's not important' when a reporter asked him how he was voting," Solvang resident Gerald Ehresman related. "He gestured at the other voters in the room and said 'What's important is how they vote.'"

"After the film was developed in the *Valley News* darkroom, managing editor King Merrill whipped out the huge magnifying glass he used to look at negatives, disdaining the linen tester/loop favored by darkroom rats."

"Yeah, you got 'em there," he said of one shot, showing RR flashing his smile, waving, with Nancy, Ed Meese, other 'kitchen cabineters' and Secret Service men alongside. It ran four columns wide on the front page."

"Of course, King Merrill fought a valiant but losing battle to call it Reagan's Santa Ynez Valley, not Santa Barbara, ranch."

"One of his gift horses, this one from the Mexican president of Mexico, was kept on a Valley ranch. We saw him speak at the dedication of the Avenue of Flags (there's a photo on the wall at Pea Soup's). He was a friend of screen writer Vince Evans. They set up tents outside Evans' Danish Inn when Reagan came to fundraisers there as governor."

"I heard him at Stanford in 1978 and 1980. He connected in a Lincolnesque manner, in that he spoke plainly, and to the people," said Bert Etling.

Ambassador Ulrik Andreas Federspiel and his wife, Dr. Birgitte Federspiel, visited Solvang's Elverhoj Museum, mingling with about 50 Solvang residents at an informal champagne reception. The ambassador, who was sworn in as Denmark's Ambassador to the United States in May of 2000, was right at home in this Danish valley of the horse. Dressage aficionados, the Federspiels brought Samir, a magnificent Danish Warmblood, with them to Washington. "I've seen some lovely horses here," said Birgitte Federspiel.

"Before Samir, my wife had a horse that was given to President Reagan," noted the Ambassador. That was an Andalusian named Numantino, a gift from Spain, donated by the President to the National Center for Therapeutic Riding in Maryland, where Birgitte Federspiel took riding lessons.

The couple have been in southern California visiting Danish manufacturers and Danish cultural institutions.

Ambassador Federspiel promised to pass on an invitation to Solvang's centennial in 2011 to the Queen. "That should be enough lead time," he laughed. "Actually, I was the Queen's secretary, so I'll just tell my successor she already agreed to it."

"The city is much bigger than I expected," the Ambassador told the crowd.

"We took him to Los Olivos and Santa Ynez," quipped Mayor Smyser.

"I think the most famous remark about Solvang in Denmark is from 1995," the ambassador related.

"Our prime minister paid a state visit to President Reagan in the White House. In a speech, President Reagan said 'Actually, we are neighbors.'"

"The prime minister thought he meant the Atlantic Alliance."

"Then President Reagan said, 'Only a small river divides us, not a real river.'"

"The Prime Minister was still puzzled."

"Then President Reagan said, "I am looking down at you every day, and I voted at your place.'"

"The Prime Minister thought this was really off the mark."

"Then Reagan explained, 'I live above Solvang.'"

# 20. Saddlemaker To The Stars

"What's the most important thing in a saddle?" I asked a man who made thousands.

"The customer," laughed Art Hugenberger. He spent a lifetime in the trade.

When he made Ronald Reagan's saddle, the ex-actor was running for governor. "I made him a western saddle, with a little design on it, some flowers in the corners," recalled Mr. Hugenberger, a 40 year Solvang resident.

The most decorated American soldier of World War II, hero Audie Murphy, rode a custom Hugenberger saddle, after mustering out. "It was a little a-fork saddle, if I remember right, a little rough-side out. It was for movie work. I tried to make it look something like they were riding back in the old West."

Mr. Hugenberger had his own World War II experience, earning a Purple Heart on March 6, 1945. "I was in Italy. I was a quartermaster, in the 10$^{th}$ Mountain Division. We were about eight miles from Bologna, still in the mountains, going forward, but it was slow."

"We were just doing some odd jobs up there at the time. They were dropping shells everywhere we were at. And I happened to get in close to one."

The shrapnel wound sent him home. He laughs about it now. "I was in the wrong place," he concludes.

He crafted saddles for many Hollywood riders and stars during his career, including "High Noon" star Gary Cooper.

"We had San Fernando Valley Saddlery, and we did a lot of work with the stunt riders and riding extras. They used to hang around there when they weren't working, and get their calls through our phone."

Western matinee idols "The Singing Cowboy" Rex Allen, versatile actor Joel McCrea, and Dale Robertson (63 films!) were clients.

Born in 1919, Art got the cowboy bug early, while growing up in San Diego.

"I grew up right in town, close to Mission Valley, which at that time was a rural area, farms and dairies and so forth. I used to go after school and hang around a stable there. That's where I got my start with horses."

Just out of high school, he signed on with Montie Montana's Western Road Show and hit the dusty trail.

"We traveled all over the western United States to different rodeos. That was quite interesting to me, 'cause I hadn't seen any of those places, you know."

A versatile jack-of-all-trades, the young adventurer sometimes filled in as a stunt rider. Crafting and repairing tack for the show, he gleaned secrets of leathercraft from master saddlers all over the country.

They even played the Aloha State. In 1939, at 20 years of age, he was in Hawaii for three weeks with the wild west show.

"We put on a rodeo. A few of the local Hawaiians got into it. They were good cowboys, some of them," he recalled.

In the mid-1950's, he moved to Santa Barbara and worked for Jedlicka's Saddlery. In 1964 he set up shop in Solvang. For many years, he made the prize saddle for the Champion Stock Horse of the Santa Ynez Valley Horse Show.

Saddle making is a collaboration.

"You use a saddle tree to start out," Mr. Hugenberger explained. "There's different styles. I ordered mine from Kenny Haws, in Utah. That's all they do, is saddle trees. You give them the dimensions and they're specialty made. They're pine, to be lightweight. The strength is in the rawhide cover that they put on the tree, not in the wood."

"You buy the saddle leather from a tannery. You order the silver from the silversmith, the pieces the customer wants, and then you mount it."

A working saddle takes from 25 hours up. When he retired five years ago, $2,000 bought a basic model.

"And it goes up from there, whatever you do to it."

Robert and Debbie Esser recently donated a Hugenberger saddle to the Santa Ynez Valley Historical Society Museum.

"It's kind of a fancy saddle, not real fancy, but it had a lot of flowers on it and a quilted seat. Kind of a trail saddle, I would say, and you could show in it also." He made it around 1994.

It can be seen at the Santa Ynez Valley Historical Museum and Carriage House, 3596 Sagunto Street.

# 21. Living the Tuskegee Legacy

"Memorial Day celebrates Americans who fought and died to preserve our freedom," said Arthur Hicks. "As a Tuskegee Airman, Memorial Day, 1945, had particular meaning."

"The Tuskegee Airmen, who had disproved the predictions of the pre-World War II War Department by their highly decorated performances for escorting bombers over Europe, returned to the segregated society that they fought for," said Mr. Hicks. "In part, President Harry Truman integrated the Armed Forces in 1948 in recognition of that performance."

Honored guests Arthur and Edith Hicks rode in a convertible in the Santa Maria Elks Parade Memorial Day Parade in 2004, representing the unit Mr. Hicks was in at the war's close, the $477^{nd}$ Composite Group, made up of the $99^{th}$, $301^{st}$, $302^{nd}$, and $477^{th}$ Bomb Squadron.

They're better known as the Tuskegee Airmen. Sixty-six pilots in the separate, all African-American unit were killed in action or accidents as they flew 15,000 combat sorties and earned 150 Distinguished Flying Crosses, 744 Air Medals, and 14 Bronze Stars. They never lost a single bomber under escort.

Ironically, in 1989, there were no African-Americans in local Elks lodges. Elks voted by dropping white (yes) and black (no) balls in a jar. Just three black balls overruled any majority. It was Art Hicks, in his quiet, persistent manner, who triggered a change.

"I believe that positive social change is the foundation of our democratic nation," said Mr. Hicks. Born in Sparta, Georgia in 1922, a middle child in a family of four boys and five girls, Arthur Norris Hicks grew up in the segregated south, riding on the back of the bus, using separate drinking fountains, separate waiting rooms in train stations, buying special socks before he could try on a shoe, handed a special cap before he could try on a hat.

"Segregation was based on hatred, and I mean absolute hatred," he remembered. "Rocks were thrown through our windows with notes, saying "Move out, Niggers!'"

Just out of high school, Mr. Hicks saw a poster in an Atlanta Post Office, recruiting mechanic trainees for a program at Tuskegee Institute, founded by the famed Booker T. Washington. In 1943, he soloed in a little yellow Piper Cub, training to become a civilian flight instructor for the Army Air Corps.

He graduated from the cadet corps at Tuskegee Army Air Field in May of 1945, just missing the action.

"I was disappointed," he remembered. "I wanted badly to be a part of the action." He served in Ohio, Tennessee, Alaska, Texas, Nebraska, California. As the years went on, he found himself fighting a lonely war against bigotry in the military.

In Murfreesboro, Tennessee, "Blacks could only use the pool on Wednesday,' said Mr. Hicks. "On Wednesday night at closing time, the pool was emptied, scrubbed down, and refilled, and blacks couldn't go into it again until next Wednesday. It was necessary to speak out."

"It's been a seemingly never-ending battle," said Mr. Hicks. "On arriving at Vandenberg AFB in 1963, family housing on base was limited and off base housing for blacks in the local area was non-existent." He served for 28 years in all, retiring as a Titan II missile guidance superintendent in 1971.

He began a second career in education. He taught at Cabrillo High, earned his master's, worked on a PhD, taught at Allan Hancock and Chapman College. He was on the Board of the Lompoc Unified School district for 12 years.

In 1989, angered by the treatment of an African-American policeman who had worked with the Elks on barbeques and in the kitchen, yet was denied admission to the Lompoc Elks Lodge, Mr. Hicks and his wife and son began a letter writing campaign to clubs, churches, schools, city councils, newspapers, county supervisors, and state Senator Gary Hart.

"My motive was to change a pattern in the institution that denigrated African-Americans," says Mr. Hicks. "I taught social institutions at Allan Hancock. The Elks' membership criteria effectively barred African-Americans, Jews, Mexicans, Indians, all but white Christians. After having served 28 years in the military protecting our freedom, I questioned why I was doing nothing to change this type of practice in such a highly regarded social institution. It was a wake-up moment. I had to get up and do something."

He banged out countless heartfelt appeals on his battered Apple computer, but hit a brick wall. The local Elks pointed their finger at the national rulebook. Gary Hart referred Mr. Hicks to Santa Ynez attorney Michael Balaban.

The controversy now involved the National Association for the Advancement of Colored People (NAACP) as well.

Mediator Balaban suggested that Mr. Hicks and the NAACP agree not to boycott the Elk's parade, if the Lompoc Elks attending the upcoming national convention would attempt to have the voting rules for membership admission changed.

It was a long shot, but at their 1989 New Orleans gathering, the Elks eliminated the three vote "blackball" nationwide.

Mr. Hicks is selection chair for the Tuskegee Airmen's scholarship fund, which grants $60,000 a year to deserving students. His daughter and her husband are attorneys, with two kids at Harvard. One of his sons is Director of Design Engineers for a Silicon Valley firm, another an artist in Seattle.

"One cannot know what life holds in store until one acts," he believes. "Such is the legacy of the Tuskegee Airmen."

## Part 2. A Roll Call of Honor, Written In Blood

American Legion Post 160 holds three services on Memorial Day, including honor guard and three rifle salute, starting at 10 am at Solvang Cemetery, 10:30 at Mission Santa Inés, and 11 at Oak Hill Cemetery in Ballard. Veterans of Foreign Wars Post 7139's program is at Solvang Park.

"Memorial Day is a sacred day to all war veterans. Sacrifice is meaningless without remembrance," said VFW Senor Vice-Commander Ed Jorgensen. "Please come, bring your children and join us as we remember and pay honor to our fallen comrades."

Loved ones have honored the fallen since time immemorial, but it was a walrus mustachioed General John Logan, National Commander of the Grand Army of the Republic, whose General Order No. 11 prompted flowers to be placed on the graves of Union and Confederate soldiers at Arlington National Cemetery on May 30, 1868.

What we now honor as Memorial Day was originally known as Decoration Day.

At Arlington, 1,200 soldiers of the $3^{rd}$ U.S. Infantry place American flags on over 260,000 gravestones. They have maintain a 24 hour guard to ensure that each flag remains standing, a tradition started in the late 1950's.

At Fredericksburg and Spotsylvania National Military Park, Boy and Girl Scouts place a candle on 15,300 soldier's graves.

In the Valley, 730 graves of deceased veterans are decorated by the SYV American Legion and Auxiliary and the VFW.

Helen Fitzgerald, Ann Flynn, Bill Hufford, Jim Poggione, Gladys FitzGerald, the Santa Ynez Band of Chumash Mission Indians Elders Council, and historian Jim Norris compiled the list of veterans.

I wish I could tell the stories of all 730 veterans buried in the Valley. It's a roll call of honor, written in blood. A sampling is below. We thank them for their sacrifices.

Richard Dee Henrey (1948-1967), USMC PFC Robert Lee Pacheco (1948-1968) and Army Corporal David R. Tibbetts (1949-1969) were all killed in Vietnam.

David Tibbetts lived down the street from me when I was in high school, and his death cast a pall over the neighborhood. Suddenly, Vietnam was only half a block away.

Cyril James Miranda (1948-1997) received a Purple Heart.

Air Force Reserve Corporal Charles Daniel Bellows (1912-1953) and William Alvarado Valdez (1930-1950) were killed in action in Korea.

Private George T. Downs, MP (1924-1944) died in service in World War II. Robert B. Forbes (1922-2001), Joseph T. Martinez (1922-1998) and Orville Lane Nicholas (1914-1997) received Purple Hearts.

Army 1st Lieutenant Paul Clay Willis (1919-1973) served in WWII and Korea and earned a Bronze Star. David M. Maturino (1921-2001) earned a Silver Star in WWII. Frank H. Spearman III (1921-1998) earned a Battle Star.

The VFW hall is named for John Pedercini, lost in WWII. His body was never found.

Joseph Betalin Derrington (1920-2002), Army Sgt. Ronald Arthur Smith (1916-1989) and Army PFC Thomas Edward Donahue (1910-1985) were prisoners of war in WWII.

Army Colonel Durward James Wilson (1893-1964) served in WWI and WWII. USMC Adolph C. Buchardi (1895-1918) died in the Argonne Forest in WWI. Ernest E. Cota died in service in WWI.

Karen Mary Jensen (1883-1971) and Magda Mary Jensen were both Army nurses, Karen during WWI.

Jason F. Bloodgood (1834-1898), Peter R. Gott (1845-1893), Edmund J. Fields (1830-1903), Marion S. Foster (1837-1907), and John W. Hartley (1846-1923) were Civil War veterans.

Seven hundred thirty lives. A million stories. Veteran James P. "Jimmy" Pace (1930-1996) was a friendly face at Solvang Hardware for decades, a soft-spoken, eloquent voice for the Chumash.

Charismatic Dunn School Headmaster John Pettley (1912-1988) was an armed forces meteorologist in WWII, making critical weather forecasts.

So many memories, gone to the grave.

## 22. David Crosby, Noah Wyle, & Bo Derek Rip Community Plan

Emotions were running high in Solvang in June of 2003, as General Plan Advisory Committee member Jan Crosby quit in a wrangle over proposed "Design Residential" cluster housing sites, and management of the planning process.

Crosby was appointed to GPAC by Supervisor Gail Marshall a little over a month before.

"ER" star Noah Wyle backed her up, saying "I do believe that the community has not been told all the facts about this particular issue, and once they are told, this will be a unanimous decision, to stop this in its tracks."

The tense scene played out before a standing room only crowd of over 200 people packed into a hot Veterans Memorial Hall annex like sardines in a sauna. The marathon meeting began at six pm with Crosby's resignation, and wrapped up around midnight with a recommendation to staff to restudy the parcels for lower density.

A host of irate citizens, including actress Bo Derek, roundly denounced the plans for hours.

Rancher Nancy Crawford-Hall said "The type of programs being proposed, as usual, have not included the entire agricultural community and their opinions. We spent two years giving opinions on what would work for us and what wouldn't. They were summarily ignored."

"The whole thing is a disaster, because they don't take the community into account," said Crawford-Hall. "They've got a political agenda in mind and they're trying to ramrod it through this Valley. And it's not going to work."

"They ramrodded it on us," said Los Olivos veterinarian Doug Herthel. "I've heard county staffers say "Deception is our friend.""

"I'm still shaking,' said Jan Crosby, after she walked out.

"It's a very emotional thing," said music legend David Crosby. "This is an old story. This is the people who live here versus the developers. These people, who are supposed to be the representative body to hear us, who live here, have ignored us, shut us up. Doug Herthel had a half hour presentation (at a prior meeting) with visual aids, witnesses, everything. It didn't even go in the minutes. We've been coming to these meetings, hundreds of us at a time, for a year, 33 meetings. At no time have they listened to us."

David Crosby said plans for clustered homes are a mistake. "They're not going to be affordable housing, they're going to be much more expensive housing as soon as they're built, and it means that the guys who are building them will make tens of millions of dollars. No one else will benefit. And the communities where they want to do it—Ballard, Los Olivos, Santa Ynez—will be ruined by it."

"This is the lie," said David Crosby. "They portray DR (Design Residential) zoning as a lovely thing. And what it is, is something real scummy. Why are they not listening to that roomful of people?"

"What they're doing now is pretty much a charade," said Jan Crosby. "They're just doing this because the law says they have to. Over and over again, they've demonstrated what their true intentions are. They're going to DR zone this entire town, and they're just going to build whatever they want. What they're up to isn't good for our Valley, and it will totally change the character of this town and Los Olivos forever and ever. There won't be any turning back at all."

"Over and over again I've asked questions, and over and over again I've been gaveled down. It's one thing to be in a position of power, and use it correctly. People are going to disagree and I don't mind that. It's another thing to be in a position of power and abuse it, and be abusive to the public. I will not let my name be associated with the way that board is proceeding, because they are behaving badly. I think they are just going through the motions. We're asking for an oversight committee to watch their shenanigans from here on out."

"We will not be silent," Jan Crosby promised. A petition drive is underway.

David and Jan Crosby's tireless efforts over the years have raised hundreds of thousands of dollars to support school music programs here, with concerts featuring David Crosby and his friend Graham Nash, Neil Young, Melissa Etheridge, Jackson Browne, and others. Crosby was a veteran of The Byrds, and Nash of The Hollies, when they teamed with Steven Stills of Buffalo Springfield fame to play their first gig as a trio, at Woodstock, in 1969.

## Part 2. Dude, Where's My Zoning?

(November, 2003) Awash in a sea of controversy stirred up by the hurricane formerly known as the General Plan, Supervisor Gail Marshall has announced she will not run again. So where does that leave the first Santa Ynez Valley zoning revamp in over twenty years?

Dead in the water for now, although planning staff are still tweaking allegedly minor items before the Board of Supervisors tackles the mess again in January, 2004.

Delay suits a lot of people just fine. So far there's one sure consensus: Nobody's happy.

To recap: After 35 arduous meetings, including a brouhaha over the flag salute that lifted eyebrows nationally and sparked a recall election, the General Plan Advisory Committee (GPAC) process lurched to a cacophonous, bitter halt in the summer of 2003. Supervisor Marshall called for a six month time-out after a near revolt at a town meeting June 25.

The 14 public spirited GPAC members who gave up countless hours of their lives at endless meetings only to encounter a firestorm of public opposition inches from the goal line feel frustrated, abused, and misunderstood. Those who were veterans of the Valley Blueprint process had been through three years of meetings prior to this round.

On any day, it's a thankless job. These rough seas were sheer hell.

Why all the hubbub? Hundreds of millions of dollars are at stake, plus quality of life issues. The ambitious proposed GPAC plan both raises and lowers density, ensuring attacks from all sides. Big landowners may lose their potential to subdivide. Some small land owners, to their surprise, may gain it.

Celebrities Bo Derek, Noah Wyle, David Crosby and John Forsythe turned out to protest high density projects. Beside them stood ranchers aghast at the potential loss of their 100 acre zoning, which will change in many cases to 640 or 320 acre zoning if the plan goes through, vastly diminishing potential land values.

Planners argue that since the County won't let the massive parcels be split smaller than 400 acres today anyway, that the proposed changes merely acknowledge planning realities. 400 acres is considered by planners to be viable for a cattle operation.

Ranchers say this overlooks the possibility that a new supervisor, or a county split, might allow property owners to actually get what they paid for, that is, parcel splits that match their zoning. They point out that no one can pay today's real estate prices and profitably raise cattle.

The matter of newly created "non-conforming" parcels is another thorny issue. Today's legally zoned parcels will become tomorrow's non-conforming parcels under the proposed plan. That makes them subject to penalties if owners try to remodel or build.

Supervisor Marshall's environmentalist following are shocked that her GPAC has proposed high density in-fill projects. Other citizens claim that "tops down" density requirements, dictated by a state planning entity, smack of socialism. GPAC chair Lansing Duncan said state requirements have nothing to do with the proposed plan.

Residents already riled by the Chumash Casino's impacts are petrified at the prospect of higher density on parcels such as the "Corner Farm," where the proposed zoning goes from seven to fifty-one units. It's currently a popular roadside farm, selling produce grown on-site, run by Steve Loyal.

The puzzled owner of the Corner Farm, Jim Lopez, said in a town meeting "If you want to make me rich, go ahead. But I haven't said it's for sale, and it isn't. I have a long term lease with Steve and he's done a beautiful job."

Many hapless property owners will be saddled with a "D" overlay zoning that makes any exterior change in their property at all subject to the Board of Architectural Review, an expensive, time consuming process. In the past, "D" zoning was one of the prices subdividers paid for approval. Now it's being inflicted on the general public.

Two citizen's organizations, Preservation of Los Olivos (POLO) and Preservation of Santa Ynez, have risen to meet the development threat. They've also challenged the accuracy of the minutes. A huge fight over approval of minutes of past meetings left participants shaken and the issue tabled.

POLO members Doug and Sue Herthel took the controversial 24.9 acre Montanaro parcel off the table by buying it themselves, saving it from cluster homes even denser than the hapless County Housing Element planners who offered to expedite up to 175 units there, in feeble hopes of getting a few shekels from a Golden State with no gold.

Have you looked at the State Seal lately? Minerva, goddess of wisdom, has been replaced by a drunken sailor.

Will the much maligned plan twist slowly in the wind until a new Supervisor arrives? Will the outgoing Supervisor try to pass it as a legacy? Will everyone back off, or blaze away? Stay tuned.

## Part 3. Santa Ynez Valley Community Plan Rides Again

(April, 2004) Who were those masked men?

Like the Lone Ranger, mysterious *Friends of the Santa Ynez Valley* may have ridden to the rescue of the new Community Plan, quietly hammering out alternatives to the General Plan Advisory Committee (GPAC) version that sparked such rancor last summer.

SB County Planning and Development's *Issues and Alternatives Paper* hit the streets last week, and lists the *Friends*' work as "Alternative One." They tackled the eight high profile parcels proposed for significant unit increases by GPAC.

The *Friends*, a kaleidoscope of community volunteers, came up with a largely status quo approach to residential zoning, plus a suggestion to allow some residential units to be mixed into the current "Highway Commercial" zoning along Hwy. 246 in the town of Santa Ynez. Planning & Development's report calls it a "citizen-generated, 'Valley appropriate' perspective."

On the Corner Farm/Duckett parcel, for example, where GPAC might have allowed a 5.5 acre performing arts center and 44 units, the *Friends* stuck with the current zoning, allowing eleven homes on one acre each.

Then there's the big land on the periphery of the valley, huge rural ranches, thousands of acres in size. There, the Agricultural Advisory Committee had a chance to express their opinion. They oppose GPAC's planned down-zoning. Down-zoning means you can't whack your land into as many pieces as you could before.

The ranchers say it ain't broke, so don't fix it. They're not buying the county's "truth-in-zoning" argument. No wonder. In the hottest real estate market in California history, every potential hundred acre split a property owner here gives up theoretically costs them well over a million dollars.

More controversy surrounds at least 150 properties that fall into the "D" Design Control Overlay zone proposed along the Alamo Pintado and Hwy 246 corridors. Owners of "any new or altered building or structure" will have to pay $440 to trek hat-in-hand before the Board of Architectural Review. Exempt: interior alterations, decks, hot tubs, fences under six feet, solar panels, and "exterior alterations determined to be minor by the Director."

Talk about a sucker punch. Affected property owners I've talked to had no idea their zoning may change. Astonishingly, in a revealing glimpse into the county's thought process, the document states the "Board of Architectural Review (BAR) review, while another step in the process, does not significantly lengthen the permitting process. Review targets are 30 days for projects without BAR review and 90 days for projects with BAR review."

Ninety days was significantly longer than thirty days, last time I looked. Two months longer. Three times as long, to be exact. It's a lifetime when you're trying to get something done. Not to mention what an architect costs, or the interminable delays when things go badly at the BAR. BAR has a shot at many projects already. The big "D" has been pasted on all new subdivisions for years. Sixty-five parcels totaling 584 acres are tagged now.

As the county draft points out, "there are multiple instances where BAR review on a project is required regardless of the presence of the overlay, including projects in Hillside and Ridgeline areas, on a parcel adjacent to the ocean, in commercial zone districts, communication facilities, most commercial, industrial, residential, or agricultural signs, and all development plans. In addition, the Planning Commission and Board of Supervisors can require that any project they are reviewing be forwarded to the BAR for review and approval," says the report.

If this passes, the screams you hear for miles will be anguished homeowners finding out their new patio cover will cost $440 and take 90 days for the BAR permit alone.

As yet, nothing's settled. Planning Commission and Board of Supervisors review is expected to take until the fall of 2005.

As novelist Saul Bellow once wrote, "the machine carries the momentum." The farther along this planning machine gets, the tougher it will be to change course. Whatever your take, speak now, or forever wish you had.

## Part 4. All Quiet On The CP Front

(May, 2004) A constructive, civil attitude reigned at recent meetings on the SYV Community Plan, the first public get-togethers since the General Plan Advisory Committee (GPAC) meetings lurched to a uproarious, ignominious halt last summer, prior to Brooks Firestone's election in March as Supervisor. He takes office in January of 2005.

"If you want to be mad at someone, it's probably me," said Planning and Development (P&D) head Valentin Alexeeff. "There was not a practical way to end the GPAC process. It was breaking down."

The Supervisors took this to heart, offering a golden handshake shortly thereafter.

Eight volunteer community members, known as the Friends of the Santa Ynez Valley, headed up by retired Silicon Valley entrepreneur Bob Field, have worked on alternatives.

P&D's report calls their ideas Alternative 1, a "citizen-generated, Valley-appropriate perspective." It leaves most existing zoning in place.

At the Solvang Memorial Hall April 27 and May 6, 2004, numerous community groups who had loudly opposed the GPAC plan found common ground in the Friends' work. Fifty-seven speakers talked for six hours total at the two professionally facilitated meetings.

Carol Herrera said the Women's Environmental Watch (WEWatch) could get behind most of Alt 1. WEWatch also supports more trails, and less light pollution.

Preservation Of Santa Ynez, while still steamed about lack of input, supports Alternative 1, said Jon Bowen.

Former GPAC member Jan Crosby, whose resignation sparked the firestorm, wants an independent Environmental Impact Report (EIR) and more public input "to avoid litigation," plus more accurate GPAC minutes.

"The minutes never showed the overwhelming objections by the community," agreed Bowen. Alexeeff said of the independent EIR, "Legally, we can't do it."

"We have a consensus," said veterinarian Doug Herthel, speaking for Preservation Of Los Olivos. The former plan was like a horse with a broken leg, he explained.

"Lo and behold, the horse heals," said Herthel.

Speaking for the Agricultural Advisory Committee (AAC), Willy Chamberlin endorsed the Friends' housing proposals. Chamberlin had concerns about rural trails, the urban/rural boundary and downzoning of ag land. He made a case for keeping the plan out of the rural areas altogether. "You can't have a plan without the rural parcels," protested former GPAC chairman Lansing Duncan. GPAC member Dennis Beebe and Valley Blueprint co-chair Richard Crutchfield concurred. Alexeeff said existing zoning will apply if the new plan does not.

"I am very heartened," by Alternative One, said Tish Beltranena, a planning consultant representing the Central Coast Wine Growers, Buellton Chamber of Commerce, and "owners of 43,000 acres of agricultural land."

"We fully back the AAC," she added, citing mapping errors in the plan.

Jim Lopez, owner of the Corner Farm property, called the GPAC proposal for his property "extortion."

Ralph Fertig of the SB County Bicycling Coalition and Cory Evans of Dr. J's Bicycles pitched a bike trail along the state water pipeline easement, from Buellton to Lake Cachuma.

Rancher Nancy Crawford-Hall lambasted the trails and habitat portions of the plan, calling them unconstitutional and inaccurate. She cited problems with disease, vandalism, and trespassers, including county employees she found on her land as she drove to the meeting.

Rancher Bill Giorgi said the trails element "feels like extortion," and opposed downzoning, calling it "the final nail in the coffin of agriculture."

Richard Christensen said, "I do not know adequate words to express my disgust with the taking of private land."

Dean Palius, Michael Balaban, Herb Bundgen, Landon Neustadt, Chris Burtness, Bud Laurent and Puck Erickson called for more affordable housing.

Gary Woods protested the downzoning of 35 acres of Anker Johnson's Ballard Fields Ranch. Losing his five acre zoning will cost the farmer millions. Wayne Natale backed him up.

"Folks saw that as a rural separator," said P&D planner Stephen Petersen.

C.J. Jackson said, "The method for informing the public that their property was being considered was brutally flawed." Gene Ray, Dale Rossi, and Doug Herthel agreed.

Shirley Walker, Alex and Dale Rossi, Puck Erickson, and Doug Herthel thrashed the proposed "D" overlay.

"It truly is a taking of property," said Dale Rossi, owner of the historic Ballard Adobe. "You'll need Board of Architectural Review approval to build a chicken coop."

SY water district manager Chris Dahlstrom called the water information in the plan "incomplete, inaccurate and inconsistent." Fred Koval and Bruce Steel also had water concerns.

Catalyst Bob Field called on the cities to shoulder their share of the housing load. He was buoyed by the response, but noted there's plenty of work ahead.

"As P.T. Barnum said, we wash one elephant at a time," smiled Mr. Field.

## 23. The Fuss About Fess Makes *The Wall Street Journal*

They say all politics is local.

Our local land use politics made the national news in a big way on May 28, 2004, as *The Wall Street Journal* tackled the proposed Parker/Chumash project, declaring in an opinion piece that developers will "start speed dialing Indian tribes" if Fess Parker's "end run around local rule" succeeds.

In *The Fuss About Fess*, the *WSJ* predicts a backlash that will hurt the tribes if the "resort hotel, golf course and 500 luxury homes" end up on federalized land. A map of the project obtained by opponents shows homes, an equestrian center, and golf course, with a "55 ACRE RESORT HOTEL AND CASINO SITE" in the middle.

"Give the man credit for clever marksmanship," wrote the *WSJ*. "The deal he's proposed with the neighboring Chumash Indians is at once simple and audacious...If the feds approve the annexation of the land as tribal territory, it means this could all be built without regard to local and state regulations."

"The resentment this would breed—already palpable in Santa Barbara—would only make it more likely that disenfranchised Californians will respond by opening up casino gambling to others," predicted the Journal. "If tribal casinos get too greedy, they stand a good chance of seeing their prized monopoly taken away from them."

After this promising, prescient start, the Journal got a little sloppy with the facts.

"The overtures to the Chumash, moreover, came only after Mr. Parker was frustrated in earlier attempts to build on the land, which he bought back in 1998," the *WSJ* wrote.

Huh? Other than planting some grapes, there's been no known attempt to develop, unless you count Mr. Parker driving Supervisor Marshall and John Buttny around on the land one sunny day in his Hummer.

Their date is off a little. Realtors say Mr. Parker bought a total 1400 acres in July of 1999, for $6 million. He's selling a half interest in 750 acres for $12 million. Big round numbers: pay $4,000 an acre, sell for $32,000 an acre. Don't let the hat fool you—this country boy's got a gold thumb.

The WSJ couldn't resist a few shots at favorite targets, bashing bureaucrats and left-coast liberals.

"Far be it from us to oppose growth or champion regulation...Elsewhere in California, environmentalists, labor activists, and no-growthers have thwarted all sorts of projects," ranted writers in the high rise hubbub of Manhattan.

"Surely there's a workable, democratic medium between the extremes of no-growthers hostile to any business proposal and the kind of developers who would look at an ancient redwood and see only lumber," cried the venerable voice of laissez-faire capitalism.

So, Wall Street—a rich guy who wants to run a stop sign at 100 miles an hour should be allowed to run it at 50 mph in the spirit of compromise? People here still think the rules are for everybody.

"We don't pretend to know what such a resolution would look like in Santa Barbara. But we do know that people who make reasonable development nearly impossible not infrequently wake up one day to find themselves staring at something far worse," thundered the Journal.

They're probably talking about Trump Tower. From the concrete canyons of the Big Apple, I suppose anything in California looks good to them.

"There's a certain amount of bigotry here," Fess Parker told KCET's Phillip Bruce in a March broadcast of *Life & Times.*

"It's the zoning, stupid," countered a letter to the editor. The incredible activism of folks from all walks of life involved in reworking the SYV General Plan over the past three years has proven that.

Famed rock lyricist Bernie Taupin has jumped into the debate over the project with both feet, buying a full page ad decrying "Fess Parker's Obscene Dream of Environmental Assault."

"Should this atrocity go ahead, it would surely be the beginning of the end for this pastoral wonderland we cherish," wrote Mr. Taupin, a local resident who has penned dozens of hits, including the best selling single of all time, *Candle in the Wind '97*. His tribute with partner Elton John to the late Princess Diana sold over 35 million copies worldwide.

## Part 2. Sugar, Cream, Casino?

Coffee houses have often been the scene of great drama. Literary giant Samuel Johnson and his biographer, James Boswell, practically lived in London's coffee houses in the 1700s. Lenin, Trotsky and Sigmund Freud came every day (not together, as far as we know) to the Café Central in Vienna to linger over espresso, probe the dark forest of the psyche, and plot against the Czar.

Karl Marx hung out at London's Clerkenwell Coffee House. Adolf Hitler studied for his exams in Vienna's Café Sperl. And let's not forget "Friends."

So it should come as no real surprise that the latest act of the hottest drama in this town played out amidst the caffeinated.

Once famous for "Remember the Alamo!," it's "Remember the Zoning!" that valley residents shout at Fess Parker these days.

A photo is circulating of a blueprint reportedly hanging on Fess Parker's wall in his office in Los Olivos. In the center of his proposed project with the Chumash, the blueprint shows a "55 ACRE RESORT HOTEL AND CASINO SITE."

The photo, dropped off by parties unknown, was parked by the half-and-half, sugar and non-dairy creamer in the Roasted Bean coffee shop in Santa Ynez for a few days. That is, until Mr. Parker came in, grabbed it, and walked out with it.

"He was fine," said the young lady who happened to be at the counter that day. "He brought it over to the counter. He said it was incorrect. He wanted to know who brought it in," she related reluctantly, asking that her name not be used. "He didn't yell at me; I'm sure he could have. I'd rather just stay out of the whole thing."

*Remember the Alamo: It's been fifty years since local hotelier Fess Parker was catapulted to fame as Disney's Davey Crockett, a folk hero who went down swinging on the ramparts of that adobe redoubt in Texas, crushed by overwhelming odds. Fess was back at the famed fort recently, donating his rifle, Old Betsy, to posterity, and probably feeling very much at home.

Cinematic struggle to the death at the hands of an enemy army was good practice for the actor turned developer. It's a lot like going before a planning commission, which is where he's been in recent decades, or the mammoth Solvang meeting on April 7, 2004, that stopped just short of hanging him in effigy.

Mr. Parker's plan to ace local zoning by partnering projects with the SYV Band of Chumash Indians has cost the affable octogenarian considerable karma here.

Popping up on Valley "STOP" signs: a sticker that changes the message to "STOP FESS."

Parker played Daniel Boone as well, and the dad in *Old Yeller*.

## Part 3. Tribe Dumping Davey?

(August, 2004) Fess Parker's proposed residential resort partnership with the Chumash is losing ground within the tribe itself.

The zoning busting development plan provoked a ferocious negative outcry from valley residents who have spent the last five years hammering out the *Valley Blueprint* and proposed revisions to existing zoning.

Some tribe members are also quietly opposed, afraid the ambitious project may turn into a long drawn-out financial boondoggle. It's already a public relations fiasco.

Years of delay are probable before the 745 acres will even be considered for annexation to the reservation. About three acres of the 6.9 acres across the street from the casino just now coming up for annexation were purchased by the Chumash in January of 1997, over seven years ago.

Mr. Parker is 80 years old. Locals are already lobbying in Washington against the plan.

It's an issue with global appeal. The Parker project has turned up in the Manchester Guardian, the prestigious international *Economist* magazine, and on websites as varied as the Adam Smith Institute and kidsnewsroom.org. Associated Press articles plastered it all over the US.

*The Wall Street Journal* declared in an opinion piece that developers will "start speed dialing Indian tribes" if Fess Parker's "end run around local rule" succeeds, predicting a backlash that will hurt the tribes.

"The resentment this would breed—already palpable in Santa Barbara—would only make it more likely that disenfranchised Californians will respond by opening up casino gambling to others," predicted the Journal. "If tribal casinos get too greedy, they stand a good chance of seeing their prized monopoly taken away from them."

The *Journal*'s backlash argument gets a boost from Dr. David A. Yeagley, a published scholar, composer, and an adjunct professor at the University of Oklahoma College of Liberal Studies. He's also a direct descendent of Comanche warrior Bad Eagle (1839-1906).

"As an American Indian, a Comanche from Oklahoma, I care about the public image of the Indian. I value being Indian. Though my tribe isn't guilty of encroachment on anyone's rights, it is a vital concern to me that, nationally, the "Indian" casino industry is destroying the pride and meaning of being Indian," he wrote in FrontPageMagazine.com, May 17.

"It's really an internal war, not between Indians and whites, but between whites and other whites. It is a desperate power struggle, and Indians are being used by liberals as the arrowhead to strike deep into the heart of American values," Dr. Yeagley claims.

"Casinos are ruining Indian country and America. Casino politicians and businessmen are the ones who are anti-Indian and anti-American," says Dr. Yeagley.

The thought that there are better, less headache-prone investments available has begun to sink in on the reservation.

On February 25, 2004, Chumash tribe member Edward Alex Valencia penned a letter to all tribal members, opposing the project.

"There are too many unknown factors in this deal," wrote Mr. Valencia. "We should pay off some of our debts before entering into such a large and uncertain venture…"

"This will no doubt create a large public outcry. We may one day need the public's support; I do not believe it's wise to have them against us…"

"Who is really going to profit from this deal?…We won't be on this earth forever, and it past time to consider the 1/8 members of this tribe before we all are gone…"

"I have mixed emotions about entering into a partnership with anyone I know nothing about except that he was an actor and is now a vintner. Sure he owns a hotel. That in my book does not qualify him to be a partner with a sovereign nation, besides the fact that he will have 'control' in this venture…I strongly believe there is more information about this 'deal' that we are NOT being told about," cautioned Mr. Valencia.

## Part 4. Boone-doggle: Fess Flops

(October, 2004) It's official: the Parker/Chumash escrow folded weeks ago. Oddly enough, both sides claim that doesn't change much.

Humm. Any time an escrow ends, there are significant, unresolved differences in the negotiating positions of the parties involved. On one issue or many, they're standing on opposite rims of the Grand Canyon. Otherwise they'd be proceeding on course, all smiles, hunky-dory.

Occasionally parties to a bombed escrow can patch things up, and put together a new deal. But more often than not, a crashed escrow is like a divorce: chances of a re-take, slim to none.

The Parker project was approved by just 72 votes. That's less than half of the 153 tribe members eligible to vote. Thirty-seven voters said no, and 44 abstained.

You can bet Mr. Parker and the Band have been discussing financing, the development plan in general, and the roles of the partners in particular, regarding management, financial obligations, and prospective returns.

More than a hundred interested parties have a role in this deal, if you count only the voting band members. Just imagine how long easy issues, like trying to decide what color to paint the houses, could take.

One King Kong thing, a massive monkey swinging from the chandelier over the whole deal, is financing. Bagging bucks for "fee to trust" deals gets weird in a hurry.

Because the federal government controls land put in trust for any tribe, there is no way a lender can foreclose on it if payments are missed. Normal banks won't even touch the pole. They have no security for the loan.

That's why the Mashantucket Pequot's Foxwoods casino in Connecticut, the largest in the world, was financed by Malaysian gambling money through Chinese national Lim Goh Tong's company, Genting Berhad, with an agreement that the moneymen could step in and run the place if the locals proved inadequate, according to Jeff Benedict, author of *Without Reservation*. Financing any trust land project without a casino's powerful money mill is iffy.

An educated guess: They've reached an impasse on critical issues, perhaps due to declining support for the fiasco within the tribe, as reported here earlier. They're putting the best face on the delay, while quietly trying to paste Humpty back together again.

Keep the champagne corked. A run at about 1,000 acres of the pristine Gainey Ranch, next door to the reservation, could be next.

## 24. Reservations About Tribal Annexations

The Santa Barbara Board of Supervisors heard about the labyrinthine federal annexation process for reservation land on Nov. 23, 2004, as Bureau of Indian Affairs speakers James Fletcher and Kevin Bearquiver gave a presentation, and took a few public comments. Regional BIA Director Clay Gregory sent his regrets.

It wasn't a public hearing. The Bureau of Indian Affairs doesn't hold public hearings on annexation requests, although they do solicit public input. And it wasn't supposed to be about the 6.9 acres currently up for annexation to the Chumash reservation.

It was billed as a generic information session about the process by which land held "in fee" by tribes becomes held by the Federal Government "in trust" for tribes. Hence the term "fee to trust" used to describe the process.

Overall, it was an enlightening presentation of the arcane regulations and numerous court decisions that continue to shape Bureau policy. The rules originally came from the Indian Reorganization Act of 1934.

The Supervisors nevertheless made their feelings clear. They're concerned about loss of control. Supervisor Centeno asked "How much weight is given to a county position as opposed to a tribe's position?"

"The further the distance from the reservation, the more weight is given to the county," replied Mr. Bearquiver. "Once you start getting several miles from the reservation, we give greater concern to governmental bodies."

Mr. Fletcher, who is responsible for 29 of the 103 federally recognized tribes in California, momentarily shook up the crowd by announcing there were no current annexations pending in this area. Mr. Bearquiver had the unpleasant task of correcting his boss in public, reminding him of the 6.9 acre request pending.

C.J. Jackson of Concerned Citizens asked the status of other annexation proposals.

Mr. Bearquiver said the 12 acre Walker/Davidge annexation has been approved. The 1.17 acre Condit/Daniels parcel was pulled. The Condit/Daniels proposal is adjacent to a 20,000 square foot vacant lot on Numancia Street the band just purchased from GTE California in October.

There were about 60 persons in the audience, including Fess Parker. Mr. Parker did not speak. The BIA noted that they had received many letters from opponents of the Parker project, but no proposals from the band or Mr. Parker as yet.

Audience members Nancy Eklund, Robert Etling, CJ Jackson, Bob Field, Jan Crosby, Steve Pappas, Nancy Crawford-Hall, and Jim Marino expressed concerns.

"It is the conversion of agricultural property to other uses that concerns me most," said Nancy Crawford-Hall, whose land shares a property line with the 750 acre Parker property.

Nancy Eklund asked the BIA position on partnerships with non-Indian developers. Mr. Fletcher noted such partnerships are common, pointing out that the Agua Caliente tribe own much of the land in Palm Springs.

"Define contiguous," requested Jan Crosby.

Mr. Bearquiver said the BIA considers land separated from a reservation by a state highway to be contiguous. That's an important definition, which will aid the Chumash in their 6.9 acre annexation bid.

Off-reservation annexations must pass more stringent guidelines than contiguous requests. Any non-contiguous acquisition must be "necessary to facilitate tribal self-determination, economic development, or Indian housing."

Gaming can only be established on after acquired non-contiguous land, as "a settlement of a land claim," or on "the initial reservation of a newly acknowledged Indian tribe given Federal recognition...," or as "restoration of lands for an Indian tribe that is restored to Federal recognition," noted Mr. Bearquiver. Gaming also requires the governor's concurrence.

Bob Field of the Friends of the Santa Ynez Valley questioned the relevance of applying depression era standards today.

"What's the BIA view of the test for economic development?" he wondered.

Supervisor Marshall echoed his concern.

"A tribe need not be suffering," explained Mr. Bearquiver. He cited a court case from Avoyells Parish, Louisiana, where the court said "A financially secure tribe might well need additional land in order to maintain or improve its economic condition if its existing land is already fully developed."

"We are not utilizing 1934 regulations," said Mr. Bearquiver. "Regulations are constantly changing. Our policies are continually changing."

"How will you protect the integrity of the local area General Plan?" asked Robert Etling.

"We do address those issues," asserted Mr. Bearquiver, citing the National Environmental Policy Act, Endangered Species Act, Clean Water Act, Safe Drinking Water Act, and Clean Air Act as safeguards.

Attorney James Marino said the process was never intended for evading taxes and regulations.

Steve Pappas of POLO asked questions relative to a rumor that the SY airport might be annexed. "Will the BIA permit land to be taken if the land contains contaminants?" he asked. Mr. Bearquiver said acquisitions must be cleaned up.

"That's county property," Supervisor Marshall said. "The county has no plan to sell the airport property."

"How can the BIA be a catalyst for bringing individuals and tribal members together in a community?" asked Supervisor Marshall, as the meeting drew to a close.

"Sometimes it's difficult to bring these things together," said Mr. Fletcher, who offered to try.

"We recognize our tribe as a sovereign nation," said Supervisor Naomi Schwartz, "What we need is a means of building mutual respect."

Leapfrog annexation of land by tribes has sparked national concerns. US House of Representatives Speaker Dennis Hastert, Majority Whip Roy Blunt, Majority Leader Tom Delay, and Eric Cantor, Chief Deputy Whip, wrote to Secretary of the Interior Gale Norton in June of 2003 on the issue.

Their letter said "We write to express our concerns over recent attempts of certain Indian tribes to develop off-reservation casino sites. We strongly believe that these attempts run counter to Congressional intent and pose a serious threat to the current regulatory scheme that governs Indian gaming.

"When Congress passed the Indian Gaming Regulatory Act (IGRA) in 1988, they did not intend to authorize 'reservation shopping' by Indian tribes. Indeed, IGRA presumptively prohibits gaming on all after-acquired lands and only permits off-reservation gaming under extremely limited circumstances...

"We strongly urge the Department of Interior to enforce IGRA and to carefully scrutinize all efforts to acquire off-reservation land to acquire a favorable casino location. This matter has received a great deal of attention recently because of the ongoing attempt by the Jena Band of Choctaw Indians to take off-reservation land into trust for gaming, but there are many similar attempts already in force across the country with more certain to come," wrote the Reps.

## 25. Follow the Money—Politicians Hit The Casino Jackpot

It came as no real surprise to most community members following the drama, when the 6.9 acre annexation to the Chumash Reservation was approved by the Bureau of Indian Affairs in February, 2004.

Property adjacent to an existing reservation is practically guaranteed approval, the BIA's Kevin Bearquiver explained during his presentation to the Supervisors Nov. 23, 2004. The BIA solicits written input, but there's no public hearing process. The decision is made behind closed doors.

The surprise was the seventeen pro-annexation letters from high-powered, out-of-town politicians, among those cited by the BIA in their approval.

Compare that with the total letters to Third District Supervisor Brooks Firestone to date in favor of annexation: exactly one, from the Chumash. (Since this writing I learned of one more, from the Coalition of Labor, Agriculture and Business, of which the Chumash are a member.)

Six hundred and thirty letters have arrived at Firestone's office opposed to annexation in general. Thirty of those, plus 74 e-mails, specifically opposed the 6.9 acre add. And they're from people who actually live here.

So who are these strange politicians bucking the tide, and why their sudden interest in sleepy Santa Ynez?

None of them live here. Only three have local ties. Yet many of their campaigns received contributions from the tribe in recent years. Cynics see a connection. Numerous citizens have brought me dollar figures and cried foul.

Lawmakers who wrote the BIA in favor, and contributions to their campaigns by the Chumash since 2000, include La Puente Assemblyman Ed Chavez ($30,000), Santa Ana Assemblyman Lou Correa ($7,000), Los Angeles Assemblyman Marco Firebaugh ($3,000), Montebello Assemblyman Calderon ($3,000), Carson Assemblywoman Jenny Oropeza ($6,000), Senator Richard Polanco of Los Angeles ($10,000), Fresno Assemblywoman Sarah Reyes ($17,000), Monterey County Assemblyman Simon Salinas ($45,200), Senator Nell Soto of Ontario ($12,000), Assemblyman Herb Wesson of Culver City

($8,000) and Los Angeles Assemblyman Tony Cardenas ($130,000). All their titles are from 2002, when the letters were written.

Closer to home, *Abel Maldonado for Assembly* collected $15,000 from the Chumash on Nov. 1, 2000, $1,000 on Sept. 18, 2000, and $10,000 on Nov. 18, 2002. Assemblyman (now Senator) Maldonado wrote a letter in favor April 24, 2002.

Senator Jack O'Connell (now Superintendent of Public Instruction) wrote in favor on April 30, 2002. Unlike the others, O'Connell had a reason to write. The project was in his district, and his comments were specifically solicited by the BIA. *O'Connell for Superintendent* received $50,000 in contributions from the Chumash on Feb. 25, 2002, and another $50,000 on Oct. 16, 2002.

Senator Tom McClintock, who now represents the district due to boundary changes, wrote in favor May 1, 2002. *McClintock for Senate* received $3,000 from the Chumash in 2000, *McClintock for Governor* received $20,000 in 2003, and *McClintock and the Car Tax Committee* received $15,000 in 2004.

Campaign contributions from the Chumash to politicians statewide since 2000 total at least $798,900.

All dollar figures are from the California Secretary of State's website, which only tracks electronically filed contributions. Donor dollars shown here are not a complete total. The website is a bit of a jumble, and finding all the bucks is like an Easter egg hunt.

Despite all that generosity, Representatives Cardenas, Correa, Firebaugh, Reyes, Wesson, and Polanco are no longer in office. I e-mailed all the others, and the Chumash, seeking insight.

The Chumash, via a spokesperson, wrote, "It's routine for us to ask politicians to show support for the annexation."

Senator Nell Soto's press secretary stoutly insisted it's not about the Benjamins, saying "Senator Soto has long been a strong supporter of a number of tribes, and as a forceful advocate for Indian self-reliance, she has frequently weighed in on controversial issues. She believes it is our duty as a nation to continue to rectify the historical injustices perpetrated against America's Native populations. As an employee of the Legislature, I am not privy to the specifics of campaign contributions, but I know that Senator Soto has, over the years, received money from a range of groups and individuals who support her efforts—including fire fighters, teachers, health care providers, Native Americans and grocery store owners.

"Senator Soto agreed to write the letter you referred to after Chumash representatives explained the details of their annexation request in a meeting in her

Capitol office. She has yet to visit the annexation site but plans to do so sometime in the future."

From the Chumash General Council meeting minutes of October 14, 2002:

"Some bills defeated this year were the Gabrieleno and the fire fighters bill. Most of what we do is accomplished not by letter but very silently with friends. Jack O'Connell got up and left the floor when the bill came up."

Afterword: Schools take the biggest tax hit from annexations. Ironically, Jack O'Connell, who penned a letter in favor of the Chumash's 6.9 acre annexation, is now State Superintendent of Public Instruction.

"If developed as proposed in the Draft Santa Ynez Valley Community Plan, the total amount of property taxes projected to be levied on the parcels is $5,551,929 in 10 years, $12,319,700 in 20 years, and $42,885,004 in 50 years," the Supervisors noted of the 6.9 and 5.8 acres annexations.

All that will be lost if the land is annexed. The estimated amount is based upon the future value of the property developed as C-2 Limited Commercial and C-2 Mixed Use Overlay as per the Draft Santa Ynez Valley Community Plan.

Losers include College Elementary School District, Santa Ynez Valley High School District, Allen Hancock Community College District, Education Revenue Augmentation, and the County School Service Fund. The County's General Fund, Santa Barbara County Fire Protection District, and Santa Ynez Community Services District will also be affected.

## Part 2. Fighting Annexation

The Santa Barbara County Board of Supervisors voted 4-0 in February, 2005, to continue the matter of an appeal of the Bureau of Indian Affairs' approval of a 6.9 acre addition to the Chumash Reservation, while concurrently trying to negotiate a compromise with the tribe. Brooks Firestone, disappointed in his attempt to move forward with the appeal process, if only for negotiating purposes, abstained.

During two hours of testimony before a packed house at the Betteravia Government Center in Santa Maria, former Old Mission Santa Inés curator William Warwick, Luis Villegas of the Santa Barbara Hispanic Chamber of Commerce, Mike Flint of Santa Barbara, Andy Caldwell of the Coalition of Labor, Agriculture and Business, Larry Stidham, general counsel for the Chumash tribe, and Ted Ortega, business manager for the tribe, argued against an appeal.

Santa Ynez, Solvang, Los Olivos and Buellton residents favoring an appeal included Seward Webb, Mary Puchetta, Michelle Griffoul, Nancy Eklund, CJ

Jackson, Curt Moniot, Carol Herrera of Women's Environmental Watch, Alexander Power, Jody White, Michelle DeWerd, Doug Herthel, Kimberly Kunkle, Steve Pappas, Sara Jenkins, Jan Crosby, Sandy Focht, John Poitras, and Robert Woodruff. Greg Simon read a letter from Nancy Crawford-Hall, and Bob Field read a letter from Frank Blundo, both favoring an appeal.

"At what point do you tell someone they've achieved certain reliance or certain wealth?" Supervisor Carbajal asked Nancy Eklund. "I just think that's very un-American."

"This is America. Everyone should be able to do that," replied Ms. Eklund. "It's just that we believe everyone should do it under the same rules and a level playing field."

"There is a compelling case for appeal," said Supervisor Firestone. "There is no benefit to the county by annexation."

"As we know, this property is taken off the tax roles. Under annexation, this property would not be under the constraints, and the planning process, that everybody else in the county lives under. They would be exempt from that. And that just seems unfair, and unreasonable, to the people of the county."

"I think this annexation should be appealed. While we're talking, to lose this option, means we lose any negotiating ability, not only now but in the future. If we don't appeal we lose this, and there is no guarantee it will ever happen again."

"If the negotiations are successful, and we gain a memorandum of understanding, we have won, both for the county and the tribe. I think it's entirely reasonable that we go into negotiations, but with some leverage."

"Also, most importantly, there has been some discussion here that there is no case. We have heard to the contrary. There is a basis for the appeal. The BIA failed to address the need for the tribe, the financial or any other imperative need."

"It did not address the cumulative impacts of annexation."

"It did not address the potential for gaming under annexation."

"These are all very relevant points to this annexation. Other counsel has represented that this was not addressed adequately in the BIA considerations and statements."

"As an aside, I am very troubled by the letters from various California politicians that were submitted, without any real connection with this. I think that's also a basis for appeal."

"So as there is a basis for appeal, if we don't appeal, we are then compromising any ability to appeal in the future. Because by not appealing, we've said these points, which I just enumerated, are otherwise acceptable, or reasonable."

"So, both by the fact of negotiating with the tribe, and negotiating from the position of an appeal, firstly, and secondly, setting a precedent for the future, by not addressing the points that are the basis for an appeal, and by simply allowing this to go unanswered, I think we are doing a great disservice to the County of Santa Barbara for the long term."

"I think there is a compelling case for appeal. And I urge my fellow members to vote for an appeal, because not to do so would be to cut off this avenue forever, to our great regret," concluded Supervisor Firestone."

Supervisor Salud Carbajal suggested continuing a dialogue with the Chumash without an appeal. Supervisor Joni Gray agreed, suggesting "jet-tracking" the proposed Chumash project through the County planning process."

Supervisor Centeno said that in his view, the decision was not precedent setting. He also noted that schools, hospitals and non-profit organizations were all off the tax rolls."

Mr. Centeno emphasized that neither he nor anyone associated with him had accepted funds from the Chumash or anyone associated with them. "I think that's important for you to know," he stated.

"I did receive financial contributions (from the Chumash) during my campaign," said Supervisor Carbajal.

"I received no money. Nor was I contacted by any of the legislators who wrote letters to the BIA, and that surprised me," said Supervisor Firestone.

"It's time for all of us to find a way to respect each others' wishes," said chairwoman Susan Rose.

"We're talking about a government to government relationship here," said Mr. Centeno. "I would hope that we could get together with the Chumash, with their elected chairman, and sit down with some of our elected people, this next week, and see if we could accommodate each other with some kind of memorandum of understanding, if you will, that will make us all happy."

"If we can't do that by next week, then we'll make the tough call," concluded Supervisor Centeno.

Supervisors Firestone and Gray and representatives of the tribe will meet this week. The deadline for an appeal is Feb. 21, 2005.

## Part 3. The Annexation Heard Across the Nation

From Stonington, with sympathy: We're famous. However, as Monika Lewinsky told a young autograph seeker, that may not be a good thing.

News of the 6.9 acre Chumash annexation has traveled across the nation. Betty Perkowski of North Stonington, Connecticut, a total stranger, wrote when she heard of the turmoil here. Her story may foreshadow things to come, if an appeal is filed.

"I see nothing has changed in the 12 years since we in Connecticut first heard the word 'annexation,'" she said in an e-mail.

"Faced with the annexation of 247 acres by the tribe which runs Foxwoods casino, we were told there would be no public hearing on the matter.

"(Assistant Secretary for Indian Affairs) Ada Deer actually came here to 'listen,' but made it clear anything said could not be used in making her decision.

"We forced the issue to be decided at the highest levels of the Department of the Interior, after being told at the start that it was a routine administrative procedure that happens all the time, and we were the only ones who ever objected.

"After two years of public outcry, and despite the support of our town governments, plus State Attorney General Richard Blumenthal and Sen. Joe Lieberman, Interior Secretary Babbitt decided that the wealthy tribe needed this land to be in trust more than the three small surrounding towns needed the taxes.

"We kept appealing, and finally, after 10 years of legal expenses, a win in federal court, then a loss in federal appeals court, the tribe inexplicably withdrew the application to annex. They said they would annex land at a later date," said Ms. Perkowski.

*Rumor control: During his presentation at the Supervisor's meeting, Ted Ortega, business manager for the Chumash, announced "We have not been approached to buy Michael Jackson's ranch."

*Don't touch that dial: National Public Radio was just in town, doing a series on the impact of Indian casinos nationwide. They talked to Fess Parker, Vincent Armenta, Brooks Firestone, CJ Jackson, Bob Field, and David Crosby, among others.

*Seven year itch: Four months have passed since an informal deal was reached on the Chumash land annexation. Now the Chumash want to limit their agreement to forego gambling at their proposed 6.9 acre museum/commercial project, across Highway 246 from the casino, to a seven year term.

At the June 21, 2005 Supe's meeting, Nancy Eklund, a board member of the Santa Ynez Valley Concerned Citizens, asked Supervisor Joni Gray, a family law attorney, what her advice to a young bride would be if her new husband suggested revisiting the deal in seven years, "claiming that certain details of their vows had been left open for future negotiation."

Supervisor Gray stoutly defended the tribe in February when the much heralded handshake agreement was announced, dismissing the need for an appeal by the Board. Now they won't return her phone calls, she complained to Tribal Administrator David Smith.

*Have gun, will travel: Tragic irony—Louis Calvin, arrested in the road rage shooting in Buellton of a father of six, Wayne Shaw, is a craps dealer at the Chumash Casino, who moved here from Las Vegas. His address there last June: 7067 Gunslinger Street.

## Part 4. Gambling On Annexation

"I was afraid this evening would be negative, and it hasn't been, and I'm heartened by that," said the Rev. Chuck Stacy of St Mark's Episcopal Church in Los Olivos, up on the stage at the July 18, 2005 meeting on tribal annexations.

That said, he is still concerned about family problems and teen gambling at the nearby casino.

"There is a basic disconnect between the casino and the rest of this community," he noted, suggesting that letting go of some of the sovereignty issues might put the community as a whole back together.

"Most of the social problems that are now arising out of the casino and out of the community are because of this disconnect." said Rev. Stacy.

"I'm seeing this year what I haven't seen before; gambling issues, where the husband goes out and loses money. He's ashamed, goes out and gets drunk, has all kinds of family problems. Wife comes into my office; says how can I leave this relationship, so I don't have to go to court and lose the kids?"

"And thank God for the shelters," he continued.

"There's absolutely no social backup for any of this," said Rev. Stacy. "I called 211 the other day and acted as if I had a gambling problem and said I needed help. It's a good number and they were very encouraging. They gave me the number for Gamblers Anonymous, but it was a dead number."

"I phoned them back, and they were surprised, too. They referred me to a counseling service in Santa Ynez, but that was for fee, and I said, well, I don't have any money, because I lost it all.

"Also, it is a fact that our 18-year-olds are at the high school go over to the casino, and then go back to high school. I don't think that's a very healthy environment. There again, the casino is a part of the community, and lots of things have to work together, and here again is that total disconnect."

"I could go on and on and on with things like this," said Rev. Stacy. "Historically, we had ten freezers in our parish for ten years, and we did a food program, because we were concerned about the welfare of the people in the tribe and in the valley."

"Historically, there's been respect. But when they claim sovereignty, and they hide behind this and hide behind that, there's a disconnect, and therein, more than anything else, stems the problem."

Rev. Stacy was part of a six member panel convened to discuss issues related to the already approved 6.9 acre and pending 5.8 annexations, along with C.J. Jackson, Nancy Eklund, Jeff Benedict, attorney Guy Martin, and Jan Crosby.

Jan Crosby noted that Virginia Congressman Frank R. Wolf petitioned President Bush on June 23 for a two year moratorium on new tribal casinos. Wolf also cited teen gambling as part of his argument.

"There is no doubt that gambling is destructive. It ruins families. It ruins businesses. It ruins communities. Gamblers often neglect their families and lose their jobs, careers and marriages to the habit. Gambling preys on the weak and exploits the poor. Study after study shows that when a casino opens in a community, crime, suicide and bankruptcies all rise," Congressman Wolf wrote in his letter to the President.

"Even more sadly, it's not only adults who are being seduced by gambling. According to a recent PBS NewsHour report, recent studies indicate that more than 70 percent of youth between the ages of 10 and 17 gambled in the past year, up from 45 percent in 1988. The National Academy of Sciences says almost one in three high school students gamble on a regular basis. The Council on Problem Gambling estimates 200,000 American teens are addicted to gambling," wrote Wolf.

Fairness was the mantra at the meeting, where attendees were cautioned in writing and by the speakers to show respect.

"ABSOLUTELY NO derogatory or negative racial comment(s) about ANY person or ANY ethnic group will be tolerated. Any person(s) making such comments will be asked to leave immediately" read a handout, entitled Required Rules of Behavior and Decorum for Attendees.

"We want fairness," said Nancy Eklund.

"We want fair land use rules," said C.J. Jackson.

"Your effort is to confine growth," summed up featured speaker Jeff Benedict. "Never mind the million-dollar lobbyists. A million one-dollar lobbyists is better."

## 26. Rural Ranchers Speak Out

A crowd gathered at the Solvang Vet's Hall in April of 2005, to hear speakers at the Valley Planning Advisory Committee (VPAC) meeting discuss preservation of agricultural land.

VPAC Chairman Bob Field's opening comments included slides depicting how a hypothetical 1,000 acre ranch could become one acre parcels, through lot splits to accommodate six generations of heirs.

To avoid such splits, while preserving the landowner's asset value, County Executive Officer Mike Brown said "My idea, not the county's," was to allow a developable building envelope, perhaps five acres in size, on larger ranches, where additional homes and guest houses could be built.

Mr. Brown envisioned a value benefit to the land owner and affordable housing through renting out the guest houses, plus tax revenue for the county, with little impact on existing schools, roads, and public service infrastructure.

Willy Chamberlin, whose family owns the 8,000 acre Los Potreros Ranch, agreed more housing on large ranches is needed.

However, "the Williamson Act, and present zoning, won't allow what Mr. Brown suggested," he noted.

Mr. Chamberlin also favored cluster housing scenarios, and urged zoning changes to give farmers and ranchers "more tools to realize economic value." He cited as one example a proposal to allow bed and breakfast operations on property under Williamson Act ag preserve contracts. "You're talking about somebody's life savings," he pointed out.

Nojoqui Falls Ranch has been in Bill Giorgi's family since the 1800's. He said national issues include estate taxes, and the Free Trade Agreement.

"I don't consider us a large landowner, just a typical family farmer," Mr. Giorgi explained. "We don't have any source of income other than what we make off the ranch, and I have personally worked the land the last thirty plus years."

"Locally, we have urban planners trying to apply urban plans to our rural landscape, without listening to the stewards of the lands who have lived there for years and cared for it," he said. "It is now time to stop this adversarial approach of regulating away our private property rights, which are one of the main principles that have made our country so great.

"We need to look at incentive based approaches, instead of punitive regulations, to achieve our goals," said Mr. Giorgi. He cited several programs in San Luis Obispo as good examples. "We shouldn't be at war with people who own the resources we want to protect."

"One of the main problems we have in Santa Barbara County is that there is no truth in the zoning," said Mr. Giorgi. "This creates many problems for us, such as not being able to build new houses for our children who want to continue the family farming operations, obtain production loans, do estate planning, etc."

Nancy Crawford-Hall manages more than 10,000 acres at San Lucas Ranch. She could not attend, but sent a written contribution, read by a friend.

"Every day is Earth Day for a farmer," she wrote. "You cannot expect farmers and ranchers to give up the value of their land simply for your viewing pleasure."

She cited excessive permitting, bureaucracy, and "an environmental movement hijacked for political gain," as major issues.

Speaking for the 10,000 acre Alisal Ranch, C.J. Jackson said there is not "a meaningful income" in the 1,600 head of cattle they run.

"There is preservation of agriculture, and there is preservation of the attributes that we have come to enjoy as the attributes of agriculture," he said. "In our haste to protect the attributes, try not to kill the patient—the agricultural entity that provides those attributes."

The Alisal was purchased in 1943 by his grandfather. "You have in Solvang the benefit of one of the agricultural attributes of cattle ranching, that is, the north boundary of our property" he explained. "It extends from Refugio to all the way beyond Solvang. You see the visual element of our ranch at that point."

"But the Alisal ranch is significantly more than that, and we pride ourselves on the fact that it is a very unique property. Beyond what you can see as you look out that vista, are investments in various elements of construction that we have done, looking toward the future."

"You all know that we have two golf courses. You know that we have a guest ranch program, and a housing subdivision around that golf course."

"Our objectives for the future are relatively simple. We want to retain the ownership of that ranch, and we want to retain it intact. We want to preserve the rural ranch environment, we want to maintain the high quality of services and facilities that we have over the last near sixty years."

"We are a recreation oriented development, and we wish to be a financially self sufficient development. We are a hybrid—we are a symbiotic relationship between an agricultural operation, which is the cattle business, and a resort operation."

"Realistically, although we at times run as many as 1600 head on the property, cattle, for us, with the requisite costs to feed, and the additional costs that are associated, in addition to property taxes, in addition to other urban services, etc., is a limited business, in terms of its ability to make those 10,000 acres self sufficient."

"What we have found, however, it that a symbiotic relationship between a cattle operation and a resort, that focuses on a western theme, and is, in part a dude ranch, is a workable model for integrating both the agricultural operation and a business operation that will allow us to continue to sustain ourselves on that property. And that is what we are attempting to preserve."

"As you go beyond the visual landscape that you see from Solvang, you don't see that we have a significant investment in topography that is unique, that has a great deal of potential for utility. We have a hundred acre lake that we constructed and completed in 1970, and that area is surrounded with an area that is completely removed visually from what you can see from here."

"It is an area that we may look to in the future, at some time, to develop, along the same lines of our recreational resort philosophy. That is the element and the direction in which we are headed."

"We don't have a plan right now for current development, but it is something we're thinking about," said C.J. Jackson.

Michael Feeney of the Land Trust for Santa Barbara County explained the mechanics and uses of conservation easements, some 22 of which the Land Trust has successfully negotiated in the county.

High land values have hindered enacting more such deals, as few landowners have sufficient income to take advantage of the enormous tax benefits common in such donations.

High land values also mean that many thousands of acres can be protected in more rural areas for what it costs to protect a few hundred acres here, which affects donations.

## 27. Land Trust Saves Endangered Species: Farmers & Ranchers

Farmers and ranchers in the Valley sometimes feel like they have bull's-eyes painted on their backs.

Bad news: they do. And it's not just a local problem.

The US Department of Labor publishes a list of twelve jobs with no future. Number One: farmers and ranchers. 328,000 of them are expected to disappear by 2010, the largest single job decline in the USA.

Locally, spiraling land and equipment costs and ever increasing regulations have put farm and ranch families on the economic ropes.

It's a problem that exists in communities nationwide, and it raises a thorny issue: How to preserve the jobs, products, open space and beauty provided by agriculture and ranching without obliterating private property rights.

The Land Trust For Santa Barbara County has three solutions: voluntary donations, fundraising for public purchase, and purchased or donated conservation easements. Conservation easements in particular offer a way to keep land in agriculture while easing financial strains.

"We work with willing landowners to preserve environmentally sensitive open space, wildlife habitat and agricultural land from development in Santa Barbara County," said Michael Feeney, Executive Director. The Land Trust is a membership based non-profit which serves as a bridge and a catalyst between owners and preservation entities.

Erik Gregersen, a descendant of one of the three founders of Solvang, is on the Board of the Trust and still lives on land in Ballard Canyon that's been in his family for close to a century. "We had a 2,200 acre ranch in the family, and 11 heirs. When the last generation passed on, we had to sell 1,600 acres to settle the estate. If we had the ability to do then what we can do today with conservation easements, I believe we would still have 2,200 acres."

The Trust acquires land and conservation easements through negotiation with willing private property owners, and solicits private donations and grants from government, corporations and foundations to support land preservation.

They promote habitat protection and educate the community with field trips with experts in ecology and agriculture.

The Land Trust led the drive to save the spectacular, historic Sedgwick Ranch, raising funds to purchase 782 acres. The entire 5,896 acre ranch was ultimately deeded to the University of California Natural Reserve System.

In the Santa Ynez Valley, the Trust's success stories include conservation easements donated on Walter Thompson's 313 acre Rancho Felicia, the 1,126 acre Great Oak Preserve, 70 acre Marcelino Springs, and 900 acre Rancho Las Cruces. More land will stay agricultural as a result.

Other North County work includes 130 acres at Point Sal, 17 acres at Mackie Mountain and 86 acres at the Tom Briggs Memorial Preserve.

At 1,400 acre Rancho Dos Vistas, next to Reagan's former ranch high atop the Santa Ynez Mountains, the Trust helped acquire conservation easements that cut the number of developable parcels from 14 to 3.

On the Gaviota Coast, the Trust raised $7.3 million to purchase J.J. Hollister's spectacular 782 acre Arroyo Hondo ranch for a preserve. Easements on 660 acres of Freeman Ranch and 750 acre La Paloma Ranch plus 650 acres of El Capitan Ranch were negotiated as well.

Projects on the South Coast run or aided by the Trust include 35 acres on More Mesa, the 25 acre Modoc Preserve, 52 acre Carpinteria Bluffs, 44 acre Ennisbrook Oak Woodland, 134 acres in Mission Canyon, 880 acre Rancho San Roque, and 12 acre Fairview Gardens.

The Trust frequently partners its efforts with like minded groups. In the case of the 230 acre Carpinteria Salt Marsh, they worked with UCSB, the City of Carpinteria, the State Coastal Conservancy and adjacent homeowner's associations for twenty years to restore the coastal estuary.

Millions of butterflies were saved when the Land Trust spearheaded a drive to purchase the 9.3 acre Coronado Butterfly Preserve. Funds came from individuals, government, private foundations and corporate grants.

Executive Director Feeney laments the recent loss of powerful ally—tax credits. A bill sponsored by Senator Jack O'Connell, the "Natural Heritage Preservation Tax Credit Act," provided up to one hundred million dollars in state tax credits for donations of qualified land. It became law January 1, 2001. About $38 million was awarded, including $3,025,000 in Santa Barbara County, before the program was put on hold by the current budget crunch.

## Part 2. Erik Gregersen

"I will leave this valley, and Santa Barbara County, a better place for my kids." That's Erik Gregersen's goal, and it's why the descendant of one of the founders of Solvang is promoting the work of the Land Trust for Santa Barbara County. He's the Solvang Vice-President of the Board of Trustees.

Countywide, the trust has protected over 14,000 acres through easements and acquisitions. They're working on conservation easements for two Valley properties totaling 2,000 acres. They'd like to do much more.

They've formed a partnership with the California Rangeland Trust, a group governed entirely by ranchers, whose mission is to conserve the open space, natural habitat, and stewardship provided by California's ranches. Together, they're focusing on conservation easements.

"Our first effort is always to get conservation easements, because that works better for everybody," said Mr. Gregersen.

"When we first got started, people in agriculture had a lot of misconceptions about what we did and how we did it. Now there are a lot of ranchers who are involved. Jim Poett, Willy Chamberlain, Kevin Merrill, and Brandy Branquinho, among others, are on our advisory committee," he said.

The conservation easement simply prevents development of the land. "Most people have the misconception that you actually give up ownership of your land. Of course you don't. And the misconception that you give up privacy," said Mr. Gregersen.

"People think they're going to have people wandering all over their property doing whatever, but unless they agree to that, there's no public access. If they decide to have a trail for some reason, and that's something all parties want, they can do that, of course," explained Mr. Gregersen.

Estate planning prompts many inquiries to the Trust.

"When people think about what they can do for the future of this valley, which is such a beautiful place to live, they say 'We should look into this,'" said Mr. Gregersen.

"You can set up your easement so you get some cash, and donate the rest, to make it tax neutral. In the case of a lot of ranchers around here, I think that's an attractive thing for them do if they want to pass their land on to the next generation. They can get enough cash to pay off any heirs who don't want to go ahead on the deal, and enough tax credits to significantly reduce their tax situation," he said.

"And there is money available these days to buy conservation easements for properties, especially those valued from a wildlife or a scenic point of view," he noted. "One thing we stay away from completely is any kind of manipulation of zoning. And we only work with willing landowners, who are positive about what they're doing."

Land buyers may also benefit. "If there's a conservation minded person out there looking for a ranch, sometimes you can give them some significant benefits in doing a conservation easement in conjunction with the sale," said Mr. Gregersen.

The synergy of common goals helped the Trust when they acquired the spectacular 782 acre Arroyo Hondo Ranch near Gaviota from J.J. Hollister and his family.

"One focus is writing grants that complement one another, so that if there is, for example, a habitat for steelhead, as in the case of Arroyo Hondo, then various groups that might fund that preservation can get involved," said Trustee Maurie McGuire. School classes or youth groups can schedule a visit to the historic ranch by calling Chris Chapman at 567-1115.

"On occasion we work with a developer, accepting an easement for open space within a development. That gives them a credit and gets something set aside," added Ms. McGuire.

"I think people are waking up to the fact that we're running out of time to do this kind of thing," said Mr. Gregersen.

*Cold Danes found town: We have harsh Iowa winters to thank for the founding of Solvang, revealed Eric Gregersen. His grandfather was one of the three men who made it happen.

## 28. West Pointer Katie Smyser

SY High grad Katie Smyser will graduate from West Point, commissioned a Second Lieutenant, with a bachelor's degree in literature, and a minor in environmental engineering.

She had on her class ring. West Point was the first school to create class rings. New ones are made in part of gold from old rings bequeathed by alumni. It's one of many traditions of the long gray line of West Pointers.

There was another ring, too. She's planning a summer 2005 wedding, to First Lieutenant Severin St. Martin.

"He graduated two years ago," said Katie. "We met each other on the equestrian team. He's from Minnesota, an infantry officer, in charge of a Bradley platoon in Germany. He's going to Iraq in November."

Katie's brother Tim is a junior at SY High. Her brother Joe is in the Peace Corps, in Swaziland. Mom Sandra will soon be taking over as superintendent at Las Virgenes Unified School District. Her father, David, is an attorney, Solvang City councilman, and Brooks Firestone's chief of staff.

While visiting here, Katie talked to students at SY High about West Point.

"I tell them the truth, I really do," she said. "It's a great school for academics, and it does open doors for you."

"I got the opportunity to go with the Army Corps of Engineers down to Panama and Honduras. We did humanitarian civil engineering. We built schools and clinics, deep into the jungle. I did that in the summer."

"This past summer, I took over a military police unit in Alaska, at Fort Richardson, very close to Anchorage. I was in charge of 30 military police. We went into the field and trained. My unit was going to Afghanistan in a couple months, so I got to train my soldiers for five weeks. It was pretty intense."

"Last semester I became a captain and served on the brigade staff, which is the highest level, which runs the entire school. I've actually been coined by three generals already, in only four years. In the army, if you're recognized for something, every general has their own coin. It's their own personal award. You can only get it from them. So I've had opportunities to meet these kind of people."

"It's a big commitment to make as a senior in high school. Four years in that kind of environment, and then five after that, and four in the reserves, for sure, at a minimum. That's a big commitment for a 18 year old to make, and you really have to be aware of what you're doing."

"As a plebe (first year student), you have no time that's your own. Nothing, ever. You're in uniform constantly, no civilian clothes. You're not allowed of campus, ever. No summer time off. You get the holidays off to come home. Other than that, nothing."

"It starts out pretty rough, with basic training the whole summer prior to your freshmen year. Your whole freshman year is really rough. I think being in the academy remains tough all four years, but your first year is especially physically and mentally challenging."

"I think it's hard, especially if you're a woman, getting used to the physical rigors of the army. You have to be on a par with the men. I think it's a common misconception that our rucksacks are smaller, or something like that. They're all the same, and the standards are the same. You have to be able to keep up."

"I say all the fun stuff, too. But it's a small school, 4,000 students, so you know everybody, and it's a tight knit group. Alumni are real serious about it. It's an awesome group to be a part of, but you've got to realize that you're really there to serve."

"I think sometimes people see it as this great thing, and don't realize it's a five year commitment to the army, possible for a lifetime, and you really shouldn't go for any other reason."

"There are, of course, a lot of athletes, and you can get recruited to play on the football team, or golf team. We have a large amount of women, and because we want to have competitive teams, most women at the school are varsity athletes."

"But I think you really have to know that the reason you're going there is not to play football, it's to be an officer in the army, and that's pretty huge. Lots of people go there because their fathers and their grandfathers went there. You really need to go because you want to serve the country."

"One thing kids need to know: The process for getting into the military academy is very lengthy and very difficult. It involves interviews with alumni, a nomination from a Senator or a representative. It takes a long time, and you're in competition with people. I had to go down to Port Hueneme and get physically and medically cleared. There are physical tests you have to take.

"Your whole freshman year you learn all the Army basics, like how to shoot, marching, throwing grenades, tanks, all that stuff. Later on, as you progress, your academic year is really rigorous, division one academics, a lot of core classes.

You're taking everything from physics, chemistry, calculus, all the way through to the engineering track, because in order to have a minor in engineering, you have to have those science and math basics."

"In the summer you advance on to actual Army schools. Not West Point schools. They move you to Fort Knox and Fort Campbell, and you train with real army people."

Her happiest moment: "Honestly, it was the day I graduated from air assault. I cried." She was in the 10th Mountain Division's school at Fort Drum, NY. "That's the hardest thing I've ever done, rappelling out of helicopters."

"The rappelling is quite easy. It's the rigors of the school that's known for being really tough. There're not very many women who've graduated. I graduated at the top of my class."

She was one of the first women to be the "honor graduate" of the class. Most women fail out.

"The rappelling is the final test," she remembered, "after you've been beaten up for two weeks. Up in the morning for a 12 mile march in three hours, in full gear, carrying a rifle, helmet, all the straps, four quarts of water on you, and two quarts in your backpack, probably 60 pounds altogether. Which to army folks sounds pretty easy, but after not sleeping for two weeks, it's pretty rough."

All things considered, she made a smooth transition from SY to West Point.

"I felt really prepared for West Point. Taking all of the advanced placement classes I took really helped, as well as Mr. Morris, who did a great job with the massive application paperwork. I took classes over at Hancock during the summer. At West Point, you have to take classes in things you're bad at. You can't take elective classes in the first two years."

"West Point classes are tough. They're taught by military officers, as well as professors. It's very regimented. They walk into a classroom, and the class stand to attention. Very small classes, maybe eight people, very competitive. Being able to go out on the weekend is completely dependent on what grades you got. It really matters."

She emphasized the value of high school sports.

"The physical rigors are tough, but if you come from a background of competitive high schools sports, you can make it, and you can do fine. Even as a small person, if you have the stamina of something like long distance running, you can handle it, and you can hack it with the guys."

She ran track and cross-country at Santa Ynez.

"At West Point, I think more so than at the other academies, running is essential. I completed my first marathon last November. I did the Philly marathon. It was really fun."

"I never thought that I would use my horse riding at school, but I just walked right onto their team. Now I do three foot jumping on thoroughbreds with the team." She's captain of the equestrian team. "We do western as well as English. We've competed on the national level, with intercollegiate teams."

She has two roommates, but didn't get many opportunities to see much of the 100 other women in her class.

"It takes a long time to get to know other girls, for no other reason than you just don't see them. For the first two years of school, I was the only girl in every class, the only girl at the table at every meal."

That makes the ties she has forged very special.

"My friendships with my girlfriends there will last forever. They're my bridesmaids, I went to Air Assault with them, I crossed the finish line at the marathon with them, I ride with them. We're very close."

She's off to Fort Huachuca, in Arizona, for six months, then to a posting in Germany.

"After you graduate, you go into different branches," Katie explained. "We have gotten tons of training on how to be an officer at West Point, but it isn't specific to branches. I'm going to Fort Huachuca for six months to learn everything there is to know about military intelligence, before I go to take over a military intelligence unit."

"I'm posted to Germany. Posting is based on your class rank. Class rank is not like normal schools. Your academic grade, physical grade and military grade are all put together. I'm 148th of 952, altogether."

She's hoping to be at military headquarters, near Heidelberg.

I asked about her long term goals.

"I could see myself staying in and working in military intelligence. A lot of my mentors have been military attaches. You work in conjunction with the State Department. There's a military attaché for each country."

"When I was in Honduras and Panama, I met the military attaches. They send you to get your graduate degree from the Monterey Language Institute. I could totally see myself following that path. If I got out, I would always be working for the government. I could see myself going the intelligence route, something like the National Security Agency, or Central Intelligence Agency, something like that."

One thing she'll always remember: "At the moment that the seniors march up to the football stadium to graduate, everyone else has a formal promotion ceremony. You become the next rank, and take the place of the people who've left. When I became a sergeant, which is a junior, that was great."

"You're not really an upperclassman until you're a sergeant. They take your bars and turn them over, and you have your new ones underneath. It symbolizes a lot, because when you come in as a new kid, a plebe, at the very bottom, the cadets that are training you are of the rank of sergeant."

"So it's like, Oh my gosh, I'm it, I'm the person who was yelling at me a few years ago."

"I thought, man, I've made it. That was awesome."

## 29. Home, Home On the Range

*Friends* star Matt LeBlanc, who played the lovably exasperating Joey Tribbiani on the number one ranked show in America, purchased property in Los Alamos in 2002.

TV Guide voted *Friends* one of the "Greatest Shows of All Time." In November 2002, AOL subscribers voted LeBlanc and Jennifer Aniston the award of *Best Couple on TV*. *Friends* hit the nine year mark in May of 2003.

In addition to his hit role on the top comedy series, LeBlanc's film credits include *All the Queen's Men* (2002), *Charlie's Angels* (2000), and *Lost in Space* (1998). In 2003 he was in *Charlie's Angels: Full Throttle*, reprising his role as clueless boyfriend to Angel Alex (Lucy Liu). Then he got his own show, *Joey*.

LeBlanc was said to make $1,000,000 per episode on *Friends*. At that rate, it took him less than seven shows to pay for his ranch, which had a reported $6,500,000 sale price.

The 1,052 acre ranch has forests of valley oak, coast live oak and blue oaks, meadows of poppies and lupine, several ponds, seasonal streams, miles of dirt roads and abundant wild life, including deer, red-tailed hawk, dove, quail and wild pig.

There's a five bedroom, four bath ranch home, plus a two bedroom, two bath pool house, tennis court, and a three bedroom, two bath manager's quarters, all nestled in a setting of oaks, rolling hills, and verdant grasslands known as excellent cattle country.

Three barns, working corrals, cattle chutes, grain silo and numerous pastures give the ranch the feeling of an authentic turn of the century homestead. Not far away, rows of grapes disappear into infinity over pastoral hills in this pristine area of large ranches.

Originally part of the Rancho de La Laguna Mexican Land Grant acquired by Jose Ramon Rodriguez in 1840, the property has been owned over the years by Otaviano Gutierrez (Nov. 14, 1845), Los Alamos town founder Dr. J.B. Shaw, Fred Wickenden, Louis Bourdet, Steve and Bonnie Tetrick, and Richard and Tina Broida.

Nearby Los Alamos, founded in 1876, awakened from decades of benign neglect and transformed itself into a vineyard village during the 90's. It's now surrounded by grapes owned by major companies including Kendall-Jackson, Sutter Home, Byron, Beringer, Mondavi, and Meridian. Other vineyards supply boutique wineries such as Longoria, Bedford-Thompson, Chimere, Lucas-Lewellen, and Clendenen.

TV's Friends hung out at a coffeehouse called Central Perk. Los Alamos' version of Central Perk is charming Café Quackenbush, the hot spot for lattes and dining in the newly gentrified village.

When they opened a few years ago, manager John Morley wasn't sure what kind of reception they would have in a still-rough-around-the-edges town, more used to biker bars than biscotti.

There was a defining, *High Noon* moment early the first day. Just after the doors opened, a battered pickup screeched to a halt in the dusty street outside.

A big cowboy, complete with ten gallon hat, boots, and rodeo belt, barged in the door and strode to the counter. His broad shoulders blotted out the sun as he looked Morley right in the eye and — ordered a non-fat latte.

Just across the street, the 1880's vintage Pacific Coast Railway depot, now an antiques mall, is the largest business in this town of 1,400.

LeBlanc is not the first star to pioneer this territory. Kiefer Sutherland sold his 800 acre ranch just over the ridge in 2000 for $3.2 million, to concentrate on his hit series *24*.

Fess Parker's winery, James Garner's former ranch, and producer Ray Stark's ranch are just a short hop down the Foxen Canyon wine trail. In Santa Ynez, Jimmy Stewart's former Little Wine Cup Ranch, some 900 acres of great beauty, sold for around $10 million in 2004.

As the world now knows, Michael Jackson's 2,676 acre Neverland ranch is a few miles away, in Los Olivos. Jackson bought in 1988 after filming the video *Say, Say, Say* at the Union Hotel in Los Alamos, with Paul McCartney.

LeBlanc has kept a low profile here, not jumping into community fundraisers and events like his Charlie's Angels co-star, a man much loved in the Santa Ynez Valley for his open, down-to-earth manner, the genteel John Forsythe.

Other stars with homes here include Cheryl Ladd; Bo Derek; singer Ed Ames; songwriter Bernie Taupin; Kelly LeBrock; Jimmy Messina; Noah Wyle; David Crosby; celebrity journalist Rona Barrett; Efrem Zimbalist Jr.; James Arness (*Gunsmoke*'s Matt Dillon), author Thomas McGuane, musician Jackson Browne, film maker Bruce Brown (*Endless Summer, On Any Sunday, ES2*); and comic Ellen DeGeneres, who bought a Tuscan villa on 100 acres in June of 2005.

Former residents include Jimmy Stewart, Dean Martin, Steven Seagal, Michael McDonald, President Reagan, Ginger Baker, Ray Bradbury, director John Ford, Jimmy Connors, Rod Laver, Fred Astaire, David Cassidy, Whoopi Goldberg, "Bowser" Bauman of *Sha Na Na*, Warhol film star Edie Sedgwick, and producer Douglas Cramer. 1976 Olympic gold medal decathlete Bruce Jenner owned 100 acres in Happy Canyon, but did not live here.

*Cream* drummer Ginger Baker first rented here in Buellton. He lived in a modest A-frame home near what is now the new Oak Valley School.

Local mortgage broker Fraser Botwright was astonished to bump into the one-time superstar as Baker tacked flyers offering drum lessons on telephone poles around town. The two expatriate Englishmen became friends.

Baker moved to a small house on ten acres on Edison Street in Santa Ynez, shortly before his 1993 Hall of Fame induction. Later, complaining no one here knew how to groom horses properly, he left for Colorado, then South Africa.

Baker's passion was polo ponies. He rode with former Monkee Mickey Dolenz, and several physicians, on a team dubbed "Drummers and Doctors."

Rona Barrett was a heavy hitter in Hollywierd, dishing up the foibles of the stars for years, before she moved here and launched a line of lavender products from plants grown on her own land. A former Miss Universe, Meryl Tanz, followed suit. Ms. Tanz was once married to David Cassidy. They lived on a ranch on Roblar Avenue known as Clairmont Farms, which she purchased from author Ray Bradbury.

After almost thirty years, the Ray Stark era in the Santa Ynez Valley officially ended January 17, 2004, when the fabled producer passed away in his sleep at his Holmby Hills home in Los Angeles. He was 88.

The moving vans rolled at his picturesque "Corral de Quati" ranch near Los Olivos. Sotheby's catalogued the contents of the handful of homes. Some of his Monet, Braque, and Rodin works went on the block in New York City. Modern art masterpieces by Henry Moore, Alexander Calder, Noguchi, Elisabeth Frink, and Ellsworth Kelly that dotted the front lawn have been carted off to the new Fran and Ray Stark Sculpture Garden at the LA County Museum.

Ray Stark was already a veteran agent and producer when he discovered Barbra Streisand in New York's *Bon Soir* nightclub in 1963. She paid back his faith with a hit Broadway musical and an Oscar winning role in the film *Funny Girl*, telling the story of Frances Stark's mother, comedienne Fanny Brice.

*Funny Girl* was Stark's first project with his fledgling Rastar Productions. Many more followed. It was only one of countless coups for the legendary dealmaker, who cobbled together alliances between mercurial, demanding, prodigious talents and the writers, directors, and money men who gear up the Hollywood dream machine.

The low profile Stark is credited with making over 125 films, including the Redford-Streisand hit *The Way We Were*, the John Huston directed Richard Burton-Ava Gardner classic *The Night of The Iguana*, and *The Sunshine Boys*, for which George Burns picked up an Academy Award. In 1993, he made *Barbarians at the Gates* for HBO. Hollywood considered him the last of the great independent producers.

His films grossed more than a billion dollars at Columbia Pictures alone. In 1984, Forbes magazine estimated his net worth at over $175 million.

Born in 1915, he attended Rutgers and New York University, dabbling in law and journalism, before heading to Hollywood in 1938. He first found work as a florist at Forest Lawn cemetery, then moved on to livelier clients at Warner Bros.

Producer Julia Phillips, of *The Sting, Taxi Driver*, and *Close Encounters of the Third Kind*, credited Stark in her catty Tinseltown tell-all *You'll Never Eat Lunch In This Town Again* with rescuing her from a self-destructive spiral of cocaine abuse, with a job offer.

Astounded visitors to his ranch, nestled between the Firestone and Fess Parker vineyards on the gorgeous Foxen Canyon wine trail, saw an open air museum of priceless works as they drove up Stark's split rail fenced driveway to a cozy enclave of vintage ranch homes and barns.

Like a wagon train stopped for the night, the many rust-red buildings at Rancho Corral De Quati circle a spacious center lawn formerly studded with statuary. Classic barns and numerous low slung, shake-roofed cottages are nestled below a sheltering ridgeline, shaded by towering oak trees. It's an Old West atmosphere, and it comes by it honestly. Stark's 256 acres are the heart of a 13,300 acre land grant of the same name made to Augustin Davilla in the 1800's, and home to horses, sheep and cattle ever since.

From the mid 1940's to 1952, Edie Sedgwick's family owned the ranch. Insiders say Bob Dylan wrote *Just Like a Woman* with the Vogue model and Warhol actress in mind. Some former employees swear Edie still visits, even though she's been buried in the Oak Hill Cemetery in Ballard since a barbiturate overdose claimed her life on November 16, 1971, at age 28. Edie's troubled odyssey from sleepy Santa Ynez to Warhol's wild New York scene, where she starred in Andy's bizarre art flick *Ciao! Manhattan*, was chronicled by Jean Stein and George Plimpton.

I went to Edie's grave to check dates. There on the ground by the tombstone were two fresh pictures of her, with the Manhattan skyline in the background. Someone still cares.

Stark bought the property in the 1970's and made it a getaway and a home for his thoroughbred racing stable. He was named California Breeder of the Year in 1982 and 1983. His horse Cacoethes shook up the English race world as the first California-bred to place in the top three in the historic 1989 Epsom Derby, and was California's outstanding turf runner in 1990. Casey, the horse who co-starred with Walter Matthau in 1978's *Casey's Shadow*, lived to be over 30 on the ranch.

# 30. For Whom The Bale Tolls

I am at an old ranch in Happy Canyon. The ranch houses cry out their history. Twisted boards of pioneer wood are worn witness to sweat and revelry, boredom, carnage, birth, death, desire, all the instincts of a life on the land.

In the bunkhouse, leather chaps hang on the wall. The long, dull steel hooks next to them, their worn brown wooden handles smoothed by sweat drenched leather gloves grabbing and throwing a million golden bales of hay, are screaming to be released into their element.

Summer's here. Bronze rectangles dot the fields like cast-off shredded wheat biscuits, cute little leaden cubes stretching in uniform rows to the horizon.

I hauled hay summers during college, here and as far afield as the Lost Trail Ranch in Marion, Montana. There, over a month, our six man crew collected and stacked some 29,000 hay bales on a ranch that stretched as far as the eye could see.

Now rare, such back-breaking hay field labor was universal before the mechanized hay loader, or "harrow-bed," was invented in the 1960's. In 1975, with two other UCSB students, I made a 12 minute documentary film shot here called *Broken Arrow-Valley Hay Haulers.*

The film follows a day in the life of a two man hay hauling team. Hot west winds blow a cloud of swirling oats, and as the whirling chaff clears we see a hay crew sweating in the fields.

A flatbed truck with loader clumsily attached to the side slowly trundles along a hillside of endless 120 pound oat hay bales, in the bright light of a spectacular morning. The truck bumps and yaws over the sloping, rough terrain. A bale bounces off the back of the truck.

The hammering, clanging, smacking, ever-spinning cruel hooks of the hay loader, driven by a deafening gas engine, drowns out even shouted voices. The man on the back of the truck bangs his steel hay hooks on the top of the battered loader to get the driver's attention. The truck lurches to a halt.

The driver leans out of the cab and looks up. This is easy, for the cab door has been removed so he can use his hooks on bales stuck in the loader on the ground to his left while in motion. Shards of oat straw are stuck to the man on back of the truck, in the rivulets of sweat coursing down his bare skin. It is seven in the morning.

"We lost one. Hold on."

The loader man moves to the back of the truck and rearranges the stack. He grabs the water cooler and takes a long drink.

The rig trundles on, each little bump on the hillside unbalancing the heavy load a little more.

Shortly thereafter, loaded with about five tons of hay, stacked five rows high, a modest jolt tilts the load, still jiggling along the hillside, once too often. In slow motion, about forty bales fall from the truck back onto the field. Bales spin in space; dusty, frolicking golden pinwheels.

The man on the back bangs on the cab roof. Hard.

The truck stops. The driver gets out and looks at the topsy-turvy mess on the ground. He lays down on the field, arms outstretched, a discouraged human "X" on an endless expanse of stubble.

The loader man kicks off more unstable bales. He begins again. The driver rises and pitches in. They tie the re-stacked load down and lurch off to a stack by Armour Ranch Road, about a mile away, and unload. The day gets hotter, and the dance begins again. They've been at it since 4 am. They'll move 30 tons today, five truckloads. Driver and loader switch roles each load.

Fortunately, only one or two loads a season ended up on the ground. It was a minor miracle that we caught it on film.

The work was intense and dangerous, but it yielded hard muscles, a tanned confidence in oneself and a relatively good paycheck. It was a tortuous but beautiful life, its truths as real as being in a golden field at sunrise swinging work shined curved steel hay hooks, bright arcs glinting in the sun. More than my own past, it is a door into all those summers past when machines were not equal to muscle.

Some fields are still too steep for the harrow-bed. And on those sun-splashed slopes, the bales are waiting.

## Part 2. A Land Of Dreams

*"Man is born unto trouble, as the sparks fly upward."*

—Job 5, v. 2

Kalispell, Montana, 1971: The traffic lights now have Polaroid lenses. Shopping malls are displacing the pines. The bars get new owners, but the town always seems the same, a dusty, two-bit patch of cowboy asphalt in the shadow of the fiercer Rockies.

Only the names change as the generations rise quickly to an overconfident maturity, amid crushing boredom. They marry at 16, or leave for either coast, only to return with the babies for another cycle.

Woolworth's, J.C. Penney, street lights, parking meters, power wires, old truck, new trucks, courthouse in city center forcing traffic around it into greener residential streets; burger and fried chicken joints; the town drizzles away, dying with a dirt motorcycle track, an auto wrecking yard.

Scarred trees edge warily into the forests beyond, up to the mountain ridge bathed in clouds, against a perfect sky.

The cherry factory at the town's west edge boxes millions of fruit nonstop in the season. High school labor, romancing on breaks in the parking lot, thinking seriously about leaving cherries and Kalispell behind forever, like a bad dream in the swamplands and marshes of memory.

The Lost Trail Ranch lies sprawled across a wide green Montana valley, bordered by logging scars which climb the hillsides to the sky, pale blue with a sprinkling of airbrushed clouds in the summer, white with snow in the winter months, when the hay bales freeze and the foreman has to go after them with an axe.

The cold dulls his reflexes. His cortisone shots fade into pain.

Anaconda Copper has logged in this area since before the turn of the century. Before the road was built, the railroad moved their logs out of this secluded valley. The rails were pulled up during World War II and recycled into munitions.

The loggers clear cut. Acres of wasteland dot impenetrable forest. Abandoned logging camps stand haunted in the overgrown clearings. Rusted giant saw blades, shattered log cabins and stables, huge mounds of sawdust.

There is a horse skull; a Pennzoil can with a prop plane and the legend "Pride of America's Fleet" barely visible; some broken bottles.

Wildflowers wave amidst the tall green grass of July.

The ranch is fourteen miles from the nearest town, Marion.

One gas pump beside the oiled gravel road; candy wrappers and tinfoil lodged in the weeds outside the tiny store/post office that is the sole commercial enterprise. The postmaster's daughter dreams wearily in pine forested desolation.

The old railroad tunnel off in the canyon on the way to the ranch was dynamited shut, but the years have opened its mouth. Water covers the floor, several inches deep. A cold wind slips out over the shrouded mound of earth that once blocked the entry.

There is an ID card left years before on a rocky ledge by a faceless explorer. It is found by flashlight in the doomed atmosphere of decay, badly deteriorated, but legible: Kalispell High School. Footprints on the beach.

The road out to the ranch from the main highway is a fourteen mile long rut, a washboard made worse daily by the logging rigs that dominate it, demanding ditch licking subservience from the pedestrian pickups and beaten family sedans.

Occasionally a pickup sails into the canyon above the deserted railway tunnel, where perpetual water drops grow four foot thick crystal columns in winter, and wandering cows disappear, prematurely iced.

Other travelers fall into the swamp of forest/lake muck, where water dammed by the construction of the road has collected around the tangled trees.

Cowboy casualties are easy to replace. The Lost Trail's foreman hits the Stockholm Bar in downtown Kalispell, where ranchers and the transient farm population mingle in feudal drinking; a convivial atmosphere of crew cut, snap-button, leather booted wrangling, all reflected by the room length mirror at the back of the bar.

Entire hay crews have been recruited from the Stockholm Bar. In forest fire season, the green Forestry trucks pull up outside and invite every male who can walk to earn smoke pay.

The foreman picked up the new bailer boy there, after the local boy ran one too many fence posts through the John Deere.

Johnny would have driven his '58 Chevy home in a huff, but it had a dead battery. So he walked the fourteen miles to Marion, too proud to call for a lift.

The Lost Trail always has three crews, they said in town. One coming, one going, and one on the ranch.

The signposts that flank the entry stand stark against the blue sky. Two wooden wagon wheels flank the cattleguard. There is no sign up where the portal board once read "Lost Trail-Elliott." The mailbox bears no name or number.

A blue Corvair Monza pulls dustily to the cattleguard that begins the long dirt driveway to the headquarters of the Lost Trail. Three men, in their late teens and early twenties, emerge and stretch beside it, surveying the valley and the complex of buildings below. In a moment another car arrives; a faded metallic red Plymouth Fury with chrome wheels, in which three more young men ride.

The drivers confer for a moment. The Ponderosa pine forests loom behind them. Then both autos move down the driveway. Weeds growing on the driveway's center hump lick at the universal joints.

The ranch house is a battered, two-story Victorian. The weather beaten barns are devoid of paint.

They left the Santa Ynez Valley on a sunny morning in June, just after Bill's high school graduation, and motored to Cayucos to pick up Elliott at his beach house, where the sea moaned through the plate glass, and wind-blown spray licked the doors.

Elliott and Bob and Roger and Barney had scrambled eggs while waiting for Dave, who had gotten lost somewhere along the way. Bill found a small coyote skull, and stuck it on the hood ornament of Elliott's Plymouth. They looked like a down-at-the-heels country band.

The snow on Mount Shasta was white as a benediction.

The Corvair slid to a halt beside the bunkhouse, a low shed-like building shabbily converted for human housing.

Uninsulated, it has a sliding barn-type door that is closed only at night. There are eight beds, ranging from a metal framed one with head and footboards, mattress and box spring, to an army cot that sags at the end of the room, next to an open sink and doorless shower.

The refrigerator is full of horse and cow vaccines, serums, and syringes. The faded white walls are peeling fiberboard. A leaking hot water heater stands in one corner, a shaky table with a broken Wollensak ¼" tape recorder on it, in another. Coat racks line the walls, in lieu of closets. A box of used house paint leaks beneath the tape player table.

Two stubby, mutt dogs follow the foreman as he makes his rounds. Each has three legs. They leap from the ground to the moving pickup with practiced agility, adapted to their crippling. Each moves his remaining rear leg twice as fast as before the foreman ran over them.

One was maimed by the bailer, the other with the pickup. One is bereft of his right, the other his left rear leg, cut off at the thigh.

They follow him everywhere, stepping on his face at midnight as he curses the broken bailer, lying flat on his back in the darkness of the lower fields, wet with the dew.

They run away when he starts in fright from his mechanical stupor, cutting his forehead on the machine, thinking in his harried disorder a coyote has attacked him.

They return soon to chase each other in the path of the bailer, somehow evading the slicing knives and the falling bales, which threaten to squash their haunted bodies.

They dance through the bailer headlights, as the foreman argues with himself in the frost-laden, moondark cold.

The man himself is gaunt, like his dogs. He is waiting for the end as the foremen of the Lost Trail, stumbling through life short-changed in competence, savagely trying to make amends, always at the expense of those around him.

The Stockholm Bar (motto: No Home Like the Stockholm) bailer boy was from Central California. He was religious at the breakfast table, a big beer drinking fellow when it came to hoisting a few, and he didn't know too much about machines. He had the face of an idiot Pope.

His bunkhouse buddy was from "Flawrida."

"Where we bailed sawr grass, twelve feet high, and yer was in fear of alligators, allus runnin' over 'em, cause you couldn't see where yer was goin'."

He claimed to have once owned a Corvette Sting Ray in his glory years, before his wife left him and took the car and its built-in reel-to-reel tape player with her.

Florida was a pathological liar. He looked like a crude Clark Gable; came to breakfast with his cologne wrapped around him like a blanket, dug into his overeasies and cold toast with a sack full of coarse dreams spilling from his kerchiefed throat.

He wore a black embroidered shirt and boots with stiletto heels. His receding black hair, greased back, looked like a skullcap.

The Bailer smiled benevolently and spoke of his abandoned wife and three children only as a bargaining chip in wage arguments.

The foreman's wife, and her junior cook sidekick, heaped greasy food on the table for eleven hands.

She pocketed the difference between bacon and salt pork, along with most of the t-shirts, whenever she could be persuaded to do the laundry. She had not spent years running a Nebraska bar without learning the art of rolling the hapless.

Much of her free time was spent in searching for affronts to her womanhood. She found in this field a ripe harvest. Her husband was the Lord High Executioner of her neurotic whims, derived from twisted loneliness. Their lives were led in scrabbling intensity, and their scars were many.

The junior cook was a replacement of the cute one. The cute one had suffered incurable hysteria after a trail ride alone with the foreman.

The valley is watered by a snowdrift lake, filled with leeches. It floods the fields, like a pre-Aswan Nile in miniature, after spring thaw, and the wheat grows without irrigation in its plain.

Two Minneapolis-Moline tractors, like bulldozers in design, alternately pull each other out of the soft ground that surrounds this receded pond. They prowl about the fields all year with a diesel snarl, their stacks dull rust brown in the daytime, cherry red at dusk, plowing, disking, seeding, and sledding hay.

The hay sleds are like reinforced billboards laid flat, big 8' by 20' boards dragged on the ground behind the Minnes while the hay bucks pull bales in from both sides, stacking them three or four high on the moving palettes from back to front. The bales are two wire hot dogs of 120 pounds each, gathered at the rate of 200 to 1,000 a day, seven days a week, at the rate of six cents a bale, as long as the foreman can put them out. But he keeps breaking down; physically, mentally, morally, mechanically.

The crew hit the fields. It was a five mile drive to the broad valley floor where were scattered the first few bales of a projected thirty thousand. Bouncing out of the pickup, after a week of drinking and driving, Bill was driving one Minne, even though he had never driven a tractor before. Dave and Barney were on one sled, Bob and Elliott were on the other, Roger at the wheel.

With a shove of the hand clutch, the Minnes lurched off across the level valley floor between the rows of bales. The men on the sleds pulled in bales from either side with their hooks and began a wall at the rear. Ninety-five bales apiece later, the sleds returned to begin the stack.

The ungainly pile the new haulers built earned local notoriety as the ugliest production in the county.

It seemed to want to get up and lumber away, and from time to time it would spontaneously quake and fall over, until propped up with 2 x 4's.

It was too wide, too high, and built with soggy, uneven bales of various density, from sheer bricks to bales you could put your foot through, in assorted shapes and sizes. The foreman had selected the site, the only slope in the entire field.

Reeling with nausea from the flaming sun, exhaustion and the effects of accumulated alcohol molecules, they built on, throughout the afternoon. The elevator was brought up to raise the higher levels, after the foundation work was through.

As the stack grew taller, the first signs of grief became obvious. The softer bales on the bottom were far lighter than those above, due to one of the foreman's malfunctions. They flattened under the weight, and tilted the stack precariously.

Thousands of bales and several avalanches later, the monolith was abandoned. The next outside stack was a carefully built square that fell down rather magnificently, almost exploding, apparently from a combination of intense heat and moist bales.

Dave and Elliott were dispatched to garner design tips from stacks about the countryside. They returned with a three wide design which became the hauler's standard. Atop the final, solid, tapered-for-snow rectangle, the crew posed for pictures.

The foreman breaks down again. The hay crew sits idle, thinking of ways to avoid the bad food, get a few beers, and spend the money they're not making.

Beer foamed up the neck and spilled out. Dave took a long hit, and passed the bottle.

The Minneapolis Moline gargled throatily and lumbered off. From the wide fender, the night spotlight threw a dim circle on the sled behind. Bob and Bill alternately slid into it in knee-drop Al Jolson stances, arms flung wide, singing *Swanee* and *Old Man River*, mugging furiously as they rocked towards the bales.

Dave bounded over as they crossed the second crew's path, danced in their midst, stacked a bale, hooted, confided something unintelligible, and sped away, leaping mad ellipses across the golden field.

It was over an hour's drive back to the ranch from Kalispell, so they didn't.

The only place the crew could find to sleep was an open church. The doors were closed but unlocked. The empty pews gleamed dully in the moonlight.

Their voices echoed from the silent altar, shrouded in the shadows of dusk.

He laid down on a pew.

Not real comfy, he concluded.

What little conversation there was, decreased in volume, until it stopped altogether.

"Is this legal?"

"Puritan superstition," declared Barney. "The church can't throw you out. They're tax exempt."

Out of the gloom came notes from Roger's harmonica. He was busy breaking into the refrigerator downstairs.

It was too weird. They ended up in some girl's parents' backyard, in their sleeping bags.

"If they're here again tomorrow night, you can leave with them," her dad told her.

It rained. The bales must be turned to dry, or they will rot in the stack, or smolder in slow oxidation until spontaneous combustion takes the barn down in flames. The crew agrees to flip every bale in the field for four cases of beer. They ran like elves through the lines of bales, deftly spinning them in half-circles.

The foreman reneges on his pledge when the job is done, and will not honor the credit at the store.

By the time they left, they'd stacked 29,000 bales. They made up stories of imaginary pioneers as they stacked, taking on the personages and exchanging spontaneous reactions.

Bill's grandmother sent a box of grotesquely colored imitation sugar orange slices. It would have been a perfect present for the foreman's wife, but Roger burglarized it.

"Give it to Roseanne," Barney suggested. "Oink Oink. Tell her it's for doing the laundry. Maybe she'll stop stealing our shirts."

It might have avoided what happened later. They probably could have bought her off that cheaply; with a two pound box of candied crud they wouldn't touch themselves. At least, five out of six wouldn't.

"Jesus, I'll pay for them," offered Roger, when they discovered he had opened the box and eaten two.

There wasn't another such box in forty-five miles, and they didn't want to spend any money on the ploy, anyway. The oranges had come unbidden, like a broad hint from fate.

Mrs. P. ran the thrift store. They always stopped there to see what sorts of exotica Montanans considered dispensable. There were some fine hats to be had for 50 cents, and one time, an oil painting. He bought some leather shoes. The soles were slick.

Mrs. P. said the local rumor was that the foreman was selling off pregnant cows in a kind of cowboy swindle. His buddy bought the cows and got free calves. Elliott thought this was jealous talk, inspired by revenge. Mrs. P. and her husband had run the ranch before the current foreman took over.

He wore the antique shoes on the hay sled. They felt pioneer-like and mysterious.

As the stack neared the front of the sled, where the dust rumbled up from the Minneapolis Moline's huge wheels, and they were pulling in the last bales to finish up the load, his soles lost their grip on the iron runner which lipped the sled.

His foot hit the field. The sled ran over it. It ran over his ankle too, and bent it flat to the ground. It ran over his lower leg. It slapped him on the ground. He hit hard, flopping sideways as the sled ran over his thigh. His left leg was on top of the hay sled. His right was underneath. The sled was planning to cut him in half.

As the iron lip hit his crotch, his whole body lurched forward. He was being shoved along the hayfield at the speed of the tractor on his side, with a hay sled weighing tons pushing and holding down his body. His entire right side, from the shoulder on, was being scraped along on the stubble and rocks and dirt of the field.

He and Roger were both screaming. It seemed like they had been screaming for a long time before Barney heard them over the roar of the tractor, looked back, saw him down, jerked the clutch out of gear, and stopped the rig. Another moment, or a snag of any kind in the field, and he would have been broken in two. The sled would have snapped his pelvis, swiveled his left leg up around his ear, and rolled over him like a knife over soft butter.

As it was, the weight of the sled was crushing his leg as it lay trapped. He could feel it being pushed into the earth, crushed by tons of hay. Barney and Roger tried to lift the loaded sled. They got it up a few inches, and dropped it back. That made it worse.

"Take off some bales," he suggested.

Roger threw a bale twenty feet. From his perspective on the ground it looked like a rocket going to the moon. He had never seen a bale go so far so fast before. The front corner of the sled was empty in a few seconds. Roger and Barney tried again.

This time, as they lifted, he could pull himself out.

He got to his feet and surveyed the damage. His shoulder was bleeding, where the earth and stubble had clawed it as he was pushed along the ground. His crotch was painfully sore. His leg was scratched under his jeans, but not badly.

He wondered if he could still make love.

They talked, laughed, screamed; relief and adrenalin surging. They relived each move. It seemed an eternity had passed.

After a few minutes, he said "Let's go back to work."

Barney was still walking in circles, hyperventilating.

"You might be ready," said Barney, "But I'm not."

The foreman's excuse for kicking them off the ranch: Barney's bare bottom.

The shower in the bunkhouse quit. They had to walk one hundred feet to the bailer boy's cottage to shower.

On the way back one day, Dave took a picture of Barney pretending to ride the Jawa 350 in his boxer shorts.

Barney mooned the camera.

Mrs. Foreman, it turned out, was intently observing this comedy from the kitchen.

They went to town, except for Bill. He heard a truck come up to the house. A few minutes later, the maniacal foreman stepped onto the porch with a shotgun and fired it once in the air.

"I'll kill that son of a bitch!" he screamed.

In the bunkhouse, Bill prepared. He pulled on his red Oshkosh headband, to look fierce. He grabbed Roger's Marine knife, and opened his own pocketknife. He had never been in a fight in his life.

The foreman darkened the door.

He seem taken aback to see Bill sitting on his bunk, stroking the knife blades against one another. He had left the shotgun behind.

"What are you doing?" he asked.

"Just sharpening these knives."

He was cautious.

"You boys have got to get off the ranch. I hate to tell you, 'cause you've always been all right, but some of these guys are no good."

He walked out.

The real reason: having people there who knew how badly he was screwing up was a worse gamble than firing the owner's son.

He found them at the Powder Keg. They had a pitcher of beer. They were mildly surprised and indignant, but they recognized the comic aspects of it. Elliott called his dad, who made plans to fly in and fire the foreman.

"Boys," said Mr. Elliott, "How would like to help me run the ranch?"

They would be delighted.

He made his way to the fairgrounds. The carnival was at full tilt, neon pinwheels spinning across the sky. He jumped the fence, and walked out on the crowded midway.

She was there, too, with some cowboy.

They told him he was hanging almost out of Dave's car shouting, "The Sons of Norway want you!" to passing pedestrians, but he didn't remember anything, except the cold metal car door against his cheek.

Mr. Elliott went out to the ranch. The foreman had just had his little finger amputated. Damaged by the cold and the cortisone, it was gangrenous.
Elliott Sr. took pity on him.
"I couldn't do it, boys," he apologized.
He wrote out their final checks, and disappeared into the darkness.

Midnight. A diner in a parking lot, under a single harsh streetlight; made from a train car.
One man sat at the single row of fixed stools, talking to the guy behind the counter.
Ordered mushroom soup. Cook opened the world's smallest Campbell's can, dumped it in a pot, slopped it in front of him.
Ate.
There was a fly-specked calendar on the wall.
It was his 18th birthday.
Left.
He stepped back into the cold darkness, and walked away from the pool of light.
He was 1,000 miles from home, in a strange city in the middle of the night, with no idea where his friends were.
You always think everything is so great, said the little voice. I hope you remember this.

## 31. Mission Santa Inés

(2004) The tranquil beauty of the Santa Ynez Mission today gives no hint of the turbulent currents of history that have swept it for two hundred years. Named after Saint Agnes, a 13 year old girl martyred in 304 AD, the stately edifice has survived natural, political and financial disasters that repeatedly threatened its existence. Zephyrin Engelhardt detailed its history in the book *Mission Santa Inés*, published in 1932. Following are some highlights of the last 200 years.

Founded by Franciscan Estevan Tapis in 1804, to minister to approximately one thousand Native Americans, the structure sat on a nearly treeless bluff, as arid in summer as a lunar landscape.

An aqueduct solved the water problem, but the ambitious improvements begun by the padres suffered a major setback from the 1812 earthquake. Eighty adobe dwellings had just been completed when the tremor came.

On December 21, 1812, at 10 am, two earthquakes at 15 minute intervals made "a considerable aperture in one corner of the church" and "threw down the said corner, and a quarter of the new houses contiguous to the church collapsed to the foundation." The permanent replacement structure was not completed until Friday, July 4, 1817.

By 1824, 564 Indian men, women and children worked at the mission. In February of that year, simmering anger, fed by years of abuse from the soldiers they were forced to maintain, was unleashed when one Corporal Cota ordered the flogging of a neophyte from Mission La Purisima.

On the afternoon of Saturday, February 21, a number of Indians, armed with bows and arrows, attacked the soldiers, who retreated to buildings at the rear of the church and returned fire. Two neophytes from La Purisima were killed.

The attackers then torched the building in which the soldiers were hiding. When the fire spread to the roof of the vestry in the rear of the church, however, the rebels did all they could to prevent the church from burning down.

From the Mission log: "All the workshops, the soldier's barracks and the habitations of the guards were destroyed."

Reinforcements from Santa Barbara rescued the besieged soldiers and put down the remnants of the rebellion the following day.

Friar Baldomero Lopez wrote "the revolt was not against the missionaries; on the contrary, the revolting Indians wanted to have the Fathers go along with them, and told them they would care for them. The revolt came about because they were made to work in order to maintain the troops, and nothing was given them in payment…"

In 1834, the Mexican territorial government confiscated all the missions. On June 15, 1846, just days before the end of Mexican rule, Governor Pio Pico sold Santa Inés to his niece's husband for $7,000. It literally took an act of Congress to get it back. The final declaration was signed by Abraham Lincoln himself, on May 23, 1862.

Around 1870, as Father Juan Basso celebrated Holy Mass, the pulpit, which was mounted some six feet high on the wall, fell to the floor of the church with a resounding crash. The priest was not injured, and completed the service. The pulpit was not replaced.

Ballard pioneer Grace Lyons Davison saw an abandoned structure on her first day here, in 1882.

"It was unoccupied at the time, and had the air of being deserted. The wagon road ran directly through the fallen arches, and in front of the venerable structure," she wrote.

Shortly thereafter, the Donahue family moved in, invited by Father Michael Lynch. Donahue, a carpenter, stonemason and blacksmith, lived at the Mission with his wife and five daughters from 1882 to 1898. He advertised his services over the ninth archway.

Father Alexander Buckler ended the long decline in February, 1904. Buckler "encountered solitude, ruin, and abomination of desolation everywhere. A disagreeable old Methodist couple occupies a portion of the house and it is very difficult to induce them to move out…Dirt and neglect stare at me all around."

He recruited his niece, Miss Mary Laura Goulet, age 23, from Minnesota to aid him. She wrote, "Vandals must have entered the buildings when no one was around, and then played havoc…no one who visits the Mission today for the first time can conceive of the appalling condition it was in at that time…We found the beautiful old oil painting of St. Francis in the old tank house under the water tank…"

Snakes sunbathed in the halls, slept in the sink, hung from the gutters, and inhabited the walls.

In 1911, heavy rains damaged the mission so badly that the *Santa Barbara Daily Press'* March 9 headline read "NO CHANCE TO SAVE SANTA INES MISSION."

The bell tower and three of the massive buttresses on the cemetery side of the church had collapsed into a pile of adobe mud. T. W. Moore of Santa Barbara mourned the presumed passing, writing "The century-old monument lies in a heap and her bells are buried in the ruins."

Bishop Thomas J. Conaty of Los Angeles found funds for repair. Father Buckler and Miss Goulet stayed on at the Mission until 1924.

## Part 2. Mending the Mission

Historian Mary Louise Days of Santa Barbara has more to add about the Donahue family who moved into the Mission Santa Inés in 1882. She should know—they were her great-grandparents. Their new home was collapsing around them.

"For 16 years they resided in the southern half of the rectory and, despite a lack of funds, set themselves to the task of making repairs and re-roofing. However, the scope of repairing the quickly deteriorating structures was beyond any one family," according to the Mission's history.

"The southern section of the front corridor collapsed in 1884, and soon the adjacent building fell into ruin, leaving only the buttressed arch, currently preserved within the parking area," says the church's website, www.missionsantaines.org.

"Thomas James Donahue and Mary Condron Donahue arrived in the valley in November, 1882, with their nine children," said Ms. Days. "They arrived by sea at Refugio from Gilroy, California, and all of them were USA born except the father, who was born in Ontario, Canada."

Even then, real estate was a tricky business.

"The family was invited to live in the Mission buildings because the church ranchland that they had hoped to buy had been taken off the market just prior to their arrival," Ms. Days explained.

She has a simple answer to an identity crisis that has puzzled scholars since 1932.

"Friar Zephyrin Engelhardt's book misspelled the family's last name 'Donohue.' I can understand how this happened, because I have seen the original letter written by my mother's Aunt Katie Donahue to Father Engelhardt, and she wrote the 'a' in the center of her surname in such a way that it looked like an 'o.'"

It was quite a clan.

"The Donahues had four sons and five daughters," said Ms. Days. "The oldest son had died in Sacramento as a very young child, so originally there were ten children. My grandmother Elizabeth was the youngest child, so she literally grew up within the mission."

Everyone pitched in to help out.

"The family repaired the buildings as best they could, the males being skilled carpenters and stonemasons. My great grandmother provided hospitality for the priests and for visitors, and the family was well-known. For a time, some of the sons had a threshing business," recounted Ms. Days.

In 1898 the Donahues built a ranch house on a bluff near the junction of the Santa Ynez River and Alisal Road. The ranch's flat farm land is now the Alisal's River Course.

"My mother grew up on the ranch, and I spent my growing-up weekends and summers there," said Ms. Days. "It was sold in the mid-1950s, after the last of the children, Miss Nellie Donahue, died."

"She and Aunt Katherine had helped raise my mother and her sister, along with Mary Condron Donahue, who died in 1929 at the age of 90. Thomas had died in 1904 at the age of 70. The two maiden daughters had been school teachers in S.B. and S.L.O. counties. Nellie was the mission organist for years."

Family members are mentioned several times in Mamie Goulet Abbott's book, *Santa Inés Hermosa*, reprinted by the Mission Gift Shop lin 2003. Donahue descendants live in Lompoc, Las Cruces, Santa Ynez, Santa Barbara, and around the country.

Ms. Days promised, "Sometime soon, I will write a paper about the store which was next door to the mission church over 100 years ago, and which was patronized by the family."

## Part 3. The Bells of Santa Ynez

As part of the Mission's bicentennial celebration, *The Bells of Santa Ynez* will be performed. It's a chorale depicting a day in the life of the people of Mission Santa Inés during the Mission era, written by Paul Weston and Marilyn and Alan Bergman.

On September 17, 1804, Padre Estevan Tapis first dedicated the Santa Inés Mission. "I blessed water, the place, and the great cross which we planted and venerated," he wrote.

The High Mass was attended by cavalry officers from Santa Barbara, soldiers from the local garrison, "various white persons, many neophytes from the Missions of Santa Barbara and Purisima, and more than 200 gentiles (Indians) of both sexes and of all ages." Twenty-seven children were baptized, and fifteen Indian men came forward for instruction, including three chiefs.

Some perspective: on the same night, Meriweather Lewis and William Clark, four months on the trail at Thomas Jefferson's behest, were camped near a prairie dog town on the Missouri River.

The show repeats on Saturday. Bob Raleigh will direct. Dramatizing the score was his idea, over forty years ago. Mr. Raleigh was at Solvang School for 38 years, retiring as superintendent. He was a music teacher at Solvang and College Schools at the time.

"I heard this music in Santa Barbara in a county office," said Mr. Raleigh. "Someone said it was Paul Weston's *Bells of Santa Ynez*. Paul Weston and his family always came up to the Alisal every year. His wife was singer Jo Stafford. I told the foreman at the Alisal, Lynn Gillam, to tell Paul I would like to do a program with this music."

"Next thing I know, Paul calls me, and he's all for it. I wrote the script, I did the choir rehearsal, musicians volunteered. We staged the thing, got the lighting guys, did the whole package, and whole community came out. We had all kinds of people. The Skytts brought bleachers."

"I think it was August, 1963; we did it in a full moon."

"Paul got a standing ovation. Then the folks from Danish Days came to me and said "Will you do this program for Danish Days? We did it for 15 or 20 years."

"It was performed at the Theaterfest, and other places in California. Richard Overstake and Marty Paitch did it with the Allan Hancock Chorale. Bob Eubanks did the narration once, Pat Boone did it once. It was a big hit," said Mr. Raleigh.

"My old friend Bill Brendle, who is musical director for Sergio Mendez, was going to be musical director this year. He did one rehearsal, then they got a booking for the 17th, so I'm in the saddle. Fossemalle Studio will do the dance sequences. James Edward is preparing the orchestra. I will be directing it."

"Helen Townsend is doing the rehearsal piano. Doug Stewart will play for the performance. Jim Richards is doing lights and sound. Talented young vocalist Tivoli Evans will sing at intermission. Bill Warwick wrote the script. Local musicians and a choir perform. The narrator is Ron Iverson."

"To me, it's a celebration of the Mission," said Bob Raleigh. "It's a community-wide event."

Mr. Weston passed away in 1996. but his daughter Amy may be on hand for the performance. Amy sang here with her mother at a seminal benefit for the arts at the Solvang Memorial Hall.

"After we had done *The Bells* a couple of times, Paul said, 'What else can we do for you?'," recalled Mr. Raleigh. "We set up a show of local talent, with the highlight being Jo Stafford singing."

"We raised $5,000 on that show," said Mr. Raleigh. "That was seed money for SYV Arts Association, under which Theaterfest came in, from Santa Maria. Other arts outreach programs came out of that, too."

"I'm not saying *The Bells* created those things, but it was a pathway," noted Mr. Raleigh. "It was a means of getting it together, and things blossomed by themselves. *The Bells* and the money raised by the Arts Association allowed us to do these other things.".

1993 Dartmouth College economics grad Paul Weston began his long, successful musical career with Rudy Vallee's Fleischman Radio Hour as an arranger. In 1935, Tommy Dorsey hired him; in 1940, as a conductor and free-lance arranger, Weston conducted newcomer Dinah Shore. Hollywood beckoned, and he worked with many top names.

Weston married singer Jo Stafford and backed her on some of her biggest hits, including *Shrimp Boats* and *Day by Day*, which he also composed.

After the CBS radio series *The Paul Weston Show* in 1951-52, he appeared regularly on television with *The Jo Stafford Show* in 1954. Many years as a musical director for top TV shows followed.

## Part 4. The Reluctant Pirate's Daily Grind

*"Among all the earliest pioneers of California, there was no more attractive character, no more popular and useful man, than Joseph Chapman, the Yankee."*

—H.H. Bancroft, the dean of California historians.

It was daybreak in the Islands. Tiny pink cotton candy clouds drifted dreamily over graceful palm trees in the Oahu dawn. The moist tropical air was fragrant with the perfume of exotic flowers, and the salty freshness of cresting sea foam rushing to the Honolulu shore.

Alone on a sweeping crescent of powered sugar sand, Joseph Chapman looked out to sea, and glimpsed a tall white sail. He was a long way from Boston, and in 1818, there were not many ways home. When the ship docked at the waterfront, he was there.

A month later, when he was captured in a pirate raid on Monterey, Chapman claimed that Argentine pirate Hippolyte de Bouchard had forced him to join the crew.

Chapman was second mate on the *Santa Rosa*, Bouchard's second ship, a 300-ton vessel, with eighteen cannon and 100 men, under Captain Peter Corney. Together with the 260 men on Bouchard's *Argentina*, the pirates were a formidable force on the sparsely populated California coast.

Merciful, practical, and in need of talent, the authorities spared Chapman's life, and sent him south, to work at the Mission Santa Inés.

His shipmates, meanwhile, sailed down the coast, raiding the Nuestra Senora del Refugio rancho, on December 4, 1818. Bouchard lost three men in the raid on Refugio, but got them back by threatening to pillage the sleepy village of Santa Barbara, if they were not returned.

On December 10, the captives were given up by the prudent Barbarenos, and the pirates weighed anchor, off to less fortunate San Juan Capistrano.

There, miffed by a chilly reception, they plundered the town, and got so drunk that Captain Corney wrote in his log, "We had to lash them to field pieces (wheeled cannons) and drag them to the beach."

Twenty men were formally punished by Bouchard, for conduct unbecoming to pirates.

At Mission Santa Inés, Chapman went to work, designing and building a mill.

As a boy, he had been apprenticed to a shipbuilder, and was taught both carpentry and blacksmithing. A ship's carpenter on his first voyage, Chapman had a Yankee ingenuity for design and construction that would serve him well in this strange land.

He built a grist mill, for grinding wheat and corn, in 1820. He also constructed a fulling mill, used to process wool from the 5,000 sheep at the Mission, in 1821.

Water was supplied by Alamo Pintado Creek, and an aqueduct tapping Zanja de Cota Creek, about two miles to the east.

Both mills are still standing, near the south bank of Alamo Pintado Creek, about 1,500 feet south of Mission Drive. Modern restoration has turned the clock back on their almost two hundred years of age.

The Mission Santa Inés marriage register, item 326, notes that on November 5, 1822, Chapman married Maria Guadalupe Ortega. Her family was from Santa Barbara. One of her uncles owned the rancho raided by the pirates.

Chapman converted to Catholicism in June of that year.

The reformed pirate spent the rest of his life in southern California. He supervised construction of another mill at Mission San Gabriel, and the first church in Los Angeles, Nuestra Senora de Los Angeles.

He built a house in Santa Barbara, behind what is now the Episcopal Church. He also bought a house in Los Angeles, and planted a vineyard.

Throughout this time, he stayed in touch with the friars, who declared it marvelous that "one so long in the darkness of Baptist faith, could give such example of true Catholic piety to older Christians."

At the turn of the twenty-first century, representatives from Chapman's sixth generation of descendants came to a dedication of the Mission Mills.

The lonely structures, and 37 acres around them, are now owned by the Santa Barbara Trust for Historic Preservation.

## 32. Lost Art—Cave Paintings of the Chumash

From Point Conception to the Carrizo Plain, from Tepusquet Canyon to Ojai, the enigmatic paintings color secluded sandstone hollows.

There are bizarre anthropomorphic spacemen, geometric designs, condors, bears, mandalas, beheaded figures, men on horseback, perhaps eclipses.

Mysterious images by the thousands, scattered across hundreds of miles of the Central Coast.

Are they the work of Chumash shamans, idle artistry, or historical records? Is this ritual hunting magic, an astrological observatory, a vision quest, or a diary?

Scholars have debated their meaning for years without consensus. One fact is sure: they are a fascinating glimpse into a lost world.

Campbell Grant's 1965 book *The Rock Paintings of the Chumash* is still the definitive tome on the subject, although traditional Chumash groups hotly contest Grant's conclusions regarding the destruction of their culture. Large paintings recreated from his book can be found at the Santa Barbara Museum of Natural History.

The mountains ringing the Valley abound in rock art sites. Most locations are carefully guarded secrets, due to the fragile nature of the art. As the Forest Service notes, "one person, in one day, can do more damage than centuries of natural erosion." Dust alone is a threat to the paintings.

The speed of erosion in normal conditions is depressing. Pool Rock is a secluded painting site, shaped like a wisdom tooth, 75 feet high and 500 feet around. Two generous depressions on top fill with water in the spring, from which it gets its name. There's a shallow painted cave at the bottom.

I took pictures at Pool Rock in 1975. Comparing them to Campbell Grant's shots of ten years before, it was clear that paint had flaked from one of the central drawings, revealing an older painting beneath the first. Worse yet, thoughtless campers had recently built a fire in the cave.

Rock art scholars present and future got a huge assist in the 1970's and 80's when William Hyder, formerly of UCSB, and artist Mark Oliver, now of Solvang, extensively documented the fragile artwork. Mr. Hyder went on to become president of the American Rock Art Research Association, among many other professional accomplishments.

The dedicated duo spent countless hours capturing art in sandstone crevices and hollows, not to mention the travel time to the far flung secret spots, which seem almost invariably to require a lengthy trek through impenetrable chaparral, excruciating even when you're not lugging bulky camera equipment. For years Mr. Oliver and Mr. Hyder trekked and snapped, amassing an unparalleled body of art featured in numerous exhibitions.

The best known, most easily accessible site is, of course, Painted Cave. If you haven't visited that magical, spiritual cavern two miles off San Marcos Pass on the Santa Barbara side of the eclectic community of the same name, go now. You will return a wiser, more thoughtful person.

The shallow cave, a State Historic Park, is marked with a sign, and located a few feet up the hill, just off Painted Cave Road. There's a gate to prevent vandalism, but the paintings are easily visible. Take a flashlight to see more details.

Look for the black disc with white border, thought by some to depict a solar eclipse that occurred November 24, 1677.

## 33. As San Andreas Said, It's Really Not My Fault

Niagara Falls plunges 167 feet straight down. Ho hum. The Goleta Slough can top that. At one time, a waterfall there cascaded 200 feet to the sea.

Dr. Robert Norris, Professor Emeritus of Geology at UCSB, captivated a packed house of 60 at the Solvang Library, discussing his book, *The Geology and Landscape of Santa Barbara County, California, and Its Offshore Islands*.

A dramatic rise in sea level doomed Goleta Falls.

"With the post-glacial rise in sea level called the Flandrian Transgression, this gorge was backfilled with river and beach sediments, so that apart from a shallow lagoon at the river mouth, there is no longer any surface expression of this former deep channel," explained Dr. Norris.

It's just one of myriad mysteries disclosed in this fascinating, readable book. Among other classes, Dr Norris taught introductory geology during his 40 year tenure at UCSB, starting in 1952, and his prose sparkles like a well polished jewel.

Road logs detailing formations along the highway are a bonus. You'll never look at San Marcos Pass the same way again, after following this geological detective as he deciphers the clues hidden in the road cuts.

Our mountains are mainly uplifted sea bottoms, tilted, twisted and contorted by the collision of the Pacific and North American plates. The Channel Islands have spun nearly 80 degrees over the eons. In geologic terms, the Islands may as well be teacups on the Mad Hatter's ride at Disneyland. There are Torrey pines there, identical to some found in San Diego.

Gaviota Pass was carved when a persistent stream cut through a landscape rising around it. Volcanos, like Tranquillon Peak near Lompoc, died out 10-15 million years ago.

"Widespread volcanic activity affected most of California during Miocene time," writes Dr. Norris.

The equestrian estates in the Santa Ynez foothills are built on eroded rock and clay, Paso Robles formation, that rolled down from the San Rafael range over eons.

"Few, if any, of our local landscape features are more than two to three million years old," Dr. Norris revealed. "Even notable earthquakes, such as occurred in 1925, 1941, 1952, and 1978 may be seen as relatively infrequent, but at that rate, there would be 40,000 earthquakes every million years. If each quake was accompanied by only a few inches of displacement, in a million years there would be rather large changes."

That blue-green serpentine up on Figueroa Mountain was scraped off the deep sea floor. There's even a 100 million year old "black smoker" up there, a high temperature submarine steam vent such as occur along active spreading centers on the sea floor.

"The Figueroa Mountain example includes a small copper deposit, pillow lavas, and fossils of organisms that look very much like the life that surrounds modern black smokers," relates Dr. Norris.

"The county's oldest rocks (150 million years old) were formed from sedimentary and volcanic material deposited during the heyday of the great dinosaurs," writes Dr. Norris. "As far as the earth's history goes, about 96 or 97 percent of it had elapsed before our oldest rocks were even formed."

Isla Vista and More Mesa were abruptly (in geologic terms) elevated from sea level in a series of shocks. The first ten foot rise happened so fast that the clams living on the beach at the time are still embedded in the rocks.

"Dating has shown these clams to be about 40,000 years old," says Dr. Norris. So much for "happy as a clam."

$41,000 in gold and platinum was gleaned from beaches between Surf and Point Sal in 1889. And back then, gold was only $20 an ounce.

And why is local landmark Grass Mountain so bare?

"Rincon mudstone," said Dr. Norris. Its characteristic poor drainage is okay for grass, but not many other plants.

Chemistry's loss was geology's gain, when budding chemist Robert Norris decided camping out sounded more interesting than lab work, and switched his major. His field trips in a 1926 Dodge sedan converted to pickup truck, top speed 40 mph, turned into a career. He survived Iwo Jima unscathed, went to grad school at UCLA, then forged a career at UCSB, starting at the Riviera campus.

His book was published by the SB Museum of Natural History, and can be purchased there.

## 34. Rancho De Los Olivos

Sometime around 1880, on a bluff overlooking Alamo Pintado Creek just north of the tiny town of Ballard, a house was underway.

It was a two story structure, with a wide covered front porch and neatly symmetrical arched windows in the center gable, on prime farmland.

Twenty-two year old Alden March Boyd, of Albany, New York, paid $8,000 for "157 acres, more or less, together with the dwelling house" in 1885. He planted five thousand olive trees and named it Rancho de Los Olivos. As they matured, olive oil, ripe olives bottled in oil, and ripe mission olives in bulk were advertised for sale.

His older sister, Margaret, sketched the ranch house and numerous other local scenes on one of her visits. Her sketch of the house shows it between two massive oaks, with rows of twig-like olive trees in the foreground.

The 1880's were a boom time for California. On November 16, 1887, the Pacific Coast Railway arrived here. The developers of the narrow-gauge railway first named their town El Olivar, then El Olivos, and finally Los Olivos, after Boyd's ranch. Ever optimists, the salesmen hoped it would be the center of a new "North" Santa Barbara County, and labeled one block "Courthouse Square."

Alden Boyd married Margaret Alexander of Santa Barbara in 1889. Their daughter Joan remembered, "One of my earliest memories was putting my arm, up to the shoulder, in the large vats of pickled olives at the olive house on the creek that ran through the ranch, and gathering up a fist full of delicious olives."

Joan Boyd had a happy childhood in the house on the hill.

"...There seemed so much to do—the hayrides; the horseback rides; the picnics and swims in the Santa Ynez River and Zaca Lake; picnics to Nojoqui Falls; the trips at Christmas time in the buckboard to the upper part of the Santa Agueda Canyon to get our Christmas tree, a digger pine; the long hot summer days, lying in the hammock on the veranda and listening to the bells on the grain wagon teams as they went by on the road below our hill lost in a cloud of dust...it was such a thrill, too, listening to the eerie cry of the coyotes at night, in the hills across the road from our house—probably one or two that sounded like ten."

"When I was a very young child we went to Santa Barbara on the stagecoach over the San Marcos and I remember my mother's story of how once a prisoner was among the passengers, with a ball and chain on his leg, and how he held the baby—my sister—when mother was sick! I can still hear the stage horses' heavy breathing as they stopped at Cold Spring, after their pull up the grade."

"Later, when the Southern Pacific was built, we took the stage, which stopped at our gate for us, and drove to Gaviota and there waited many hours at the station for the train to take us to Santa Barbara. Oh, how hard those benches were during our weary wait! Once or twice a kindly brakeman let us ride to Santa Barbara in the caboose."

"Sometimes we drove our own spring wagon to Santa Barbara and I remember the thrill when the horse's feet clattered on the first pavement and we glimpsed the sparkling blue ocean at the foot of State Street."

"A high point in our lives was the arrival every year of the Chinese merchant, on foot, with a long pole across his shoulders and a big basket hanging on either end. Inside were such wonders as china tea sets, cups, silk scarves, chinese nuts and many more intriguing articles."

"In 1906, the telephone rang one day, and when my father answered the phone we sensed that something terrible had happened. When he turned from the phone, he told us that Mr. Mattei had announced that San Francisco had disappeared from the face of the earth. Later, of course, we learned that though the earthquake and fire were devastating, San Francisco was still there."

Rancho de Los Olivos was the home of numerous prominent Santa Ynez Valley citizens over the years, and the old house was a silent witness to countless moments of joy, drama and sorrow. It saw structural changes, too, as plumbing, electricity, and new rooms were added.

In 1988, the Hopson family sold Rancho De Los Olivos to the Normans, who built a home adjacent to the century old structure. And at two a.m. on Monday, November 25, 1991, the two story home, now in two massive pieces, began to trundle from its staging area in a field beside Roblar Avenue to a new site about a mile away at the corner of Nojoqui and Alamo Pintado Avenues in downtown Los Olivos.

Utility cables were relocated and numerous logistic challenges overcome before the halves met again six hours later on the foundation prepared for them. By eight am, Los Olivos had a new neighbor, just a stone's throw west of Patrick's Side Street Cafe.

Meticulously refurbished, with original hardware restored where possible, the Rancho De Los Olivos homestead is now owned by the Saarloos family and houses dentist Kathelene Williams-Turk and various offices. And possibly a pioneer ghost or two, casting wry spectral glances at life in town.

## Part 2. Phantom Hoofbeats at the Union Hotel

Fourteen miles north of Los Olivos is Los Alamos, and the Union Hotel.

The Civil War was a passionate topic when the Union Hotel was built in Los Alamos in 1880. It was a frontier town then, bustling with the excitement of pioneer hopes and dreams, grand plans and a limitless future.

The railroad was coming to town, and newcomers were flocking to California in record numbers, drawn by tales of glory and gold, anxious to make their own mark on this untamed edge of America.

The Union Hotel served travelers who came on horseback, on foot, and on the narrow gauge Pacific Coast Railway, which wound its way, in a plume of steam and oak wood smoke, from Port Hartford (near present day Arroyo Grande) past newly planted eucalyptus groves on the Nipomo Mesa, across fertile farmland by Santa Maria, to the ranch town the conductor called "Lost Almost."

The end of the line, in Los Olivos, the conductor called "Lost Altogether."

As time passed, the Union welcomed weary wayfarers in steam and gas automobiles, too, and witnessed boom and bust through two World Wars, and the relentless transformations of the twentieth century.

The old railway station still exists, as part of a rambling antique warehouse.

Los Alamos remains close to its ranching roots.

Lifetime local Chuck King, a tall, taciturn, Marlboro Man look-alike, and a direct descendant of 1839 land grantee Jose Antonio de la Guerra y Noriega, still recalls with a wry grin the day he and his brother Bill, who quit law school to run cattle, drove their herd straight down Bell Street.

Chuck personifies the enigmatic nature of Los Alamos. His favorite book is Andy Adams' 1903 *Log of a Cowboy*, the vivid story of an 1882 cattle drive from Brownsville, Texas, to Montana.

Chuck can also pepper the beeves with Latin, from his prep school days on the East Coast.

The Union Hotel looks today as it did in the 1880's. It burned to the ground in 1886, and was rebuilt in the early 1900s. A painstaking 1970s restoration gave its faded wood exterior the look of the original.

Along with its neighbors, a Victorian mansion and an antique gas station, it is a living museum of the past century, and more.

One look at these three structures encompasses the raw spirit of the frontier, the refinements of turn-of-the-century Victorian wealth, and the history of the automobile.

The gas station was built on the site of a Wells-Fargo stage stop. "Friend Tom Coe, Stagecoach Driver," is buried in the Los Alamos cemetery.

Inside, the hotel is still patterned by the past. The aura it casts of famed gunfighting towns brought Paul McCartney here to film a rock video.

From the bar, formerly in the Crystal Ball Room in Virginia City, Nevada, you can easily imagine walking out to a duel at high noon.

History still echoes in these halls. The original *Riders of The Purple Sage*, led by their founder, Buck Duffy, played here, and as the strains of *Ghost Riders In The Sky* rang out in the dark Los Alamos streets, a cold wind swept through the town like a rush of phantom hoofbeats.

The pioneer wagons have come and gone. The last train has left the station. The tracks have been pulled up and sold for scrap, and drivers look for a computerized gas station, but the Union remains.

It is a monument to the most vibrant century the world has ever known.

# 35. Cowboy Up With Jake Copass

Jake Copass was in Los Olivos, starring in a Western being made by USC film student Sonia Warren. The quintessential cowboy, Mr. Copass came here to work at the Alisal in 1945, and never left.

A photogenic, multi-faceted man, ace horseman, poet, and actor, he's by turns quiet, courtly, comical. His friends know him as a hard working man of honor; thoughtful, forthright, and fair.

Rubbing shoulders with the stars is all in a day's work for Mr. Copass, 83, who's appeared in more than 15 films and commercials, working with Slim Pickens, Faye Dunaway, John Wayne, John Malkovich and many others. He knows Western authenticity—he's lived it.

Jake Copass grew up dirt poor in Texas.

"My folks had eight kids. It was tough growing up, but everybody had it tough, so we didn't have anything to complain about anymore than anybody else. Some people walked, some people rode horses, that was the way it was."

The Dust Bowl and Great Depression didn't make things any easier.

"That was double tough," he says. "After 1929, the farm workers and the other people was all in the same line getting soup. But nobody was any worse off than nobody else, 'cause nobody had any money."

Even then, California was calling.

"That was when a lot of people came to California as migrant farm workers. Anybody who could catch a ride did. There weren't many cars in those days. Everybody had to help everybody else. We didn't know any different, we just kind of grew up with that."

At six he was driving a team. At ten he was being paid a grown man's wages for it.

"I'm old enough to know what it's like to drive one of them big old heavy wagons. We hauled our water seven miles. We'd drive out to the lake with a team, load it up by hand. When you was out of water, you was out of water. Ask somebody to do that today they'd think they're gonna die before the sun goes down."

At 17, he hired on at the Pitchfork Land and Cattle Company, a 180,000 acre ranch still in business. Visit www.thepitchforkranch.com, for incredible photos of life on the open range.

"My dad had a little farm. That was all right, but I wanted to be a cowboy. I got $20 a month at the Pitchfork breaking horses, and room and board. I had no expenses. If I had stayed there sixty years, and saved all my wages, would you believe I could have saved $14,400 by now?"

Mr. Copass rode out of Texas with the Eighth Cavalry in 1940 and wrangled 1,600 Army mules in New Guinea during World War Two before landing in the Valley.

"I was in the Veterinarian Corps, attached to a mule outfit. That was another one of MacArthur's deals that wasn't any good. They ended up sending those mules to India—they did more traveling than most people. They wrote a book, *Ghost Soldiers*, about my old outfit."

He jokes about his early days in Solvang.

"The Danes didn't want no foreigners here then. They wanted to keep it pure." One of his close friends was Sig Hansen, a rancher about whom he penned the poem *Danish Cowboy*.

He and G.B. Barry ran their own outfit, C & B Cattle Company, for over fifty years. For the last 16 years he's wrangled at the Alisal, making trail rides a memorable pleasure for thousands of visitors.

One part of his work is smoking out the guys whose pride won't let them admit they don't know how to ride.

"They say "Yeah, I've been around horses, my dad had some horses.'"

Jake's response: "My dad had an airplane. I never did learn how to fly that thing."

Mr. Copass has authored two books, *It Don't Hurt To Laugh* and *I'll Be Satisfied*. Never one to take himself too seriously, he says the latter is about "75 years of BS."

i'd call it an honest, adventurous, truly American life, well lived.

## Part 2. Dutch Wilson

"Dutch was a good cowboy, one as good as ever went down the road," said cowboy legend Jake Copass.

"All the young cowboys admired Dutch," reminisced Jake. "And I'm sure they learned a lot from him. We all learned a lot from him. Until 2002, he'd been to the National Rodeo finals every year they had them. He remembered everybody who ever won anything from 1930 on.

"In his younger days, he used to rope calves. He did the roping events, team roping, steer stopping, after he got smart enough not to ride the bulls.

"I don't know anybody in the rodeo field who admired anybody more than they did Dutch Wilson. He wasn't a contender in his later years, but he was one of those guys who just fascinates people," recalled Mr. Copass.

"When he would go to Vegas, they would haul him around like he was a king, from the hotel to the rodeo. After he got stove up, they would be sure he got to where he was to set, and got back to the hotel."

"I've known Dutch since I was in the service, in 1945," said Mr. Copass. "I met him in Santa Barbara. We kind of hit it off right off. He found out I was from Texas, and he liked to give Texans a bad time and vice versa.

"We've worked together, and done a lot of stuff together, and we've argued for 59 years. We never agreed on anything in front of anyone else, but we had our own thing in-between us."

"Dutch was the kind of guy, if he could get an argument out of somebody, well, that was his long suit. We've argued over everything, from how you rope, to when you rope, the whole ball of wax," laughed Jake.

"Dutch was one of a kind. We don't realize these things until we get older, but there went a bag of history down the deal. To see a guy who's almost 95, with a mind a like a trigger, you know?" said Mr. Copass thoughtfully.

"We've had a lot of fun," continued Mr. Copass. "I don't know where he's going, but I'm gonna find out, and I'm gonna go there too, because there's gonna be some changes made when he gets there."

Raymond "Dutch" Evertt Wilson was a Californian, Los Alamitos born, on November 22, 1909. His ancestors were from Scotland via Kansas on one side, and according to his aunt Ida Wilson, "part Cherokee, related to Pocahontas," on the other.

In 1898, the family moved to Long Beach, working for Fred Bixby on Rancho Los Alamitos, where Dutch was born. In 1910 the family moved with Bixby to the 41,000 acre Nacimiento ranch, where Dutch's father was ranch foreman.

Dutch's earliest memory, at three years of age, was standing under a huge Belgian named Golgatha, scratching the stallion's stomach. About the same time, cowboy Fred Tafaya gave the lad the nickname "Dutch," because he was so stubborn. He grew up farming and ranching, moving on to another Bixby property, the Cojo Ranch, in 1926.

Veteran local rancher and De la Guerra descendant Chuck King accompanied Dutch back to the famously windy Cojo Ranch in 1992, and Dutch showed him an enormous anchor chain attached to a tree.

"When the wind blew that chain straight out, we still went to work," kidded Dutch. "But if it was snapping links off, we stayed in the bunkhouse."

In the late 1920's, as a veterinary dental assistant, Mr. Wilson attended famed race horses Phar Lap, Tea Trader, and Flying Ebony.

Mr. Wilson worked on the Jalama and Sudden ranches in 1936-38. From 1939 on, he was a Santa Ynez Valley cowboy, starting at Dwight Murphy's Los Prietos Ranch before moving on to help Harvey McDonald on J.J. Mitchell's Juan y Lolita, getting stock ready for the use of the Rancheros Visitadores.

He worked on the San Lucas Ranch, Westerly Stud, the Lazy-G, and others. He was a lifetime member of the Professional Rodeo Cowboys Association of America, and participated in many rodeos throughout the West.

His 1993 book *Let Me Tell You—Memories of Dutch Wilson, A California Cowboy*, is a treasure trove of local lore.

He eloped with Mary Longawa in Yuma, Arizona, on October 24, 1936. They had two children, Mary Barbara Wilson and David Michael Wilson, both of Santa Ynez. He is survived by two granddaughters and three great grandchildren.

Mr. Wilson passed away Saturday, August 21, 2004, aged 94, while enjoying a meal with friends, celebrating the opening of deer season. Services were held at the Oak Hill Cemetery in Ballard.

## 36. Murder In De la Guerra Plaza

I once worked in Santa Barbara, near the De la Guerra adobe. I was back there recently, and couldn't find my favorite bench. I'm very upset.

The sycamore timber bench was constructed without nails, mortised and tenoned, ruggedly solid, and worn to a silver gray hue like seacoast cypress by years of exposure, with a soft natural matte finish, pleasant to the touch. It bore in the center of the backrest a small brass plaque that announced its antiquity, oxidized to a pale, appealing green.

It read: "This bench is made from sycamore wood timbers used in construction of the original De la Guerra House, built in the year 1826."

In the morning in summer the sun fell on the right hand corner of the bench, strong and warm. On the left hand side was a mottled shadow of the spiny leaves of the patient oak.

History shimmers everywhere in the soft Santa Barbara sun, but is especially strong in this epicenter of local life. In the 1980's, the wide porches of the De la Guerra adobe, hung with ivy, touched by orange tree branches, surrounded a small, inviting green lawn, fronted by a chest high white-washed adobe wall, with two hand-wrought iron gates. It's been restored to a patch of sand, with a mid-calf wall.

Gnarled oak and olive trees shaded the quiet enclave, which looks across De la Guerra Street to De la Guerra Plaza. The Plaza is a lovely greensward, surrounded by tall palms, ringed by quiet, white, serene, two-story Spanish-style architecture: the *News-Press* building, City Hall, small cafes and shops.

Worn red tile pave the broad raised veranda of the old estate; twelve-inch square tiles, the color of faded blood. Countless footsteps have carved their rolling surfaces; Spanish aristocrats, soldiers, mariners, politicians, artists.

Sailor and author Richard Henry Dana attended a fandango in this casa in 1836, when the main commercial trade was dried cow hides. Carried through the surf on his head, they were rowed to the waiting schooner, bound for Boston, many months away.

In August, across the street, the square fills with booths during Fiesta. Tantalizing aromas from the outdoor kitchens fill the air, and a steady stream of passersby join the throngs jamming the plaza. Music plays, to loud applause.

Other times, sitting on this quiet veranda, there is a serenity so vast it threatens sanity. It seems the very universal locus. The earth will surely split apart at any minute. The choirs of beyond will vaporize the cosmic frame in one single instant from this tiny opening in the veil.

The day is poised, ancient, silent, vibrating with life, sure in an unshakable faith in destiny, waiting. The air shimmers. Time stands still.

Perhaps it was like that the day a man was murdered here for his hat.

In the 1850's, a decade of lawlessness and mayhem, a day-tripping tourist, said to be a gambler taking a stroll from a steamer anchored offshore, met up with one Patrick Dunn in this quiet plaza.

Jesse D. Mason's 1883 *History of Santa Barbara County* says it went something like this:

Dunn: "That's a fine hat you have."
Stranger: "I don't know that it's any of your business."
Dunn: "Say, I'd like that hat."
Stranger: "You can have it if you can take it."

Dunn shot the tourist on the spot. Two trials ended in hung juries. The sheriff, judge, and district attorney were all told by parties unknown that they would be murdered if they prosecuted the case.

Dunn died in Arizona in 1866, aged 41, after serving a term in—no, not prison—the upper house of the first legislature of the territory.

*Debenched: A former Casa Committee member revealed the secret of the missing Casa de la Guerra bench I mourned recently. "Your favorite bench on the Casa's veranda was removed to ensure its safety," she wrote.

"The rest of the benches were removed for the same reason the benches, and picnic tables, which used to populate not only Plaza de la Guerra, but East Beach, are no longer there. Santa Barbara's indigent population found they made great beds, places to loiter, and perches from which to harass passers-by."

I know my jean jacket is a little worn, but I didn't think I looked that bad.

## 37. Foxen Canyon Hosts Camp Jeep

Foxen Canyon Road ends in Los Olivos, on the northwest side of town. The road is named for pioneer Benjamin Foxen, whose ranchlands a few miles to the north are still virtually as he left them, over a century ago.

Benjamin Foxen first saw Santa Barbara as the 22-year-old skipper of his own trading ship, the *Courier*. He settled in Santa Barbara in the late 1820's, and built a schooner in Goleta in 1828. His legacy there remains. In Spanish, "goleta" means "schooner."

In 1830 he married Eduarda Osuna, the lovely daughter of pioneer Jose Osuna. He was one of the first Americans in the area, a pioneer rancher on a huge 8,874 acre 1837 Mexican land grant called Rancho Tinaquac. He and Eduarda raised 18 children there.

When John Charles Fremont rode by in 1846, heading to Santa Barbara to claim it for the fledgling United States, Foxen (some say it was his son) guided the legendary soldier and his troops over rugged San Marcos Pass, on Christmas Day.

Fremont captured Santa Barbara without bloodshed, and on January 13, 1847, California was ceded to the U.S.

As his reward, Foxen was harassed by his neighbors for the rest of his life.

Foxen died in 1874. He is said to have been bitten by a black widow spider as he lay in the shade of one of the twisted live oaks.

His old homestead is now just a small mound of adobe and sandstone in a field west of Foxen Canyon Road. There is plentiful water a hundred yards away in the creek; the high bluff to the west shields the site from the prevailing winds. The fallow bottomland along the creek would have provided good grazing for cattle.

A small brass plaque on a sandstone marker marks the spot. It seems lonely and deserted. This area has changed little since Foxen carved out his ranch in the wilderness.

But when I turned over a piece of wind pocked sandstone that lay atop the ruined adobe brick, there was a sentinel here. A lone black widow, waiting to get his descendants.

Though only a few stones of his original adobe and stagecoach relay station remain, a church built by his descendants survives. The old white chapel looks out over the sprawling gravel beds of the Sisquoc River, from its bluff beside the alluvial plain.

To the west the river courses toward the Pacific; across the river the high rolling hillsides lead back through oak studded canyons to the rugged Sierra Madre Range, where mysterious Chumash cave paintings of other worldly creatures can be found hidden amid the stark ancient sandstone outcroppings.

The San Ramon Chapel was built by Frederick and Ramona Foxen Wickenden, Foxen's daughter, in 1875. Although shaped like an adobe structure, with simple lines, it is built of redwood.

It would look picturesque in a New England village. Surrounded by the dry hills and gnarled oaks of California coast, it has a determined air of great resolve.

In the quiet that surrounds this place it is easy to visualize a Sunday morning of a hundred years ago. Pioneers and Indians came to services on horses, on foot, in wagons and carriages, shivering in the chill winter mornings, sweltering in summer when the fierce California sun burned away the dew at daybreak and relentlessly blazed ever higher in the sky.

Behind the chapel is the small graveyard, about a half acre in size. The tombstones have suffered over the last hundred years; many are broken or missing. The names are a roll call of pioneer history: Ontiveros, Calderon, Mendoza, Aquirre, Arellanes, Cararra, Goodchild, Foxen. Benjamin Foxen (1796-1874) and William J.J. Foxen (1833-1891) lie by side in the farthest corner of the cemetery.

His tombstone is over ten feet tall, a truncated marble ship's mast on a Doric base with a draped wreath of marble roses, a simple cross midway down the shaft, and this inscription:

BENJAMIN FOXEN
BORN IN ENGLAND 1796
DIED FEBRUARY 19, 1874.

Camp Jeep California opened a three day run at the Chapman-Leonard Ranch in Foxen Canyon in August of 2004. It was a four-wheeler's Woodstock, held a stone's throw from a tiny pile of rubble with a brass plaque. That's all that's left of pioneer Benjamin Foxen's once flourishing homestead, in the canyon that bears his name.

Shelley's poem *Ozymandius* comes to mind. Where once great deeds were done, "The lone and level sands stretch far away."

Foxen Canyon hadn't seen this many people since Fremont marched on Santa Barbara. From Bangor, Maine, West Palm Beach, Florida, and New Orleans, Louisiana, Jeep enthusiasts converged on the first West Coast Jeep jamboree. A thousand Jeeps and some three thousand participants were expected, many veterans of east coast events.

From a distance, it looked like the world's largest Bedouin encampment. Acres of white tents, some thirty or more, with lofty center poles jousting at the sky. You could have been forgiven for thinking you were at the Denver Airport.

Beyond were acres of parked cars, almost all Jeeps. You could pull into the parking lot in any car, but only the sponsor's 4x4 gets on the four wheel drive trails.

James Kenyon of Detroit, a 15 year Chrysler vet, said "It's just for Jeep owners. You can come in and park in another car—maybe a little farther from the gate—but to get on the trails, you need a Jeep. We've got some great off-road trails, which I think the people are going to find interesting and challenging, but mainly we're just going to have a good time."

Some trails across the 1,466 acre ranch seemed vertical. Jeeps lined up eagerly for the challenge.

Ann, Mike and Stephanie Seymour of Corona came to try four-wheeling for the first time. "They show you what to do, so you didn't have to get scared," said Ann.

Dentist Howard Hamerink, his therapist wife, Sally, and their son John, a student at the University of Michigan in Ann Arbor, came all the way from Michigan for the event. "We like the region," said Dr. Hamerink. "It's a short, four day vacation." They had attended Camp Jeep in Branson, Mo.

Geordan Logan and his wife and 16 month old daughter Havana of Las Vegas were also at the Branson event two years ago. "We love it. We're Jeep owners for life," said Mr. Logan.

At the Jeep Rubicon Challenge, a short course, drivers in sparkly lime green, cherry red and lemon yellow Wranglers got a taste of four wheeling.

I jumped in and hit the trail. One moment I seemed headed for the sky; the next, straight into the Grand Canyon. I bumped over boulders that jolted the undercarriage and splashed through puddles, only a roll bar between me and the great outdoors, air conditioning and stereo blasting.

It was motor nature at its best.

Next door, ten year Jeep employee Dion Finocchiaro of Delaware, was embarrassing a Ford Explorer, Ford Escape and Toyota Rav 4 in some head to head events. "It's my job, and I love it," laughed Mr. Finocchiaro.

Pistons in cutaway engines pulsated in the tech tent, with engineers on hand to talk. Young Steven, from San Diego, was riding around on a six foot tall, talking, strobe-lit Bosch robot. Dozens of classic Jeeps, civilian and military, were displayed, some perched on enormous faux rocks, including an amphibious model and Roy Roger's NellyBelle. Sleek, glistening concept cars turned heads.

There was an astonishing variety of exhibitors, including a diving demo, complete with a large pool. Nicole Lemoine of Los Angeles was talking up Sirius Satellite radio. *Sunset* magazine reps were cooking a pork loin. *Outside* magazine sponsored a climbing wall. *Traditional Home* showed up, as did *Sports Illustrated*. The Jeep store looked to be a good 4,000 square feet. A Californiano Heritage tent made a feeble stab at local history.

Fender guitar's Jeff Livingston came from Phoenix with an impressive display of dozens of Fender guitars and amps you could try out. Orvis had a fly casting arena, complete with jumping wooden trout. The ocean kayaking, it turns out, was at Gaviota. Ski filmmaker Warren Miller had a tent. There was a video game pavilion, kiteboarding, and a jungle gym four stories tall called the Adventure Tower.

Tots raced in ovals on the Fisher-Price track. Rosanna Harrison of Santa Ynez was cashiering at the Jeep Grille.

Chris Mosher, 12, from Valencia, loved the skateboarding ramp. "It's awesome. I think it's the best thing I've done in a couple of years," he enthused.

Three county sheriff's deputies said the event was no problem for them.

"We're having lots of fun so far," one said.

"We've never had a problem, even with ten thousand attendees at our East Coast event. These people are here for a purpose," said Ron Svymanski, retired from the Jeep assembly line in Toledo, Ohio. He's been working the events for seven years.

Live music resounded from two massive sound stages throughout the day Thursday, including the rock band Clifton from Charlotte, NC, singer-songwriter Jen Chapin, and band Dan Dyer, who announced a "Rock the Vote" event.

Los Lobos played, as did bands Old Dead Bug, Tyler Hilton, American Minor, *Live*, the Rosenbergs, the So and Sos, MRNORTH, and Keri Noble.

At the end of the day, the greatest challenge for many sunburned spectators was finding their car among 1,000 similar models.

There is no camping at Camp Jeep.

*Hitting the dusty trail: The white Jeep Cherokee bounced sickeningly in a cloud of dust to the edge of the precipice. The driver furiously spun the wheel, and his female passenger hung on for dear life, gaping at the 200 foot deep canyon they were about to tumble into, as their wheels spewed foot thick powdery dust in huge rooster tails out into the canyon.

"They're going over," I told Bill Becher, adventure columnist for the *LA Daily News*, seated beside me in a once pristine, brand new slate gray Jeep Sahara loaned by Chrysler, now covered with dirt, inside and out. We had a ringside seat on a hairpin turn across the abyss, awaiting our turn at the deathtrap.

But when the dust cleared, the Cherokee was still dangling, hanging on by a whisker, saved by a sagebrush from a fatal plummet. Two Jeeps cabled together winched their fellow jeepster away from the chasm.

And this was only the intermediate trail.

Drivers paid $335 for the chance to spend three days legally four wheeling on six different trails across the 1,466 acre spread, a sinuous route across heavily grazed grasslands and through tight, winding canyons. Long lines of Jeeps of all description splashed across a creek, climbed impossible hills and descended precipitous slopes.

I was two and a half hours on a loop which probably covered about ten miles. Thirty minutes of that was waiting for the drama at precipice cliff to wrap up. Our caravan of about 25 Jeeps traveled in a long train, and all vehicles waited for their compatriots to complete the nasty spots before bouncing on.

Aside from the near fatalities, it was a lot like my day job as a real estate broker, only with less people in the car.

The Jeep Jamboree, a similar event, includes 33 stops in 2004, from Moab to the Mohawk Trail, Ouray to Appalachia. There are six events in Canada, as well.

## 38. The Longhorn Cafe

Breakfast at Kelli Moniot's Longhorn Coffee Shop and Bakery in Santa Ynez is like being in the dining room of an extended family. Kids and moms in cowboy hats, teenagers catching up with their friends, guys headed to work, or avoiding it, all casually chatting over coffee and heaping helpings of fabulous food.

"I thank my loyal customers," said Kelli. "Everyone from cowboys to celebrities." The cribbage players have been coming for 30 years.

Early is over at 4 am in the country. Kelli opens at 4:30 am, serving breakfast and lunch until closing time at 1:30 pm, seven days a week.

I sat next to Digital Instruments founder turned philanthropist Virgil Elings and that big bear of a realtor, Clarke Franke. The place had the friendly, sleepy feel of the morning after a slumber party.

Which it was, for some. Across the pleasantly noisy room, an expert on the finer things in life, personable Christie's executive Carlyle Eubank, casually presided over a tableful of about a dozen tousleheads celebrating young Winchester Eubank's birthday.

Years of selfless scout mastery prepared Carlyle for this moment, handled adroitly with his customary superdad aplomb. Mr. Eubank was flying solo. His wife, talented author/artist Patricia Reeder Eubank, was in St. Louis for a book signing at the Missouri History Museum, part of the Lewis and Clark Bicentennial. In 1804, St. Louis was the last outpost of civilization.

Yes, it's been 200 years since the most successful road show duo to predate Bob and Bing hit the dusty trail, opening the West for the rest of us. (that's Bob Hope and Bing Crosby, for you youngsters)

Except for the Spanish and the Chumash, of course, who were already here, hard at work on the Mission Santa Inés, also begun in 1804. That cad Aaron Burr shot Alexander Hamilton in 1804, too! But I digress.

If you haven't seen Patricia Eubank's best selling *Seaman's Journal: On the Trail with Lewis and Clark,* you've missed one of the best kid's books in ages. Inspired by the family Newfoundland, *Seaman's Journal* follows Lewis and Clark's epic trek from the viewpoint of Seaman, Meriweather Lewis's faithful canine companion. Patricia Eubank's consummate artistry brings the epic trek to life in magical and copious detail.

Never met a Newfoundland? They're BIG. Imagine a St. Bernard on steroids, or a bear. Down, boy. Please.

Clarke Franke said he and wife Linda Boston are toying with the idea of franchising their Heartland real estate business, to capitalize on the success of their handsome *Ranch & Country Magazine*. *R&C* is a must have wish book for avid ranch buyers and frustrated city slickers, featuring properties all over the West.

For example: *Open and bright 3BR/2BA home on 10 acres, mostly fenced. Panoramic views of the La Plata Mountains, wide open blue skies and abundant wildlife. Just minutes from world class fly fishing on the San Juan River. $139,000.*

Wagons, ho! We're off to Farmington, New Mexico. $139,000 might get you a mobile home here.

Clarke, Linda, art director Kim Heuer, and tireless distribution coordinator Dusty Rhoades (hmm) are celebrating over a million copies of R&C in print.

Clarke's tablemate, Virgil Elings, put a fabulous personal collection of vintage motorcycles on display when he bought the former Solvang Outlets complex, giving confused tourists still looking for the late, much lamented carousel there something faster to contemplate. His Solvang Motorcycle Museum includes Matchless, Manxman, Nimbus, Norton, Vincent, Velocette—75 rare cycles in all.

A man with the Midas touch, Mr. Elings put a little lavender out in front of his place because he didn't like lawns. He's now among the largest of the local lavender lovers, with over 20,000 of the profitable, pungent purple plants.

The Longhorn is at 3687 Sagunto, in Old Town Santa Ynez. Look for the bevy of pickup trucks. Local millionaires prefer old, battered ones. When genius U-2 and SR-71 Blackbird designer Kelly Johnson of Lockheed first pulled up at a local real estate office in his clunker, the staff thought he was a derelict.

He bought the 1,800 acre Starlane Ranch, in Happy Canyon.

## 39. The Way We Were—Solvang Circa 1961

"I believe some things in life belong with certain people," said thoughtful, generous Arthur Osha, "And I think this belongs with you."

Sherman, set the Wayback Machine to 1961, and cue *The Way We Were*.

Arthur handed me a 1961 "Golden Anniversary" edition of *The Valley News*, celebrating the half century since Solvang's founding in 1911. He picked it up at the mammoth sale at what was once Anker Johnson's Ballard Fields Ranch.

"SOLVANG JUBILEE HERE!" shouted the headline. Portly Aksel Elbek, official town greeter, smoking a long pipe, and Greg Henning, 2, Janelle Henning, 3, and Mindi Jaeger, 7, all decked out Danish, graced the front page. Fifty-two full pages of nostalgia, including a cute photo of my mother-in-law, Doris Christiansen Mitchell, in a kid's folk dancing troupe during World War II.

Danish Days, skipped altogether in 1959 and '60, was back.

Viggo Tarnow, ex-director of Atterdag College, was master of ceremonies at the grand banquet and program at the Vet's Hall. Hakkebof med log was on the menu.

The Danish Counsel General came to the bash, where a 40 member chorus performed, led by Leslie Andersen, principal of Solvang School. Magnus Gregersen, son of Rev. J. M. Gregersen, one of Solvang's founders, said a few words. Another son, Albert, sent congratulations from Copenhagen, where he was Gulf Oil's general representative for Scandinavia and Finland.

Herman Strandskov, "seated and singing in a horse and cart, accompanied by an accordionist," led the torchlight parade.

Years later, Mr. Strandskov, none the worse for singing in a horse, gave me this considered advice about life: "When the wagon's going over the cliff, don't try to hang on. Give it a push."

A sycamore was planted in Solvang Park at the end of the celebration on Sunday. The Gregersen family donated the land for the park, incidentally.

In other news, Grange, Pythian Sisters, civil defense and Lucky Clover 4-H meetings were announced. Palacio Del Rio was taking overnight guests. Burtness Realty advertised a three bedroom home on five acres for $23,750.

Nellie Donohue, 82, who once lived with her family in the Mission Santa Inés, remembered the arrival of the Danes in 1911. "They were fine neighbors," she recalled.

"I felt that we would be enriched by the coming of these Danish-Americans," wrote pioneering Ballard teacher, author and journalist Grace Lyons Davison, "and so it proved." She penned an anniversary song.

In addition to a healthy dose of history, this mother lode of local lore offers up a remarkably innocent slice of life. Forty-three years ago, legendary editor King Merrill printed a "Family Section," penned by Dorothy Brand and Doris Ray, that included a rundown of kids' birthday parties, complete with guest lists, plus a social round-up.

"Angus McIntosh celebrates his eighth birthday with a party at his parents' home today," read the News. "Invited guests include Debbie Laranjo, Jackie Roberts, Robin Mathiasen, Susie Pensa, Joan Robertson, and cousins Carole and Janet McIntosh. Other young guests will be Rolf Klibo, John Gruenstein, Tony Ostoja, Mark Mercer, Mark Koenig, Donald Ray, Keith McLenithan and Dean Moering."

I was in SY High with almost all those folks. No one who witnessed it will ever forget Angus' rockin' rendition of Foxy Lady at the school dance. At the last reunion I attended, rock's loss was cuisine's gain. Angus was a renowned chef.

"Little Denise Andersen celebrated her seventh birthday," the paper duly noted. "Rev. and Mrs. Ronald Holcomb and family enjoyed visitors Sunday from his former church." Rev. Holcomb married me—that is to say, he ran the show—at the little white chapel in Ballard in 1972.

On September 16, 1961, my friend at dentist Dr. Dwayne Elder's office, the former Miss Barbara Best, looking radiant indeed, married Gordon Brown, at St. Mark's.

Ellen and Peter Weber thanked guests who came to their open house at Peter's Pastries new Copenhagen Drive location. Harlan Burchardi thanked everyone for the cards and letters they sent him in the hospital. Harold and Myrtle Buell invited friends to celebrate their 50th wedding anniversary.

Give it to the intern: David Walker, a student at Grand View College in Des Moines, Iowa, spent most of his summer vacation assembling and writing material for the special edition. The founders, and many first residents of Solvang, had ties to Grand View.

What was it like to be an early settler in Solvang? A Swedish doctor visiting the Mission in 1846 noted "The great want of shade and trees does not make it a pleasant residence. The winds are very troublesome." In 1911, the first wave of Danes came to a treeless plain as dry and dusty in summer as a lunar landscape.

A land purchase in Laytonville had been considered by the Danes. On the way there, a horse, wagon, and Peter Bertelsen rolled down a hillside, breaking Bertelsen's leg and demolishing the rig. John Roth's horse got sick. J.C. Burchardi missed the train. Then the buyers got out a survey tape, and found the alfalfa field was 200 acres short. That was that. Land in Marysville, Santa Rosa and Atascadero also fell by the wayside.

Real estate broker Mads Frese saw an ad in the paper in his home town of Salinas, and tipped off the Rev. B. Nordentoft, Rev. J.M.Gregersen and P.P. Hornsyld. They formed the Danish American Corporation in October 1910, which bought around 9,000 acres of the Rancho San Carlos de Jonata (St. Charles of the wooded place) for $40 an acre.

Escrow closed in January of 1911, and Mr. Frese and the first settlers, Mr. and Mrs. Sophus Olsen, Hans Skytt, John Petersen and John Ahrenkild, arrived January 28. They planned to establish a colony patterned after the Danish college of Grand View in Des Moines, Iowa. The first hotel and folk school were southwest of the corner of Mission and Alisal, on what was then the main road between LA and SF.

Mamie Goulet was living with her uncle, Father Buckler, across the road, in the Mission Santa Inés, when the Danes arrived. She didn't think they'd stick. She'd heard that an Irish and a German colony had previously tried and failed.

Early settlers had their own doubts. When Paul Iverson arrived Nov. 20, 1911, riding in on the narrow gauge from the Black Hills of South Dakota, he thought "I won't stay in this Godforsaken country." Fifty years later, the farmer was still here.

Mrs. Johanna Albertsen arrived in 1911, coming by train to Gaviota.

"There was a wagon there with four horses. Eleven of us got in it with all our boxes and suitcases to come to Solvang," she related in 1961. "Coming up the hills the men would get out and walk to save the horses."

"I cried when I came to Solvang," Mrs. Albertsen admitted. "I liked my house in Iowa. I always wanted a bigger house, but I never got it."

Astrid Lauritzen said "We carried our water. No electricity, no plumbing, nothing. We had a meat safe in a tree."

A somewhat cheerier Axel Nielsen was 13 when he arrived in November of 1911.

"All that was there was the Mission, the hotel, the folk school, the store, a barn, the Jensen residence, and the Sorensen house," he recalled in 1961. "We had to gather the wood, as we all had wood stoves in those days. I milked the cow morning and night."

"The river bottom was our playground," said Axel, whose father, Marcus, founded Nielsen's Market, still in the family. "We swam and fished and had school picnics there. We had an old swimming hole and it makes me sick to see it go. We took our horses and dogs and fish poles along whenever we went."

"There were three or four stores in Santa Ynez then—that was the big town," he recalled. Thirteen year old Axel drove the team to Gaviota and picked up a new family.

"On the way to Solvang, I can remember the oldest Olsen girl asking, 'Is Solvang in America?' The stage passed us. The girls thought it was quite exciting."

Young Ella Albertsen Christensen waited tables at the Solvang Hotel and helped the first cook, Betty Rasmussen Skytt. They served 25 persons for dinner, "like one big happy family," she remembered.

Mrs. Skytt baked bread in two big woodstove ovens, Monday through Friday. "You wouldn't believe me if I told you how many loaves were baked each day," she told the Valley News. It was a full house. Overflow guests were sleeping on the floor between the tables in the dining room, and in the barn out back.

"I will never forget how funny it was whenever a new girl came to Solvang," reminisced Margrethe Wulff. "All the bachelors fell over each other trying to be the first to meet her."

There were deadlier country customs. Mrs. Wulff left baby Hans in his carriage outside the front door of their cottage. Some boys across the street then used the buggy for target practice. Hans was rescued in time.

"I promise never to do it again," swore Harold Campbell.

"I planted barley and oats, dry farming," said Niels Petersen. Originally from Denmark, he heard about the new venture in Fresno and drove a lumber wagon and two teams to Solvang.

"One third of our crops went to the ground squirrels. Jack rabbits ate lots of crops. Deer lived in the brush and came out at night and ate the crops. There were lots of coyotes," said Mr. Petersen.

"Quail, cottontails and lots of fish," George Scheldt said. "The river ran practically all year."

The venture teetered on the edge of bankruptcy in 1912. J.C. Burchardi nominated Pastor Gregersen to mount a sales drive through Nebraska and Iowa. The Reverend closed 3,000 acres, saving the day.

The first community mailbox stood on a post near Mission Drive and Alisal. The stage came through at 9 am from Los Olivos and 4 pm from Gaviota. Around 1913 the horses lost their job to a car.

As late as 1927, the telephones were part time. When the operator went home, the lines shut down for the day.

## 40. Ballard Pioneers

Valley pioneer Norman McDonald Davison passed away peacefully January 30, 2004, aged 97, at the home in Ballard he built in 1956.

In this family, that's the "new house."

As a Warrant Officer aboard the USS Tomich and USS Saginaw Bay in World War II, Norman Davison worked on the cutting edge of electronics, becoming an expert in the newly employed art of radio detection and ranging technology—"radar," for short.

His daughter, the gracious Nan Adams, still lives next door in the "old" family home, a quaint two story Victorian built around 1886 on the west bank of Ballard creek.

Norman's son, Don Davison, told me recently about combing the old stagecoach crossing, just a few yards away from the family home and the Ballard schoolhouse, for treasure with his childhood buddies. A rusted antique pistol found there by a family member many years ago may have bounced out of a coach as it splashed across the bumpy ford.

Born in Ballard on February 17, 1906, Norman Davison would have said the real pioneers were his grandparents G.S. and Elizabeth Davison, and his parents, Edgar B. and Grace Lyons Davison.

Grace Lyons Davison, Norman's mother, was the daughter of the Santa Ynez Valley's first justice of the peace, Samuels Lyons, and for many years she was the Valley correspondent for the *News-Press*.

My daughter, Leah, now an ace reporter for the News-Press, credits Grace Davison's books *Beans for Breakfast* and *The Gates of Memory* with inspiring her interest in the Valley's history.

As related in *Beans for Breakfast*, Grace Lyons came to Ballard with her parents and three siblings in 1882 from West Elizabeth, Pennsylvania. The title refers to her diet at her first teaching job, at a school on San Marcos Pass.

The family took the train to San Francisco, a boat to Los Angeles, and a sidewheel steamer to Gaviota, where they bedded down for the night on a pile of burlap sacks under the pier.

A grain wagon took them to the Valley the next day. As they topped the mesa that would one day host Solvang, they drove right through the Mission Santa Inés.

"It was unoccupied at the time and had the air of being deserted. The wagon road ran directly through the fallen arches, and in front of the venerable structure," Grace Davison wrote.

Ballard was unimpressive to the weary travelers, who had family there.

"Ballard was a mere handful of houses, with a school, but as yet without a school house...Papa would have gladly bought a return ticket and gone back to the land of his birth," wrote Grace Davison.

It was not, however, a town without culture.

"One of the most outstanding entertainments of the early days was *The Merchant of Venice*, in which the scholarly Presbyterian minister was Shylock," wrote Ms. Davison. An Oxford graduate played Antonio.

Grace Lyons married Edgar Davison, Norman's father, in 1902. Edgar was a forest ranger on Figueroa Mountain from 1898 through 1912, making $75 a month.

Grace and Edgar built a cabin in remote Fir Canyon, in what is now the Los Padres National Forest, and lived there for the early years of their marriage. If they were separated, grandson Don Davison related, at sundown Edgar would signal from his lofty Figueroa perch with a mirror to Grace in Ballard, flashing an all's well.

Tall trees have grown up and blocked that view. As Grace Davison wrote in 1956, "the cones (burning in her fireplace) had come from the pine tree in her yard planted over fifty years ago, when her oldest son was a baby. It was a towering tree now..."

On the last page of *Beans for Breakfast*, Grace Lyons Davison poignantly described burning her old letters before the river rock faced fireplace, still in use in the home today.

"The great-grandmother...sat before her fireplace in the old house...In her lap she held several bundles of letters, tied with faded ribbons...One by one she laid them on the coals and watched them gradually disappear..."

"...The chilling room brought her back from her dream world and she laid the last letter on the fading coals. It burned brightly for a moment then died out, and on the blackened paper she, as she leaned forward, could read the words that closed so many of the letters: 'God bless you—I love you.'"

## Part 2. He Rode The PCRY

It was April Fool's Day. The man on the phone was describing his ride on the narrow gauge steam train that once dead-ended at Mattei's Tavern in Los Olivos. Early on, passengers switched to stagecoaches there.

Skeptics could be forgiven for raising an eyebrow. The last train ran in 1934, and the tracks were later torn out and sold for scrap metal to the Japanese, who shortly thereafter shot it back at us. But this was no joke.

"It was slow and easy," said Wilfred Lyons, 92, the only person I've ever known who actually rode on the fabled Pacific Coast Railway (PCRY).

After I wrote about Wilfred Lyons' aunt, Grace Lyons Davison, my brother Bert, editor of *The Cambrian*, put me in touch with Wilfred, a Cambria native.

"In 1922, when I was ten, I went on the narrow gauge from San Luis Obispo to Los Olivos three or four different times," Mr. Lyons related.

"They had one passenger car. Sometimes I was the only passenger. It was about a four hour trip. There were a lot of stops along the road, mostly picking up merchandise.

"In Santa Maria they picked up produce, and a lot of farm products. One train car had live animals in it."

"Once we stopped at a crossing, just before we got to Los Olivos. A Model T had broken down on the tracks. We had to wait while the engineer, conductor and a couple of crew members pushed it off."

Wilfred's father was William Lyons.

"My grandfather was Samuel Lyons, who was Justice of the Peace in Ballard for over 50 years. Lot of times he'd hold a little trial in his front room," Wilfred said.

"Grandfather Lyons had six children, my dad William, Samuel, George, Jeannette, Grace and Alice. Jeannette, born in Ballard in 1886, was the only child born in California. The family came from Pennsylvania. My grandfather was affected with coal dust, and the doctor told him he'd have to get to a warmer climate."

"They arrived in Ballard in 1882. My father helped build the first Presbyterian church."

It is still standing, a classic little white country chapel now used for weddings and funerals. I was married there, in 1972.

Teaching ran in the family. After a teaching stint in Cayucos, Wilfred's father William and mother, Anna Marquart Lyons, ran Lyon's Store in Cambria for four decades, until it burned to the ground in 1951. Aunts Grace Lyons Davison and Jeannette Lyons had extensive teaching careers, and wrote valuable local histories. Visit the Jeannette Lyons room at the SYV Historical Museum to learn more.

Wilfred Lyons was born in 1912 in Cambria. He went to the Ballard School for one year, in 1922.

"The teacher was my aunt, Alice Lyons Potter. I lived with my grandfather Samuel Lyons half the year, and half with aunt Alice."

"Grandfather Lyons kept me busy, catching gophers. I got five cents a gopher. Most of what's now the Ballard cemetery was his land. He farmed, had a little orchard, planted grain."

"My grandparents were very strict religious people," Wilfred remembered. "On Sunday we weren't supposed to do anything but stay home or read the bible."

To slip the leash, he'd head over to the cousins.

"There were four boys and one girl in my aunt Grace Davidson's family, Art, Donald, Norman, Sam, and Margaret. I'd tell my mother I was going to Aunt Grace's—it was just a short distance. The Davidson boys said 'There's a ball game in Los Olivos!' Off we'd go to the ball game all day."

Wilfred Lyons and his wife Hazel worked for William Randolph Hearst from 1934 to 1942, helping the French chef, stoking the fires in the forty fireplaces, wrangling the trail rides, and chauffeuring stars like Clark Gable, William Powell, and Cary Grant up the storied "enchanted hill."

"We lived at the castle, both of us," he recalled. "I knew Marion Davies very well. She gave me two autographed pictures of herself."

Newspaper tycoon Hearst was a crabby boss.

"He was really cranky," remembered Mr. Lyons. "He was a domineering sort of person."

Wilfred Lyons' most memorable day in Ballard was Christmas of 1924.

"We had gone down to my grandfather's home for a large family celebration. While taking a bath, my uncle George knocked over a kerosene heater in the bathroom and caught the two-story house on fire."

"Everything was lost, including all the Christmas presents," Wilfred lamented.

## 41. Summertime, and the Living is Easy

Summer's here. When I was a kid, that meant we loaded up the fake-wood-grained 1958 Mercury Colony Park station wagon with my mom and dad and four boys and luggage and a wicker picnic basket full of sandwiches and provisions and a thermos jug full of lemonade, and left Winston-Salem, North Carolina, headed for Brokaw, Wisconsin, where my mother's many relatives all seemed to own dairy farms.

We usually left in the evening. Dad come home from his engineering job at Western Electric about five, but there was always a last minute brake job or tune-up or tire rotation or other damn thing that required us four boys to hover restlessly around the wagon, dancing from foot to foot, dying to get going, as a humid southern night fell, lit like the Pirates of the Caribbean by the flashes of thousands of fireflies, which we called lightning bugs, with a sound track of noisy cicadas.

After an eternity of "Get me the screwdriver...get me the crescent wrench...get me that part that just shot across the yard," inevitably there came a final slam of the porch's screen door, a leap into the sagging wagon, fierce jockeying for position, and a clamor for lemonade, as our exasperated mother resisted our attempts to finish it all off before we had even left the driveway.

We headed out into the night, on a 1,122 mile trek. Sometimes we drove straight through. Once, in the mists of dawn, I awoke, crawled over my sleeping brothers, and stumbled, rubbing my eyes, out of the parked car, to find my father sound asleep atop a picnic table in a roadside rest just off the Ohio Turnpike. A few feet away, semi-trucks hurtled through the fog, as loud as jet airplanes on takeoff.

Upon arrival in Brokaw, Wisconsin, the paper mill town where my mother grew up, we greeted Grandma Helen, snatched a fresh homemade doughnut or still-warm slice of bread, and hiked over to the stacks of peeled poplar (they called it popple) that were all over town. The mammoth stacks were fifteen or twenty feet tall and about ten feet wide, one after another, hundreds of feet long. The wood was destined for the acid-filled millponds, and conversion to paper. We would find my grandfather, Ben Prellwitz, the former mayor of Brokaw, in the big yellow crane, moving wood from railcars to the log piles or vice versa, and wave madly. He waved back. My dad filmed it every time, with his eight millimeter Kodak movie camera.

Next we boys ran away up the hillside behind the town, to three aging ski slides, towering like bony skyscrapers over the trees.

My Uncle Ken, a champion ski-jumper, leapt off these snowy scaffolds in their youth. My mother went down the landing slope, epic in itself.

They had to be nuts; suicidal; stark, raving insane. There is still a bar somewhere up around Merrill or Minocqua, with a picture of Ken sailing into the abyss on his long wooden skis.

Abandoned now to the elements, they were rotting away, with missing timbers clearly visible in the steep, curved floor of the looming towers, as we gaped up at them. They were what the legal profession calls attractive nuisances, and parents call deathtraps. Naturally, after being told repeatedly to stay off them, we scampered immediately to the top, and enjoyed the peculiar thrill known only to stupid outlaws.

It was a killer view, looking out over the wooded hillsides, past a couple of square blocks of houses in the tiny Wausau Papers company town, plus a combination post office and general store, a small school, depot, and a park. The railroad ran along the base of the hill, far below us. The tall smokestacks and sprawl of the paper mill bordered the Wisconsin River, flowing serenely by, and a scattered checkerboard of dairy farms, each with tidy homes, barns and silos, dotted the hills beyond.

Eventually, the town cut the guy wires that held up the ski-slides, and they tumbled over in the first strong windstorm.

We crossed the river to the family farm where my grandmother was born, and visited with genial cousin Jim, herding dairy cows, learning to drive the tractor and the old pickup, shoveling grain, picking up rocks, burrowing through the hay barn like human moles, eating huge meals. Down the road at Aunt Emma's we slid on their haystack, and got yelled at by crabby old Uncle Ed. At Cousin Victor's, as we were bumping across the field, taking a load of hay back to the big red barn, most of the load I was riding on top of, including me, suddenly flopped off the wagon, finishing up in a messy new pile on the ground. By some miracle, I fell between sheltering bales, and wasn't damaged in the drop, or creamed on the ground, by the bales landing all around me.

We went to the state fair in Wausau for the Fourth of July fireworks. Afterwards, we visited Uncle Reno or Uncle Henry, who had retired to town after decades of milking cows at dawn, leaving the next generation on the farm.

At the annual family reunion in Marathon Park in Wausau, the men would play schafskopf (sheep's head), a card game that evidently officially required swinging your arms wildly in a full 360 degree circle before slapping some cards on the table with enough force to shake the earth, because they all did it, with gusto.

We kids ran wild around the huge park, drinking Orange Crush and Nehis and root beers fished out of the galvanized tub full of ice and drinks, roasting hot dogs, throwing things in the fire, watching Cousin Jim demonstrate how you can really boil water in a paper cup on an open fire, and nibbling from the piles of potluck lugged in by distant relatives whose family connection I still don't understand.

The little rideable replica Union Pacific train made its oval rounds, with a host of tikes aboard, and an adult engineer in a striped hat and overalls, sitting somberly on the orange and silver engine, tooting the whistle.

The best part was the trip "up north," to the log sheathed cabin on Payment Lake, a few hours away. Grandpa went in to rent a boat there years before, and came back with a boat and a cabin on the shore, all for a few thousand dollars.

The cabin replaced "the shack," a tar-paper-sheathed, three room affair set out in a swamp with a gas lantern for light, an outhouse, and outdoor pump for water, where porcupines chewed the varnish off the outdoor icebox, and the log boatshed was covered with old license plates. It was purchased by my grandfather and three other guys (Ed Stubbe, Joe Sirney, and Mr. Schultz) during the Depression for $100 total. Call it an early timeshare.

At Payment Lake, we swam and ran around and threw things in the lake and fished up a few bass, sunfish, perch, the odd catfish, and once in a blue moon a scary northern pike or muskie, angling right off the wooden dock, or venturing out on the small, pretty, birch-tree-lined lake in the old wooden rowboat or the sleek silver Alumacraft, with a classic Evinrude outboard. There was a beaver dam, a marsh with lily pads and cattails, hidden bays and trails through the woods all around the lake to explore, and loons haunting the morning mists.

We saw far more big fish displayed in the freezer at Mercer Hardware than we ever caught. A trip to the Wampum Shop next door, chock full of tourist junk, was an annual pilgrimage.

One year, we continued on out to California to see Uncle Ken in the Simi Valley. In Yellowstone, the bears snuffled right up to the door of our car, looking for a handout. We spent that night in a wooden tourist cabin, wrapped in wool blankets against the cold.

We walked in the redwoods, admired the falls, played in the cold river, and watched the fire fall at Yosemite, where embers from a huge fire were pushed off a cliff at dusk, before the Park Service gave it up as too much trouble. We went to Will Rogers State Beach, and frolicked in the surf with Uncle Ken and his kids.

And then, we turned around, and drove 3,000 miles home.

## 42. Gathering Cattle

Vern McWilliams and Matt Dodson were at Vern's silversmith studio in the sculpture garden behind the Judith Hale Gallery in Los Olivos, looking at some striking eight-by-tens of a small stampede.

Built of seventy year old wood salvaged from old corrals on part of the old Buell place, the down-home studio is the perfect setting for Mr. McWilliams' silver business, "Coyote Casting." Some of the boards even bear cattle brands. It's very Valley.

I was there because local historian Jim Norris tipped me off to a remarkable roundup Mr. McWilliams had pulled off, capturing a dozen longhorns living large on Rancho Ynecita, an area of twenty acre estates just outside of town. The time had come for the quarrelsome, rambunctious bunch of beeves to mosey off to a new home.

"They belong to some people on Rancho Ynecita,' said Vern. "They're kind of like the deer over there. These are the wildest cattle I've seen in 25 years."

Matt Dodson concurred.

"I was hired a couple of times to catch this little yearling bull," said Matt, "But there was no way."

The bull won the preliminary rounds.

"The owner was trying to haze him out in the open," said Matt. "That little bull turned and charged him. The owner tried to run away. The bull went right over the top of him. Drilled him right in the back, and then went through the gate."

"He ran off wearing that gate," laughed Matt. "I went out there three times," he grinned, chagrined. "We never did get him."

Vern McWilliams said, "There was an ad in the paper. Some longhorns needed homes."

"I spent a week up there feeding them hay, tracking them here and there. I fed them into a little corral and shut the gate on them. We got five of them loaded out that way," he explained. "We ended up roping three, and one's still up there. He jumps out, wherever he wants to."

The wild bunch went to Buellton.

"We've been taking care of the Norman's cattle over there for 25 years, and they're in with them," said Vern.

With true cowboy humility, he nevertheless denied any expertise with cattle.

"So much of that cowboy stuff is BS," he snorted. However, he did admit, "I have no recollection of life without horses."

"I grew up in Sublette County, Wyoming," said Mr. McWilliams, "about 80 miles south of Jackson. I've been on a ranch as long as I can remember, both sides of my family, for two generations. I've gathered a lot of cattle. I've been here 30 years," related Vern. "I'm starting a colt of my own. I still ride."

"I'm doing some silver. I do things like these hats," he explained, pointing to a rack of shiny miniature western chapeaus, each about three inches in diameter.

"They're old western movie stars and famous cowboys' hats. Charlie Russell, Gene Autry, Tom Mix, Festus, Clint Eastwood's *Pale Rider*, *Gunsmoke*'s James Arness. They go for $350."

He journeyed to the Ronald Reagan museum to drop off a silver replica of the former president's hat the other day. There's still a crowd there daily.

"Cars were lined up for two miles," he noted.

"I do horsehead belt buckles, miniature horseshoe necklaces, these crosses," said Vern, pulling out beautiful samples of his work. "If the door's open, I'm open. If I'm not here, just slide the money under the door," he laughed.

His contribution to the Judith Hale sculpture garden is a slim, beehive shaped tower of hundreds of horseshoes, rising six feet tall.

"I should of counted them, but it don't matter. It's just a pile of horseshoes," said the quiet artist.

Mr. McWilliams is beginning a new wine venture.

"I have a friend who makes certified organic, sulfite-free wine. There are lots of people allergic to sulfites. I met him when I was on the board of directors of the California Certified Organic Farmers, when we were in the organic cattle business." A distribution deal is in the works.

"I'm not much of a businessman," Mr. McWilliams claimed. "A lady asked for my cell number the other day. I told her I was out on good behavior."

## 43. It's Never Too Late To Honor Heroes

When he was a 21-year-old Army Medevac pilot, flying Dustoff #112 in Vietnam in 1968, Richard Lindekens wasn't concerned about recognition.

It was about saving lives. As one of his band of brother pilots said during a particularly heavy firefight when the ground troops urged him to leave, "We're not going until we have all your wounded."

"That's just the way it was," says Mr. Lindekens. "I got shot down a few times. DUSTOFF is an acronym for what we did as Medevac pilots. It stands for Dedicated Unhesitating Service To Our Fighting Forces."

Still, even though it's thirty-seven years coming, he's heartened that HR 1308, a bill establishing a combat badge for helicopter medical evacuation (Medevac) ambulance pilots and crews, is working its way through Congress. A quirk in Army regulations has shortchanged the dedicated soldiers for decades.

"Please contact your House of Representatives member, and ask them to support HR 1308," Richard Lindekens urges.

"I was with the 254th Medical Detachment, part of the 44th Medical Group. We were a small unit with six ships, that flew our missions in the Central Highlands," said Mr. Lindekens. "During the Vietnam conflict, helicopters became a vital tool used to remove the wounded from the battlefield. Not only did they rescue the downed pilots in the north, but the bulk of the flying was done extracting wounded soldiers in the south.

"The pilots and crew members of these helicopters were, for the most part, volunteers to the dustoff mission. The helicopters were unarmed, except for the crew members' personal weapons. The missions were flown 24 hours a day, no matter what the weather was like."

Kathleen Fennell served at the 12th Evacuation Hospital at Cu Chi in 1968-69.

"As a Vietnam nurse, we could NOT have saved so many of our brother soldiers, had it not been for these men bringing us our patients from the field, often minutes after they were injured," Ms. Fennell said.

"It was my honor and privilege, though heartbreaking, to place the unofficial Combat Aeromedic Badge at the black granite panels of our sacred Vietnam Veteran Memorial. Many of these men flew Dustoff ships into our hospital, and I shall forever hear the sounds of Dustoff coming in to the 12th. It is a sound dreaded even today. Not a day goes by that I do not look in terror at any chopper I hear."

Richard Lindekens, a captain for American Airlines, grew up in Pasadena, and has lived here for nine years. He's a past president of the Danish Brotherhood.

Helicopters run in the family. His wife, Raelynn, the daughter of former Viking Press owner Bo Pedersen, once landed a chopper at Solvang School to show the students. She's now a pilot for Northwest Airlines, on the Bombay route.

At the request of his former commanding officer, Richard K. Andersen, Richard Lindekens went to the Vietnam War Memorial, where members of the Vietnam Veterans of America hosted a ceremony attended by about 150 persons, dedicated to the 215 fallen crew members of the U.S. Army Medical Helicopter Ambulance units. An unofficial Combat Aeromedic Badge was presented at each soldier's panel, and later forwarded to their families.

"I went and represented our unit. This particular set of wings will be sent to Doug Stover's dad this afternoon. His dad was a World War II pilot, flying B-24s," said Mr. Lindekens. "The sad part is, I belonged to a unit that had only about six helicopters, but I presented ten of these badges.

"Not all of those guys died during my tour. Three of the crew members, that I flew with for the year I was there, died the day I left."

The first Gold Star mother of the Vietnam war was at the ceremony at the Wall, as was a former POW who spent a number of years in the same cell as Senator John McCain.

Richard Lindekens pointed to a man in wheelchair in a photo of the event.

"He lost both legs, and this arm. He went in front of Congress on behalf of this bill, and in ten minutes had everybody absolutely crying. He talked about the crew who picked him up. Everybody in the crew got shot, including the medic working on him, who got shot in the face, and still wouldn't stop working on him."

"We presented badges to 215 of our fallen friends, who made the ultimate sacrifice. They gave their lives. This bill, now working its way through Congress, will hopefully be passed, so these crew members will finally, officially, have their badges," said Mr. Lindekens.

# 44. Something's Fishy: The Case of the Missing Mermaid

Dateline: Copenhagen.

The attacks started years ago, crimes of unspeakable cruelty.

In 1998, they cut off the 85 year old handicapped woman's head.

It wasn't the first time, either.

Friends resurrected her, and helped her back onto her favorite rock. But on September 11, 2003, there was another attempt on her life.

This time the cowards used dynamite to blow her away. She was found floating off Langelinie Quay, face down.

Still she survived. Now aged 90, she's been beheaded twice, had her right arm sawn off, and suffered innumerable dousings with paint, yet she poses patiently daily for hundreds of tourists.

The victim: Copenhagen's famed Little Mermaid.

Just the facts: Sculptor Edvard Eriksen modeled the topless, girl-sized bronze after his wife Eline and ballerina Ellen Price, in 1909.

As far as we know, Eline and Ellen did not have fins.

After four years—perhaps the girls wouldn't sit still—the statue was placed on a rock in Copenhagen's harbor.

It was a bust bought with beer money. Ballerina booster Carl Jacobsen, founder of Copenhagen's Carlsberg brewery, who was rather taken with Ellen, wrote the check.

We take our mermaids seriously in Solvang. When weeks went by with no leads, I jetted to Copenhagen to help out at the crime scene.

Okay, it was a long planned family vacation. Was it Nixon who said, "We could write this trip off—but it would be wrong?" Or was that Arthur Frommer?

I checked in with Copenhagen Homicide. They referred me to Superintendent Jorgen Thomsen, who said "We haven't found the men who did it, and it will be some time before the Mermaid is back. She had quite a bit of damage. Explosives are the only way they could have done it."

Suspects: Despite the 9/11 date, al-Qaeda is not on the short list. The feminist group "Radikal Feministisk Fraktion" claimed responsibility for the 1998 decapitation, saying "Men like women better without their heads anyway."

This was later exposed as brazen head(line) hunting. Then photographer Michael Poulsen, who broke the story and subsequently "recovered" the comely bronze bust, was arrested. Charges were later dropped, with no culprits ever identified.

In Hans Christian Andersen's 1836 tale, the Little Mermaid saves the life of a shipwrecked prince and makes a deal to become human so they can wed. This sets her back her voice and tail, and she will endure pain with every step, forever. Plus, there will be disadvantages.

So far, your average marriage.

You ain't seen nothin' yet. If the fickle prince weds another (he does, the lout) the finny female becomes foam, and disappears forever.

Frankly, you don't need "Dear Abby" to sense a dysfunctional relationship coming on here.

Imagine her letter: "Abby, I'm a cetacean—that's a big headed fish—and I fell for this sailor. Now I'm invisible. Any ideas? Sign me, All wet in DK."

Over a million tourists a year trek here to see the naked maid. Maybe they're sorry for a girl who had the misfortune to live before there were helpful newspaper columnists to sort out her fishy love life.

Perhaps they're just finny voyeurs. I rather doubt it—there are more sex shops in Copenhagen than grocery stores. In any case, only Disney has made more kroner on this frail siren than the Danes.

"She's so—little!" is always the reaction when pilgrims arrive at the waterside viewing area, a shady, tree lined concourse called Langelinie Quay, quite peaceful in between busloads of Japanese tourists. The statue is about the size you'd expect your average weight watching mermaid to be in real life, roughly three times the size of the copy in Solvang's Copenhagen Square, which is also said to have been crafted by Eriksen.

In 1961 a chaste admirer dressed the little sea princess in bra and panties, then painted her hair red. (Usually she wears an algae-bra.)

In 1963 she was painted all red. In 1964 she was decapitated for the first time. Two drunks sawed off her right arm in 1984, then turned themselves, and the arm, in to police the following day.

In 1990 a lazy decapitator gave up halfway through. 1998's headhunter was successful. The explosives were a novel twist.

In Hans Christian Andersen's tale, the Little Mermaid's granny tells her "Pride must suffer pain."

I don't think this was quite what Grandmother had in mind.

## 45. The Island of the Danish Bakers

In a continuing attempt to seek out Solvang's roots and write off my trip, I'm in Aero, Denmark's Nantucket.

Third generation baker Bent Olsen of Olsen's Danish Bakery moved to Solvang from Aero in the mid 60's. He was back in Aero for a vacation. I missed him there, but Denmark born Solvang retailer Marianne Larsen said, "Bent will tell you Aero is the best part of Denmark." Mr. Olsen carries on a tradition of fine baking made famous in Solvang by Carl Birkholm, also from Aero.

Everywhere you look on this jewel of an island of 7,200 souls, an hour's ferry ride from the mainland, is a scene that should be framed. There are sweeping vistas of the sea, quaint thatched roof cottages, rich farmland and tidy homesteads painted in bold colors, complete with flocks of geese.

It was from here that young Carl Birkholm set out to seek his fortune. His journey took him to Solvang, where he put that Danish village on the map with a pastry empire that seemed to rise as fast as his dough.

In the 1960's Birkholm's Danish Bakery was a flourishing local landmark, supplying tourists, groceries throughout California, and even the airlines with mountains of fresh Danish pastry daily. Today Solvang Bakery operates out of the old Birkholm's building on Alisal Road.

The island the bakers left behind is about eighteen miles long, five wide in the middle. Ancient tombs found here are 10,000 years old. Aeroskobing, the island's main town, has a royal charter that dates to 1522. The look of the charming medieval village is protected by strict building codes. A thatched roof cottage can be bought for just $75,000, but only permanent residents may own a home in the old town.

Once a Viking stronghold, this isle has always depended on the sea. Models of sailing ships hang in the Aeroskobing church in the town square, built in 1756 on the site of a Middle ages sanctuary. Only Copenhagen had more ships in the late 1800's.

Aero mariners sailed the world from this home port in an era when Denmark owned St. Thomas and St. Croix in the Caribbean.

Shop windows shine like diamonds at night. The jeweler leaves gems in the window and the florist—"blomster"—simply ties a string around the plants sitting for sale outdoors. Perhaps honesty is made easier by the fact that there is no easy way to leave before the morning ferry.

Tiny, colorful one room cottages line the beach. Horses graze in a field nearby, flanked by giant, high tech windmills and solar panels which provide almost half the island's electricity. Bicycles abound, with riders of all ages.

After a meteoric career in California, Carl Birkholm retired to this sleepy island, memorably bringing his Cadillac along with him.

In that motorized diplodocus, he somehow negotiated the narrow, winding, cobblestone, one car width streets. Some measure less than 15' from building to picturesque building.

There's one elegant bakery in Aero now, the Hansen Konditori. A couple from Seattle were trying to decide which decadently delicious delicacies to devour, as we bought a flaky bear claw.

Mr. Birkholm passed on a few years ago, but his memory remains.

"Everyone on Aero knows Carl Birkholm," said the cashier in the Red Cross store. The island of Birkholm, just offshore, is the smallest inhabited island in Denmark.

"I didn't know Birkholm personally, but I read about him in the newspaper," said Hans Peter Petersen, an educator who has lived on Aero for 25 years. Mr. Petersen loves it here, but knows what might induce some to leave.

"On a Sunday in December you can walk through town and never see a soul. The economy is bad. Four shipyards have closed in my time here. The work is going to the far east, or Poland, where labor is cheaper."

A mainstay of the island's economy is a state run navigation school with 300 students. A plan to shut it down a few years ago galvanized the islanders.

"Everyone on the island closed their businesses, the schools closed, and we all went to Copenhagen to protest," said Petersen. The school stayed open.

Tourism helps the economy a few months out of the year.

"The tourist season is mainly June, July and August," said Maria Leth of the Hotel Aerohus. Like most Danes we met, her English is perfect. A girlfriend of hers visited Solvang this past summer. Ms. Leth was delighted by Solvang's homage to Denmark.

"Denmark is such a small country. To have an entire Danish town in California, that looks like this!"

## 46. The Happy Canyon Boys and the Secret of the Old Shaft

Was it really Unhappy Canyon? Wolcott Schley, Sig Hansen, Bob Field and the Hourihans have reached a consensus: The secret of who named Happy Canyon, and why, may lie at the bottom of a bottomless mine shaft.

The mercury mines that flourished in the mountains just beyond Happy Canyon after 1874 probably influenced the name in one way or another. One theory: the label is ironic, referring to the mountain of litigation quarried after the price of quicksilver collapsed, and the lawsuits piled up.

Another guess: the 400 miners employed in the various diggings at the peak spent their pay in a bar located in the vicinity, getting happy.

Then there's the deleterious effect of mercury itself, exposure to which causes brain damage. It was once a favored chemical of hat makers. From that toxic detour, we got the expression "mad as a hatter."

On June 11, 1874, the *Santa Barbara Index* reported "great excitement in certain moneyed and mining rings in San Francisco...in regard to the discovery of an immense ledge of cinnabar in Santa Ynez Valley."

Cinnabar is the rust red ore from which mercury is derived. The Chumash Indians used it as a primary pigment in their cave paintings.

Geologist W.D Brown predicted that, under the right conditions, "the Santa Barbara quicksilver mines will be the most valuable in the world."

Los Prietos, site of the current boy's camp, became one mining headquarters.

"There is already quite a little village of buildings, all belonging to the company...The miners are now working in tunnels night and day," wrote a reporter.

The excavated ore was toasted in a gargantuan oak wood barbeque.

"The heat separates the quicksilver, and it is carried off in fumes to a condenser...No fumes can escape to injure the miners, unless the fan breaks," the article cheerily related.

Oh, that pesky fan.

"Even if that should happen, they have only to leave the vicinity until the fires die down," suggested the optimistic scribe. Now you know why we have OSHA, the Occupational Safety and Health Administration.

At the "Santa Ynez Furnace," closest to Happy Canyon, the correspondent said, "Words fail us here, to describe the enormous mass of cinnabar actually lying on top of the ground."

This was probably near what US Geological Survey maps show as the Red Rock Mine, on private property not far from the Cachuma Saddle guard station.

"The work at this mine is done mainly by Chinamen, who make their own camp and board themselves."

Surprisingly, the writer was female, an intrepid traveler who even worked a visit with recluse Davy Brown into the story. The National Forest campground near his old cabin is named after the onetime slaver, forty-niner, and bona fide mountain man, friend to John Muir.

"Descending the trail again on our sure footed little pony, we reached the camp, where we found a dinner and a place to rest before retiring," she wrote. "Here the pioneer hunter of Santa Ynez lives, and he presented us with his photograph, we being, as he said, the first lady who ever visited his camp."

"And the pioneer hunter makes an uncommonly picturesque picture, arrayed in his hunting suit, with the deer's tail in his cap—an Indian sign that the wearer is on the warpath," related the remarkable reporter.

A grumpy C.E. Huse made a case for better roads to the mines.

"In all the territory north of the Santa Ynez range of mountains and east of the San Marcos Tollroad, and south of the boundary of Kern County, embracing an area of about 900 square miles, this county has never spent a single dollar for roads or trails or for any other object whatever," Mr. Huse complained.

"In the rainy season, the route up the river Santa Ynez is wholly impracticable, by reason of the quicksands. The road crosses the river thirty-eight times, and many of the fords are washed out every winter. All supplies for the mines during the rainy season are sent on the backs of pack animals, over a very circuitous, rough and almost impassable trail over the mountains," Huse argued, in a petition for funds.

The cinnabar boom busted quickly.

"The works have been silent since 1876," read a later article, "first on account of a suit against the company for infringement on a patent, and also on account of the low price of quicksilver, and perhaps, to some extent, on account of lax management."

Lawyers got the mine, and investors got the shaft.

## 47. The Danish Capital of America: Solvang

For many visitors, Solvang's Danish roots are like real roots, in the sense that they don't see them at all.

Tourists say "Look at those windmills! What a nice Dutch village!"

Only a few towns in America started as educational communities. Solvang's founders established a Danish folk school and built their town around it, largely with Danish immigrants already in America. They came from the Dakotas, Minnesota, Iowa, all across the mid-West, as well as Denmark.

Founding fathers Nordentoft, Gregersen, and Hornsyld had searched the state for the right spot. After an attempt to buy land in Mendocino failed, they found the Valley in 1911. The fascinating Elverhoj museum at 1620 Elverhoy Way chronicles the tale.

This is a town with a strong sense of community. Probably half the residents still have ties to Denmark by blood or marriage. Kids attend schools their grandparents built.

Superb bakeries are reason enough to move here permanently. Descended from generations of Danish bakers, Bent Olsen of *Olsen's Danish Bakery* and Torben Petersen of *Danish Mill Bakery* are up well before the sun, preparing mouth watering pastry and breads, fresh daily. Add *Mortensen's Bakery* and *Solvang Bakery*, and you're never more than a block from blowing your diet.

The Solvang shopping directory lists 190 businesses. Some truly great stores: Marianne Larsen's *Gaveaesken* ("The Gift Box") at 433 Alisal Road, is a local favorite. Born in Denmark, former Danish Maid Marianne specializes in hand made Scandinavian gifts.

Bent and Lisa Pedersen's *Ingeborg's Danish Chocolates* at 1679 Copenhagen Dr. creates old-fashioned Danish chocolates and candy, which they ship all over the globe. Sweet!

Steve Nelson's *Royal Copenhagen Shop* next door clearly shows the impact of many buying trips to Denmark in the varied inventory, including a superb Danish cookware collection. You can get your own ableskiver pan across the street at Birgitte and Steen Pedersen's *Iron Art Gift Shop*.

Kathy Mullin's *Book Loft* at 1680 Mission Dr. is a fine bookstore, with a Hans Christian Andersen Museum upstairs. They've inspired thousands of young writers with their essay contests over the years. *The Solvang Antique Center* collective at 486 First Street has an overwhelming array of fine antiques and kitschy esoterica.

Phil Grant's *First Street Leather* at 1634 Copenhagen is a model for retailers and a joy for buyers. An outstanding collection of coats, hats, belts, bags and more since 1972, plus Phil's personable presence.

*The Jule Hus*, Solvang's Christmas store at 1580 Mission Dr., is ornament heaven. Owners Lauren and David Watts often travel to Europe to seek out unique finds.

Discover *Charlie's Playhouse* nearby at 444 Atterdag for classic wood and tin toys and a charming children's clothes collection.

Don't miss Sabine Brouillet's *Pearls of Provence* at 485 Alisal for a cheery "Bonjour!" and a quick idyllic trip to the lavender laden south of France, complete with period antiques and colorful linens.

There are many more fine shops to discover—explore.

More tasting rooms are opening. *Lucas & Lewellen* debuted in June at 1645 Copenhagen Drive. Legendary Louis Lucas is one of the pioneers of viticulture in this area. Next door are *Plam Winery* and *Royal Oaks*. *Presidio Winery* is at 1603 Copenhagen. Gerry Moro's *Morovino* is at 433 Alisal Rd. *Cabana* and *House of Honeywood* are at 1539 Mission.

Summer theater, put on by the Pacific Conservatory of the Performing Arts at the Solvang Festival Theater, is one of the joys of living here, a true jewel in the Valley crown. Always professional, usually outstanding, often amazing, Solvang's theatre under the stars has delighted audiences since 1974, when townspeople and contractors rallied to construct a 700 seat playhouse modeled after Shakespeare's Globe in just a matter of months.

Overall, it's nicer than the now reconstructed Globe, set on the banks of the Thames in an iffy London neighborhood, because Theaterfest has an enchanting park-like reception area as well, perfect for intermission mingling and wine tasting. Plus you don't get mugged walking home.

At Allen Hancock College's training program in Santa Maria, the only one of its kind in the US offered by a community college, PCPA students tackle a rigorous two year curriculum, taught by a resident company of professional actors, directors, designers, musical directors, choreographers and technicians. Alumni include Robin Williams.

My own all time favorite play here was *Hamlet*, starring Daniel Davis. A riveting performance, and the outdoor setting was perfect—a chill mist swept the theatre as if on cue when the ghost arrived. *Hamlet* aficionados called it one of the best ever, anywhere. Women threw roses to the intense star. Theater professionals were awed.

My brother Bert, former editor of the *SYV News*, now editor of the award winning *Cambrian*, tells this story: "As a student at Stanford's overseas campus at Cliveden House, west of London, I took a class in history of theater design. The professor had a long career designing theatrical productions, complemented by stints as a teacher. As part of the class, we were to attend two productions of *Hamlet*, one produced by avant garde actor/director Steven Berkoff and the other by the Royal Shakespeare Company. On the bus ride into London to see the play, somehow the subject of favorite productions of *Hamlet* came up."

"I've seen hundreds," the professor said. "But the best I ever saw was in a little town called Solvang, on California's central coast."

Alan Fletcher, then head of American Conservatory Theatre's training program, directed that amazing 1979 production.

When you go, dress warm. Locals bring blankets. It's nippy after nightfall.

Solvang suffered economically in recent years. An outlet store mall built in the early 90's to strident protests drove out numerous small shops that had been here for years.

As predicted, when outlets flooded the Central Coast and profits softened, the discounters hightailed it out of town. A second mall proposed to the south was converted to timeshares.

Bright side of that debacle: Digital Instruments founder physicist Virgil Elings bought the buildings at 320 Alisal Rd. and installed his Solvang Motorcycle Museum. It's a treat, one of the best collections of classic and vintage bikes in the USA.

\*Talk the Tak: "Tak" means "thanks" in Danish. After that, newcomers to Solvang want to know—what is an Elverhoj, anyway? Or a Midten Hof, Nordentoft, Vigard, Vester Sted, or Abletoft?

The Danish street names in this charming village puzzle, confound and provoke non-Danish locals and visitors alike. We find streets named Odin, Freya, Valhalla and Esrom. Esrom?

Odin is the supreme god of Norse mythology. Valhalla is Odin's hall for slain heroes. Freya is the Norse goddess of love, marriage and fertility. Esrom is a city in Denmark. There's an esrom cheese, too.

Quite a few street names here are Danish towns, including Copenhagen, Ribe, Silkborg, Holsted, Aalborg, Aarhus, Abeltoft, Adelgade, Abletoft, Elsinore, Kolding, Nykobing, Nysted, Oxbow, Ringsted, Roskilde, Skagen, and Viborg. Hornbeck evidently refers to Hornbaek, a small town on the coast north of Copenhagen.

Castles are well represented, including Augustenborg, Fredensborg, and Hamlet's castle, Kronborg. Hindfell is a castle mentioned in the *Volsung Saga*, which was originally written in Icelandic.

"Midten Hof is not Danish—probably German," said Marianne Larsen. "Hof" means 'farm" in German, while in Danish, it would mean the Royal Court and midten would mean "in the middle of," she noted. Also, "I know there is a street called Vigard in Solvang, but it is incorrect. 'Vi' means 'we' and 'gaard' means 'farm.' 'Our farm' would be 'vor gaard.'"

The Rev. Benedict Nordentoft was one of the founders of Solvang. Vester Hof means "west ground." Vester Sted is "west place." Oster Sted is "east place." Molle means "mill." Overdel means "upper part." Kroen means "inn."

Rebild refers to Rebild National Park in Denmark. Elverhoj means "elves on a hill." Kanin Hoj is "Rabbit Hill." Bakke also means "hill." Atterdag translates to "another day."

Then there's Solvang itself. Danes pronounce it "Soul-vong." A cab driver in Copenhagen told me "Sol is sun. Vang is a very old word. Maybe a field. Better ask a farmer."

Most locals are happy with the translation "sunny field," but a few hold out for "sunny valley." "Sunny meadow" and "sunny countryside" are also-rans.

* Turkey Bingo: The sixty turkeys given away are no longer live turkeys. As the years rolled on, no one knew quite what to do with a live one. But the traditional charity gathering, begun around 1915, continues to benefit the needy, thanks to the Alpha Pi Charitable Organization.

Turkey Bingo was originally started by the "Men of Dania" to fund the building of Dania Hall, a meeting place which stood on Atterdag at Copenhagen until the 1970s. The "Ladies of Dania" took the event over several years later. Insert your own pithy comment here.

## 48. On the Viking Trail

Tracy Farhad, the new executive director of the Solvang Conference and Visitor's Bureau, announced that 24,000 visitors stopped in at the welcome center in Solvang the first quarter of 2005.

Perhaps, like Don Lago, they're on the Viking trail. Mr. Lago's book *On the Viking Trail: Travels in Scandinavian America,* published in 2004, includes a visit to Solvang, where he chatted with The Book Loft's Kathie Mullins. She's quoted in the book, and has copies on hand.

Mr. Lago theorizes that Solvang, "the most architecturally ambitious Scandinavian town in America, by a long shot," appeals to some tourist's psychological hunger for roots, in a franchise-happy, cultural wasteland.

"It spoke with an accent as strong as the Spanish of Santa Fe, the French of old New Orleans, and the Colonial English of Williamsburg," writes Lago. "People come here to feel, if only for a day, if only unconsciously, a sense of roots and community they can't find in Los Angeles."

A number of recent articles on the rise of heritage tourism and "ethno-tourism" seem to support his theory. *USA Today* featured Solvang last month in an article on the "top five Europe style destinations within North America." New Orleans, Newport, RI, Montreal, and Fredericksburg and New Braunfels, German towns in the Texas hill country, were also mentioned.

His father's Alzheimer's launched Mr. Lago on a quest to save the stories and traditions of his Swedish ancestors that ultimately took him around the world. He began in his ancestral home of Gränna, Sweden, and studied Swedish, Danish, Finnish, Norwegian, and Icelandic towns and cultural phenomenon in America, as well.

The result is an eclectic, meandering journey of discovery. Novelist Wallace Stegner, "Swedish Nightingale" Jenny Lind, Mrs. Olsen of Folger's Coffee fame, poet Carl Sandburg, and a host of other Scandinavians, cross Lago's inquisitive, intelligent path.

"Family memoir, chronicle of exemplary Nordic Americans, immigration history, travel guide, rumination on ethnicity, and a good deal more, *On the Viking Trail* is an erudite, witty, affecting read, as bracing as a cup of strong coffee or a swallow of aquavit," summed up James P. Leary, professor of folklore and Scandinavian studies at the University of Wisconsin.

Mr. Lago is a political activist, book reviewer, kayaking instructor, researcher, and author, whose essays on nature, science, and history have appeared in numerous magazines and journals, including *Orion, Astronomy, Sky and Telescope, Smithsonian, Science Digest,* and the *Antioch Review.*

I phoned him in his cabin in the pines outside Flagstaff, Arizona., for an update.

"Solvang surprised me, in a pleasant way, and really stood out," said Don Lago. "It's a sociological book, in that I'm looking behind the scenes, and a lot of the tourist-oriented towns didn't seem to appreciate that too much."

"I got a warmer reception in Solvang than I ever would have imagined," he recounted. "Some of the other towns I wrote about got really irate."

Towns discussed in the book include Kingsburg, Ca. (Swedish), Gothenburg, Nebraska (Swedish), Ely, Minnesota, (Swedish), Poulsbo, Wa. (Norwegian), St. Peter, Minn. (Swedish), Spanish Fork, Utah (Icelandic), Bishop Hill, Illinois (Swedish), Lindsborg, Kansas (Swedish), Hancock, Michigan (Finnish), Stanton, Iowa (Swedish), Decorah, Iowa (Norwegian), Moorhead, Minnesota (Norwegian), and many more.

## 49. Danish for A Day

Solvang hosts an annual party called Danish Days. Started as a community gathering in 1936, the festivities have grown to be a showcase weekend for the community. Volunteers dressed in traditional Danish togs cook ableskiver and medistepolse for thousands of visitors. Hans Christian Andersen, portrayed by Randel MeGee, tells his famous stories.

There are be three parades, a raffle for a trip to Denmark, comics, and live music, including Jonathan Wild, the Great Danes, the Police Orchestra from Solvang's sister city, Aalborg, and the Village Band, playing atop the vintage Carlsberg Beer wagon. Wave to my dad, Ben Etling, on trumpet.

Three teams of Danish dancers twirl, twist and shout. In a crowd pleasing ritual, third generation master woodcarver Mark Colp noisily attacks a huge log with a chain saw for the better part of a day, releasing the creatures within. 2003's dolphins can be seen in front of the Home Connection at 425 Alisal Road.

A charming teen descendant of the founding families is named Danish Maid, and greets visitors. In 2004 it was Nicole Rasmussen, whose great-grandfather, Jens, arrived in Solvang in 1917.

Funds raised benefit the Danish Days Foundation, which scrapes together a pot big enough to do it again next year. Foundation members include Hans Birkholm, Kevin Petersen, Max Hanberg, Ken Andersen, Brenda Andersen, Rick Marzullo, Tom Wright, Bent Pedersen, Dave Harrison, Denise Birkholm, Rose Skytt, Brenda Knudsen, Ed Hansen, Inge-Lisa Pedersen, Bruce Pedersen, Martha Nedegaard, the Jaeger family, Petti Pfau, and Donna Beehler.

If you've never had that tennis ball sized, pancake-like treat called ableskiver, and medistepolse, the chunky sausage that accompanies it, you are culinarially challenged. Some say ableskiver were originally whipped up on dented Viking shields. They're now served on a pedestrian only Copenhagen Drive Saturday and Sunday mornings, 8-12:30 am. Locals prefer early Sunday morning, when the quiet morning streets are perfect for catching up with neighbors on another year in the village.

It's a good time to reflect on what the community was and has become. Nearly a century after its founding as an educational community, this little town clings to its roots, still very Danish, still very family and education oriented.

Solvang is one of the most distinctly different, inviting, pedestrian friendly towns in the entire USA. I admire the entrepreneurial retailers, eking out a living in shops full of fascinating finds from afar, many in the same families for generations.

There's magic in the architecture. Here's an entire town with buildings yearning for a bygone European century. Savor master builder Sir Ferdinand Sorensen's windmills and whimsy, like the twisted dragon tail tower on the King Christian Tower Building at 436 First Street, a small version of the famous one on the Copenhagen Stock Exchange. Mr. Sorenson was knighted in 1976 by Queen Margrethe of Denmark for his work.

Look up to spot storks, and the real thatched roof on the Family Coat of Arms building at 1659 Copenhagen. The Round Tower at 436 Alisal is a one-third scale model of the famous Runde Taarn in Copenhagen, which houses the oldest functioning observatory in Europe.

Don't miss the Elverhoj art museum, Hans Christian Andersen Museum, and an exceptional Motorcycle Museum. The barrow stone in the park denotes the distance to Copenhagen instead of sheltering a 911 AD Viking tomb, but it's still a nice touch. The wind wafts mouth-watering aromas from numerous Danish bakeries, popping out fresh bread and decadent pastries every day. And once a year, people are dancing in the streets.

If you want to walk through a doorway into that lost America where people had a real community, and they cared about it and each other, and they went to a lot of trouble to throw a big annual party for free and were happy if you came, and you have a sense of humor and can look on the bright side of life for the cool things all around, and you don't honk the horn when there's a little traffic, and you like seeing lots of people, and you'd like to try a new breakfast, come on up to Solvang for Danish Days. You'll be glad you did.

Please leave grumps, snobs and people who tell blond jokes at home.

## Part 2. Dr. Danish Days

Can you get a University of California doctorate in Solvang Studies? Well, almost.

Hanne Pico Larsen is working on her doctorate in Scandinavian Studies at UC Berkeley. She's mining Solvang's rich lode of cultural, anthropological and economic contradictions.

"This paper is work in progress for my Ph.D. in Folklore and Scandinavian Studies," said Ms. Larsen, who was born and raised in Denmark. "The dissertation is about Solvang and tourism."

It's a shot heard around the world.

"I also want to thank participants in the international conference *Tourism & Festivals as Transnational Practice*, in Innsbruck, Austria, for many helpful discussions and comments," she said.

An earlier paper she authored explored the many facets of Danish Days. Put on your thinking caps.

"The theoretical framework for this paper is the dictum between front vs. backstage introduced by Erving Goffman, and later brought into tourist studies by Dean MacCannell," wrote Ms. Larsen. "MacCannell argues that tourists are on a quest trying to find the others' quotidian everyday life. Danish Days is the time of year when the Solvang stage is fully in use, a dressed up and smiling city.

"The tourists are invited to be on the stage with the locals. Drawing on Barbara Kirschenblatt-Gimblett's ideas on festivals, I explore what 'being Danish' means for the tourists in Solvang, and question whether that is in fact what they seek and hope for."

So much for those who thought is was all about the ableskiver.

Ms. Larsen's conclusion: "We are all Danish for the weekend."

"After having investigated the different meanings imposed on Danish Days by the different parties, as described by one informant, we have learned, that Danish Days is an event that everybody can fill with their own meanings," she wrote.

"Danish Days is referring back to Danish heritage," said Larsen. "Activities with Danish color and flavor are offered to and acted out by everybody who wants to participate, no matter what background they may have.

"People may come for a relaxing, yet entertaining, holiday. Some come to folk dance, some come because they can wear outfits that would not normally suit the everyday dress code. Some come because of the reference to Denmark, and some because it became a substitute for an old tradition; like an old LA couple who used to travel, but had now become too weak. For them Danish Days became a symbol of that used-to-travel-tradition that they had lived before. The visitors can have as many motivations for coming that we can imagine.

"As we also have heard, the festival can have other meanings for the organizers and people living in Solvang. And yes, for some, the reference back to Denmark is important, for others it is the money aspect that overshadows the event. However, the most important aspect for all is the intimate feeling and the social aspect," she related.

True scholars will want to read her sources, like Dean MacChannell's 1973 *Staged Authenticity: Arrangements of Social Space in Tourist Settings*, from the *American Journal of Sociology.*

She's presented papers in LA, at a conference of the Society for the Advancement of Scandinavian Studies, in Austria, and in Salt Lake City, at the Conference for American Folklore Society, about cultural landscapes.

"My dissertation will be on tourism and Solvang as it is now (and how it came to be like it is now)—and that is a project that usually takes 2-3 years," said Ms. Larsen.

"Solvang is indeed part of the Danish immigration history and "Diaspora", but in this paper I will be looking at the face of Solvang, the iconographic architecture as well as, the staging, exhibiting, and promotion of the Danish-ness offered as a little bit of Denmark. How does it fit our perception of an authentic cultural landscape? And what is the sense and meaning of the place for those living there, and for those just visiting?

"My research will include a two-fold perception study based on fieldwork and interviews. I will research the tourist motivation, expectation and experience, after which I will turn the focus to the Board of Commerce and other Solvang citizens, and map their attitude towards the 'business.'

"I believe my paper will be of importance to scholars of Folklore, Cultural Studies, Tourist Studies, Immigrant Studies, Museology, and Performance studies, as well as Scandinavian Studies, since many aspects of this work are essential to all the disciplines mentioned. Inspiration has come from works by Barbara Kieshenblatt-Gimblet, Barbro Klein, John Dorst, Dean MacCannell, Nelson Graburn, Eric Cohen and others."

"I hated it here when I first came," confided Ms. Larsen. "Now I want to stay."

Incidentally, quotidian means "occurring or returning daily; of an everyday character; ordinary, commonplace, trivial."

## 50. Solvang Citizens

The City of Solvang honored citizens Bob Raleigh, Hans Larsen and Renton Mitchell in 2005, issuing proclamations that officially recognize their many selfless contributions to the town over the years.

The three friends are tireless, imaginative, hands-on volunteers, exemplars of the kind of community spirit that makes this such a great place to live. They meet almost daily for coffee at the Solvang Bakery. Not infrequently, some good deed results.

Renton, Hans and Bob's accomplishments stretch over decades. I can barely scratch the surface of the things they've quietly accomplished over the 40-some years they've each lived here.

For starters, the three men are all members of the Vikings, an organization which lends a hand to neighbors with special medical needs, and children's charities. Bob Raleigh is currently vice-chief of the organization.

Never afraid to get their hands dirty, for years the trio voluntarily replaced the dead bulbs in the rows of cheery exterior lights that glimmer in Solvang after dark, illuminating a magical silhouetted cityscape. Hans Larsen restored a lift truck especially for the task, hanging banners as well.

Hans can always be found at the ableskiver stove during Danish Days. Owner/broker of Hans Larsen Realty, he's quietly been the go-to guy for behind-the-scenes private sector civic improvement here since the early 1970's.

Robert Raleigh directed *The Bells of Santa Ynez* again in 2004. Dramatizing the score was his idea, over forty years ago.

Bob was a music teacher at Solvang and College Schools at the time. *The Bells* production was an annual event for many years. Mr. Raleigh was at Solvang School for 38 years, as teacher and administrator, retiring as superintendent. He helped launch Theaterfest in the valley, as well.

In the early 1960's, Mr. Raleigh and Mr. Mitchell were both active in the Solvang Business Association. They were sought after emcees of numerous events, raising money for many local causes. Mr. Raleigh was chairman of Danish Days in 1967; Mr. Mitchell was co-chair.

I've been honored to know all three men for decades, and I have to tell you, we should clone them. Friends treasure their keen wit, intelligence and buoyant camaraderie. Bob, Renton, and Hans are people you're happy to see coming, proud to be seen with, and lucky to live near. The secret of their success: Ann Raleigh, Doris Mitchell, and Wendy Larsen.

## Part 2. Renton Mitchell

"I've always been lucky," said Renton Mitchell. He came to Solvang as a newly minted deputy sheriff in 1961.

Born in Glasgow, Scotland, in 1926, Renton grew up poor but happy, in a large family, amidst the razor gangs of Belfast, Ireland, named after their favorite weapon.

His adventurous forebears had some experience with America. Years before, his remarkable grandmother (she had "The Gift," they said—psychic power) had tracked down Renton's Uncle Duncan here, shortly after World War I.

She trekked from Scotland to see the lad, who was working for Fred Harvey at the Phantom Ranch, at the bottom of the Grand Canyon.

Her first words to her son after getting off her mule: "Are you hiding out from the law?"

Renton's father was a piano player, singer, and adman in Belfast. Renton did some design work at an early age.

"I was just a little boy, when my dad asked me to draw a picture of a loaf of bread for him. Next thing I knew, my loaf was on all the trams in Belfast."

His mother, Helen, and dad, Walter, had William, Walter, Agnes, Duncan, Renton, and Robert.

"My dad looked like Churchill. In Southern Ireland, they thought he WAS Churchill. And being an entertainer, he pretended to BE Churchill," laughed Renton.

A Hollywood director asked Walter Mitchell to be in the film version of *Brigadoon*. He declined, suggesting a friend instead.

Renton later visited the man in Hollywood, where he had done well, appearing in many films. In his dressing room, he tearfully thanked the son of the man who gave him his start.

In 1940, after Hitler launched his Blitzkrieg against Holland and Belgium, Renton's oldest brother, William, was sent to bring Queen Wilhelmina from Belgium to England. Bayoneted through the neck and captured, he spent five years as a POW, most of it working on a farm, where he was well treated.

Brother Walter was the flight deck engineer on board the convoy escort carrier *HMS Smiter*, on convoy duty in the North Atlantic, during WW II.

Renton lied about his age (he was 16 and two weeks) to enlist in the British Navy in 1942. He served until July of 1946.

A few days before D-Day, he was a signalman on a LCM (landing craft, manned), part of the invasion force at Poole Harbor, near Bournemouth, waiting for General Eisenhower to give the order.

Suddenly called out for review, he stood with about 80 other signalmen, lined up at attention, as a jeep with an American commander in it pulled up.

The American strode down the line, chatting with a few of the men. Renton, and another sailor, an older man, were pulled out of the ranks.

They'd been chosen to instruct new American signalmen. They were told to get their gear, and move out.

A few days later, his friends were part of the Allied invasion. Many never returned.

As the war wound down, he was again assigned as signalman on an LCM. He wasn't the captain, but he was in charge of the four man crew. He left the tiny LCM tied up one night, and went out with his mates. As a lark, he dressed in an American uniform and went with them to a dance in town, but the local girls weren't buying it.

"You're no Yank," they laughed.

Upon the crew's return, they discovered their boat stern down in the water.

"Some of the tides there drop 28 feet," he remembered wryly. There had not been enough slack in the lines. He'd sunk his ship.

Hauled before a board of inquiry, he was admonished. Two things saved him.

One: The war was over, and all anyone wanted to do, was get home.

Number two: "You're bloody lucky that was an American boat," they told him.

Belfast did not suffer like London during the Blitz, but it took some hits. One day a dud bomb landed on the Mitchell's roof, tore through the attic and the upper story, and rolled down the stairs to the ground floor landing.

Mustered out, he received a striped suit, shoes, and a hat.

He took a job driving a taxi in Belfast, where he was the only Protestant in the cab company. This worked in his favor with one Catholic priest, who always asked for Renton to take him on drunken weekly rounds visiting parishioners and his girlfriend.

Fabled Irish tenor Joe Locke, about whom the film "Hear My Song" was made, spent two months riding in Renton's cab.

Renton went back to sea. His first civilian ship was the *Ballyholme Bay*, an ancient, coal-fired scow, with a miscreant captain who neglected to purchase enough supplies for the journey. On the way to Finland to pick up a cargo of logs, they ran out of food.

The crew appointed Renton to negotiate with the cantankerous old Irishman. The captain had plenty of liquor on board. Renton suggested trading it for fish from nearby vessels. The fishermen were delighted, and the crew was fed.

In Finland, he was surprised to see the longshoremen were actually longshorewomen. The *Ballyholme Bay* made it home safely, where the captain was brought up on charges, and the ship scuttled.

Renton spent two seasons (October-April) in 1947-1949, aboard the whaling ship Balaena, as a bone gang man. Christopher Ash immortalized their toil in his 1962 book, *Whaler's Eye*.

He was going to the movies one afternoon, with his brother Duncan. As they passed the Albert clock tower in Belfast, Renton noted a crowd by the docks.

"Looks like they're picking men for the ship," he told Duncan. Their older brother, Walter, was an officer on board. "I'm going to see. I'll meet you at the matinee."

Of the 50 men trying to get a berth, only Renton was chosen. He was ordered to hustle home and get his gear.

He didn't make the matinee. He didn't see Duncan again for 21 years.

They sailed for the Cape of Good Hope. There was a crew of over five hundred on the massive, 400-foot-long, Anglo-Norwegian factory ship, akin to a tanker in design, which took 20,000 tons of diesel fuel aboard for the seven month journey.

Although they weren't yet whaling, they were already working. On the way south, they re-decked the entire ship.

They slipped out of Cape Town in the darkness, to get away from their fierce competitors. The *Balaena* circumnavigated Antarctica. In the land of the midnight sun, the state of the art factory ship dragged massive blue whales and other species aboard, and processed them on the spot, snatching up on average a whale an hour, 24 hours a day. Some blues were almost 100 feet long, weighing 82 tons.

In 1946-47, they carried a *Walrus* biplane on deck, to spot the whales. Renton's brother, Walter, an officer on the ship for 15 years, was in charge of the plane, which was catapulted into the air, and winched back on board.

"As it turned out, there were so many whales, there was no need for the plane," said Renton.

They plunged deep into the Ross Sea, carving a lane through the ice, then retreated with the season, to avoid being caught and crushed, like Shackleton's expedition.

They saw penguins marching from floe to floe.

"They would parade from one long ice block to another," he chuckled. "One fellow, a very strange man, caught a penguin and trained it to walk with him on the deck. Back and forth he would go, with the bird waddling after him. They took it away from him when we approached warmer waters, and released it."

"The longest whale I ever saw was about 110 feet," said Renton, tongue-in-cheek.

"A blue whale was coming on board, and a killer whale went after its tongue, which they like to eat. It got caught, and crushed by our machinery. So there was a 90-foot-long blue whale, with a 20-foot-long killer whale sticking out of its mouth, coming up the conveyor."

He cut the bones out, with razor sharp tools, on a slippery, blood-soaked, chaotic deck. It was brutal work, in a steaming sea of gore. He carved sperm whale teeth into penguin figures in his spare time.

Bizarrely enough, at coffee in Solvang one day, decades later, he met a man who sailed on a competing vessel.

"We all wanted to be on your ship," he told Renton. "Everyone was jealous."

Back in Ireland again, he took several University of Pennsylvania professors on a guided tour of peat bogs around Ireland. He owned a 1934 Aston-Martin racing sedan, a rare four-seater, high performance car.

Renton was offered a job as a Beechams Pills salesman in Northern Ireland in July of 1950, but decided instead to try his luck in America. He sold the Aston-Martin back to the company for their collection, and set off.

It was typical of this funny, generous man, that after losing most of his money playing cards on the ship over, he spent nearly his last dime taking an aunt who met him in New York out to lunch, and never mentioned his lack of funds.

He still had his bus ticket to Los Angeles, California, where another aunt awaited. There he landed his first job, at Germain, Inc., a nursery company, paying 93 cents an hour.

He married Jean Irene Frame, administrative assistant for a Los Angeles County Supervisor, and the fastest typist in LA (she won a contest). She had a four year old, Robbie. Their daughter, Margaret, was born in 1953. Renton bought a gas station in Riverside, and prospered, with hard work and a magnetic personality.

A bout of rheumatic fever at 14 had left Irene with severe heart damage. To get her out of the smog, they took a trip to Santa Barbara.

At a coffee shop there, Renton met the nephew of the county sheriff, who suggested Renton apply for a position. He took a test, interviewed, and finished at the top of the list of candidates.

He sold the gas station to become a lawman, assigned to Solvang, and the little family moved to the country in 1961. But Irene's heart troubles worsened, and she passed away in 1962.

Deputy Mitchell took the report when Jimmy Stewart found someone had rustled one of his cows, at Stewart's Little Wine Cup Ranch, down by the river on Refugio Road.

"He was really upset," recalled Renton. The thief had butchered the beeve on the spot.

He had to deal with the plane crash of a P-38 on the Chamberlin Ranch. The pilot had a chute and jumped out, only to be snagged by the twin tail, and plummet with the craft to the ground.

When Edie Sedgwick died from a barbiturate overdose, he and Sheriff Jim Webster had to deliver the news to her parents, at the ranch later donated to UCSB.

Over the years, Renton sponsored 13 of his relatives for American citizenship including his mother, brother William, William's wife and two kids, his brother Robert and his family, and his sister Agnes, and her husband.

In December of 1963, he married Doris Christiansen Doll, whose husband had died in a plane crash, and they raised Renton's daughter and adopted son and Doris' three girls together.

In the early 1960's, the personable Mr. Mitchell was active in the Solvang Business Association, a sought-after emcee of numerous events, raising money for many local causes. He was co-chair of Danish Days in 1967; chairman in 1968. King Merrill of *The Valley News* called it "unquestionably one of the best organized and most enjoyable festivals ever held in the community," attended by 55,000 happy tourists.

He was a deputy sheriff here for twelve years before launching a highly successful real estate career. Clients genuinely liked Renton, immediately and instinctively, and they swarmed to his warm personality like bees to melted caramel.

He worked with tennis great Rod Laver, and producer Jon Peters, among many others. He and Laver toured the Scottish Highlands together. Olivia Newton-John stopped in for a 45 minute chat. Bob Eubanks listed his ranch with

Renton. Richard Widmark and Dean Martin were clients. John "Bowser" Bauman of *Sha-Na-Na* bought a house.

Singer/actress Claudine Longet called him one day, in tears. She had to cancel their appointment. When Renton turned on the news, he learned that Longet, crooner Andy Williams' ex-girlfriend, had just shot her new boyfriend, skier Spider Sabich.

I married Renton and Doris's daughter, Debra. Listening to Renton's real estate stories got me interested in the business.

Renton initiated the sister city relationship with Aalborg that Solvang enjoys today. In October of 1972, he stopped in Denmark, to visit pioneering Danish baker Carl Birkholm.

Carl and Renton drove over to Aalborg, where they had lunch with mayor Marius Andersen. Aalborg is the fourth largest city in Denmark, with 155,000 citizens at the time.

The mayor discussed being a sister city to Solvang, and suggested that council members of Solvang take the first move.

Mr. Andersen sent Renton back to the States with a book about Aalborg, personally inscribed with this message: "Say hello to all our friends in Solvang—Kind regards, Marius Andersen, Mayor."

Upon returning home, Mr. Mitchell advised the council members on how to make it happen. The sistership took place, and numerous delegations traded visits.

On July 4, 1976, Solvang's Rebild Society appointed Renton to welcome former California Governor Edmund G. "Pat" Brown, plus former Prime Minister Poul Hartling of Denmark, to Solvang, as part of the July Fourth bicentennial celebration.

He operated Solvang Antique Imports in the mid-1970s, bringing antiques over from Scotland. He bought Santa Ynez Valley Printing and Lithography in 1985, and ran it for over twenty years, contributing printing services for countless charitable causes along the way. Troubled by back problems, he sold out in 2005, and retired, at age 79.

## Part 3. Over The Hump

Farewell camels, Clenets and cleavage. Peg Johnson, the over-the-top publisher of *The Santa Ynez Valley News*, called it quits in July of 2004, selling out to Pulitzer Inc.

Peg Johnson sent shock waves through this staid community from the moment she arrived in the Valley almost thirty years ago with her husband Ken, snapping up the weekly paper, and a rambling 10,000 square foot Moorish mansion known as Palacio Del Rio.

She relished her rebel reputation. "Yes, the rumors are true: I flew to Paris for lunch one day," she told the California Newspapers Publishers Association. "I have often gotten up in the morning and headed for the L.A. airport at a whim and been on my way to one of my favorite countries."

She loved living on the cutting edge of conspicuous consumption. "I am the original material girl," Ms. Johnson continued. "Madonna was in diapers when I got started. I have a collection of more than 100 Buddha statues; I collect Armani ceramic statues, the fantasy collection of ceramics by the world famous Cybis from Poland, prized collections of celestial items, a castle collection and many other interesting items. One of my favorite collections is camel saddles I rode and purchased in India, Algeria, Kenya, Morocco, Jordan and other Arabic countries."

It wasn't always that way. Husband Ken began his career sweeping the floors at a tiny newspaper. Fortune smiled, and he ended up with a string of profitable small town tabloids, acquiring the *SYV News* in 1975.

In addition to a local lifestyle that included frequent social splashes, the Johnsons maintained a Colorado presence. Valleyites invited to a lavish Christmas bash at the couple's home there found themselves in a 42 room, 20,000 square foot Tudor known as Redstone Castle, eerily reminiscent of the hotel in *The Shining*. Coal baron John Cleveland Osgood built it around 1901 for roughly $2.5 million; his visitors included John D. Rockefeller, J.P. Morgan and President Theodore Roosevelt.

Always the life of the party, "Peg was dancing on the table," said an astonished dinner guest at one soiree. Visitors to the paper were greeted by a large picture of the publisher in a daring blouse, leaning on her Clenet roadster.

A DeLorean gathered dust in the garage. She won a gold medal in the prestigious London to Brighton race in her 1904 Woolsey. Her Arabian stallion won a world championship.

Ms. Johnson dabbled in development, building several eclectic mansions in the foothills in the late 1970's, only to see them linger on the market for years. Was it interest rates? Or the black bathtubs and indoor waterfalls?

After the Johnsons divorced in 1980, Ms. Johnson took control of the SYV News, and forayed into commercial real estate. She built the log restaurant that now houses AJ Spurs, including a boudoir over the bar from which she could monitor the action.

A peripatetic traveler, she published rambling, melodramatic narratives about her odysseys. Her signature close: "And the beat goes on."

Her editors were ordered first and foremost to cover the Solvang and Buellton City Council meetings, a focus that produced a grounded, if sometimes mind-numbingly boring, sheet. At one point, to the horror of the staff, she ordered up a fawning series on the paper's largest advertisers.

She is a fan of the famous, and proud of it. "For five years I followed NASCAR racing and was personal friends with Dale Earnhardt, Richard Petty and Bobby Allison, among others," she told CNPA. "Paul McCartney was my houseguest for two weeks while he and Michael Jackson filmed the video *Say, Say, Say*." An anniversary issue honoring the long history of the SYV News featured Peg and recent Hollywood arrivals on the cover, not valley pioneers.

Things quieted down in 1988 when Ms. Johnson turned over the helm to her daughter La Cinda. Mom moved to Malibu, occasionally publishing her adventures with Richard Gere and the Dalai Lama, and travels with North Africa's "blue men" of the Tuareg tribe. She was on a camel trip in the Sahara Desert in Tunisia when La Cinda tragically died from an asthma attack in 1998. Her mother resumed the reins.

As the news of the sale broke, some relieved locals called it the end of an error. Uh, era. But something Hamlet said about another famous, forceful, fallen quixotic figure from Danish folklore—his father, Hamlet Sr.—comes to mind: "I shall not look upon his like again."

## 51. U.S.S. Yorktown Sailor Lauren Walter

About one hundred sailors who served on the USS Yorktown (CV-5), the mighty aircraft carrier which sunk after playing a crucial role at the Battle of Midway, held a national reunion in Solvang in September of 2003.

"There's not too many of those World War II heroes left," said 18-year Solvang resident Lauren Walter, 86, who orchestrated the event. "There's fewer every year."

Mr. Walter was on the Yorktown before it ever left dry dock in Newport News. He was part of the 1937 commissioning crew, and served two and a half years on the 19,800 ton ship, coming to California on it in 1939, where it was home ported in San Diego. He was a water tender second class, making the steam that powered "The Fighting Lady."

After an annual war games exercise near Hawaii in 1940, it was announced that the 800 foot long ship and its crew of 1,889 would be staying at Pearl Harbor. Mr. Walter was unimpressed by the Islands, preferring the mainland, where on July 27, 1940, he married Jeannette, his wife of 63 years, in North Hollywood.

The married man left the seagoing swabbie life behind, and went to work for Lockheed's experimental aircraft division, where another Valley figure, Starlane Ranch owner and legendary airplane designer Kelly Johnson, was gaining the knowledge that would lead to such groundbreaking planes as the U-2 and SR-71 Blackbird.

Fortuitously chasing German subs in the Atlantic during Pearl Harbor, the Yorktown steamed through the Panama Canal to reinforce the battered Pacific fleet, seeing combat in the Marshall Islands and the Battle of Coral Sea. At Midway, the great turning point of the war in the Pacific, Yorktown planes helped sink two aircraft carriers and a cruiser before dive bombers and torpedo planes took her out of the action.

A submarine torpedo attack delivered the final, fatal blows. Cruisers and destroyers nearby picked up Captain Elliott Buckmaster and the crew.

They murmured in disbelief, "The old York's going down!" as she slipped beneath the waves, shortly after a humid tropical daybreak, on June 7, 1942.

A safe berth directly contributing to the war effort wasn't enough for the gung-ho Mr. Walter, who jumped back into the fray in 1942. As an aviation metal smith, he was stationed in the South Pacific, patrolling on and repairing PBY Catalina flying boats. His first posting, in Perth, Australia, was "horrible," he candidly admits. Six months in New Guinea followed.

Eventually he landed back in the States, overhauling ships at the naval yard in North Island, San Diego. He joined the Naval Reserve after mustering out, retiring as a Master Chief Petty Officer with 38 years of combined service, and nine hash marks on the sleeve of his blue uniform.

In May 1998, UCSB alumni and *Titanic* discoverer Dr. Robert Ballard found the resting place of the Yorktown. The ship was in surprisingly good condition, after fifty-six years under three miles of salt water.

Mr. Walter and his shipmates toured Vandenberg AFB, and rambled, wine tasting through the magical oak covered back country canyons up to Los Alamos, with lunch at the historic Union Hotel.

There was a banquet and reception with General Earl E. Anderson, USMC, retired. General Anderson, who rose to be the number two man (Assistant Commandant) of the Marine Corps, was a lieutenant aboard the Yorktown when it went down. Gen. Anderson later served two tours in Vietnam and was Commanding General, Fleet Marine Corps Forces, Atlantic, from July 1971-March 1972.

A memorial breakfast was held. The roll call of sailors who have gone to the "Supreme Commander" was read, and a bell tolled after each name.

## Part 2. Naval Vet Runs Aground On DMV Reef

"It reminds me of the Gestapo," said Lauren Walter. The 86-year-old Solvang resident, who organized a nationwide reunion here for fellow USS Yorktown veterans, was turned in to the Department of Motor Vehicles, for an unknown reason, by an anonymous tipster.

"The DMV has a program where anybody can say anything about anybody," said Mr. Walter. "I got a notice in the mail about a month ago, after that Santa Monica incident. Somebody has reported me for doing something. I don't know what. It's confidential."

"Anybody can file one of those reports. The DMV has to follow-up. They said to be in Oxnard at such and such a time. If you fail to keep the appointment, your driver's license will be suspended."

He was able to get a change of venue to Goleta. Then he received a mailed notice changing the appointment to Lompoc. When the big day came, there he sat, endlessly waiting for a hearing officer who never showed up. It turned out the officer was in Goleta that day.

"I called the 800 number out of the phone book, and waded through punch this and punch that in eight different languages, and never did get to talk to anybody," said Mr. Walter. "I found a number on the form, called and said, 'Can't the officer tell me, what did I do?'"

The DMV case officer won't talk before the appointment. "He's got the file, and he's got to discuss it with me. He has do it personally, and he can't come out to see me, I have to go see him. I am totally disgusted with the whole stinking system."

"I don't want to go to Goleta," said Mr. Walter, whose appointment is now rescheduled there in October. "You just ruin your whole day when you do that. And I don't have a whole lot of days left."

I called the DMV's 800 number for some input. The first call ended when I was unceremoniously dumped into the ether while on hold. Second try: I hummed along to "Fire and Rain" for a while, then suffered through a less classic cacophony. I was dozing off when the gentlemen who answered referred me to another number.

A canny lady there answered "Driver Safety," but refused to give her name, saying "We're not going to talk to the media at all. That's it. You have to call Information Services." The glamorous truth about reporting: it's a lot of calling people who hang up on you. She lightened up enough to say "It's not going to be that easy (to turn someone in), unless you're a family member."

The Information Services number led to another long wait on hold, not bad while a snappy *Rhythm of the Night* played, but a little tedious later on, when it segued into endless white noise. At that point I gladly gave up on humans, for I had located the pertinent form at the DMV website by keying "unsafe driver" into the site search slot.

It is actually very easy to rat out, or perhaps just have a little fun with, relatives, friends, and perfect strangers. The simple form is called "Request for Driver Reexamination" and promises secrecy to the tipster, maybe, saying "Confidentiality will be honored to the extent possible under the law; however, DMV can be compelled to reveal your name if ordered to do so by a court."

Eleven boxes under "Driver Condition" and nineteen under "Driver Behavior" offer copious way to deep-six a suspect, including "Confused/Disoriented," "Drives in wrong lane," "Drives on sidewalk," "Drives too slow, or stops, for no reason" and "Falls asleep while driving." The DMV suggests mailing or delivering the completed form to any local office, or to one of 12 convenient locations listed.

The State's take: "We understand that reporting someone, especially a patient, relative, or close friend, is a sensitive issue and DMV does not want to harm your relationship with that person. However, we also want to make sure that potentially unsafe drivers are evaluated...DMV knows the importance of a person's independence. DMV keeps this in mind while at the same time weighing the safety of all drivers."

Mr. Walter says, "I'm really going to contest it. I don't know how."

## 52. Stem Cell Research Hits Home

Ron Reagan Jr.'s speech at the 2003 Democratic Convention gave stem cell research a high profile. When you're in a wheelchair, that debate is not academic.

"The controversy around stem cell research is largely because doctors are asking for public funds. If you're privately funded, you can do whatever you want. The reality is that there's a lot of misinformed people when it comes to stem cell research," said Will Ambler.

He should know. Mr. Ambler was paralyzed from the waist down in a motorcycle accident in 1992, when he was 24 years old. A friend had a new bike, and insisted that he take it for a spin.

"The idea that embryonic stem cell research is a panacea that will cure all is blatantly false," said Mr. Ambler. "It is extremely important for laboratory research, but as a clinical application, it will not be used. Embryonic stem cell research will allow doctors to uncover how things occur, but it's strictly for the laboratory.

"People don't understand that your body is filled with stem cells. Stem cell by itself is not a bad word. People automatically associate it with embryonic," he cautions.

"The important distinction is this: embryonic stem cells are good, they will allow medical research to progress, but as far as human application, the adult stem cells are the most important. That's what going to be used in the regular clinical setting," said Mr. Ambler.

"What's important to realize is, scientifically speaking, scientists are a lot further along in being able to repair damage to the brain and spinal cord There are incredible things going on. They've been going on far too slowly, and we're just trying to accelerate the process," he said.

Will Ambler doesn't remember his accident, but describes the aftermath this way: "I broke my back in seven places, and suffered spinal cord injury at the T-12 level. I spent three weeks in intensive care unit, then eight and a half months in rehab. After I escaped from rehab, I began to look into spinal cord injury (SCI) research."

He began a foundation, SCI Research Advancement (SCIRA).

"We are a group of paras and quads that are funding our own research team to bring spinal cord regeneration to humans ASAP,' says the foundation's website.

"Our group, led by Will Ambler, is funding Dr. Levesque from Cedars-Sinai and Dr. Peduzzi from the University of Alabama, Birmingham, to do sufficient rat experiments to satisfy the FDA's requirement for Safety and Efficacy. If all goes well, we are hoping to begin human clinical trials in 2005."

Drs. Peduzzi and Levesque testified recently at Senate hearings on stem cell research.

"I grew up in Walnut Creek," said Will. "My folks moved down here in 1986. My family started the girl's soccer program at the high school. I was assistant varsity coach, going to Fresno State, and planning to be a teacher."

After the accident, he became an eloquent spokesman for the new cause. "I've always had an interest in science and teaching. I guess that made it easy for me to pick up on scientific information," said Will.

It runs in the family. His uncle is an accomplished astrophysicist.

"Of the approximately $10-$12 billion spent annually on SCI care, less than $100 million is spent on cure research," says the Spinal Cord Injury Research Advancement foundation.

"The vast majority supports research that has no mandate, incentive or guidelines to actually help paraplegics and quadriplegics regain substantial function. That's where we are different," states Ambler's SCIRA.

"Our plan is to complete the final animal tests required before human treatment can begin. As soon as we have results in the animal tests, human trials can begin in as early as 16 months," they hope. You can learn more at www.linksforcure.com.

## 53. Americans Are Trailer Trash

"Sophistication is not generally an American thing," claimed travel writer Stanley Stewart in London's *Sunday Times*. "The unreliable filter of television persuades us that they are either trailer trash sleeping with their whippet on Jerry Springer, or flag-waving crazies at election rallies."

Ouch. But Mr. Stewart makes an exception for Santa Barbara.

"The hilarious bits of America—Disney World, Las Vegas, most of west Texas, any baseball game—are hilarious because they mirror these false expectations, but the best bits make us realise what dupes we have been to fall for the stereotypes in the first place."

"Santa Barbara is one of the best bits: a city so sophisticated it hurts," he allows. "The fact that it's so close to Los Angeles, home to all that is crass and wacky about American life, only adds to its poignancy."

"On the southern Californian coast, it is suspended in permanent summer, like some rare orchid in preserving fluid. Its Spanish colonial architecture consists of arched facades, muted plaster exteriors and trellised courtyards. Its citizens—modest, unassuming, well spoken—confound every American cliché."

"Above the red-tiled roofs lie the San Rafael Mountains, bordering a world of old-fashioned ranches the size of Devon. In the other direction lies the Pacific, barely five minutes from downtown, with a golden beach that goes on for ever."

"I am sure that somewhere in Santa Barbara there is a mall where fat people with pick-up trucks buy Fritos by the hundredweight, but strolling along State Street, you could be forgiven for thinking you had stepped into the American Dream as portrayed by Martha Stewart," writes Stewart.

"This city has great restaurants the way Kansas has corn...This is where celebrities come when they are tired of being celebrities."

Mr. Stewart and Cloud Climbers tour guide Lee Tomkow, a transplanted Englishman from Lancashire, jeep over Refugio Pass to taste the valley's vintages.

"We climbed through tough canyon country, the road bucking and twisting between coastal oaks and mountain laurel," rhapsodized Stewart.

"Behind us, the Pacific offered a blue background to old citrus plantations. Then the paved road ran out and we left the ocean behind, dropping through tangled woods scented with sage and spread with yellow poppies on a track meant for mules. At the bottom we emerged in the valley of Santa Ynez, a wide world of vineyards and ranches, baked yellow under a big blue sky."

His wine tasting tour is a bit too successful.

"By the time we got to the Foley Estate, I was completely plastered...Among sophisticated vintners, being plastered is not the thing...I had a sudden impulse to tell the woman pouring the wine that I loved her...The whole thing seemed upside down, back to front. I was the drunken boor clutching my glass; the Americans were the erudite sophisticates discussing the nuances of wine-making."

We accept your apology.

To assuage his distress, Stewart seeks out the simple life—at a $400 a night resort.

"The next day, I slipped away to Alisal Ranch, down a beautiful road lined with sycamore trees. Wooden fences snaked along the road. Old wagons stood knee-deep in feathery grass. Groups of ruminant steers had settled down in the shade of old oaks."

"The Alisal is both a working ranch and a guest ranch, with stylishly decorated cabins. Dinner was the usual sophisticated Santa Barbarian fare, but otherwise I felt happy to be in cowboy country. I ordered a beer with my dinner."

"The next morning, I went for a ride with one of the wranglers. We had 10,000 acres to roam around in. It was rangy, long-limbed country. Red-tailed hawks and turkey vultures circled above us in a blue sky. I spotted coyotes slinking away across wild yellow pastures. As we rode we chatted about cows and horses and a lot of other cowboy stuff. We got to talking about water, a big issue for ranchers in southern California."

"'In these parts,' the wrangler drawled, 'Bourbon is for drinking. Water is for fighting over.' Wine didn't get a mention," concludes Stewart.

The wrangler was cowboy icon Jake Copass.

# 54. Sculptor John Cody

John Cody just completed a jumping serpentine dolphin for the Santa Maria Natural History Museum. It looks alive, like it just left the water; sparking, iridescent. You would swear it's soaking wet.

The masterful Mr. Cody has been sculpting for almost forty years, starting before he came to the valley in 1967, at age 18.

He's a big mountain man, accustomed to muscling dense stones about as he finds and releases the spirits within. On this day, he's covered with pale, lime-green rock dust, from his wild, long hair to the toes of his work boots.

"That weighs 1,500 pounds, probably," he guesstimates, putting his shoulder to the serpentine like Atlas, rolling the dolphin over for a photo. "The base kind of runs into the piece, to give it the feeling like it's coming out of the water." Pegged together with hidden iron bars, the finished work will stand about four feet tall.

The remarkable, complex serpentine stones he uses, veined and speckled like living tissue, range in deep, shifting hues from greens to blues to black to brown to red. They come from Figueroa Mountain, a few miles up the road from his current home.

The Cody family lived on a remote parcel in the backcountry for years, in a home he built by hand from timbers and boulders, until one too many rattlesnakes threatened Back then, he carved by hand. After fifteen years as a purist, he decided some power tools wouldn't hurt.

There's a mottled, lichen-like pattern, in shades of beige and brown, that surrounds, entwines, and disappears into the exotic depths of the frog-green stone.

"That alteration halo in there, that's where the stone was interrupted during its metamorphic period, when it uplifted onto the mountain," said Cody.

"That gives it that great round line through the whole thing; it follows around the entire stone. That's why the other side has that triangle on it; that's why I decided to polish the whole base, too. It comes up the nose, the face."

Each new stone is a mysterious stranger. "The inside is like granite," explained Cody. "It's harder than hell." The polished stone has depth, like a pond. Gold flecks below the surface of the stone light up as they catch the rays of the sun. "That's kind of like manganese," he noted.

"That's what I love about serpentine. It's always a surprise. Marble—my Italian marble—is going be the same, always," he said. Cody trekked to Pietra Santos, in northern Italy, in 1990, bringing home twenty-five tons of stone.

"But this, you don't know what you're going to get when you're done. You're like 'Waaa!,' all blown away."

It took countless eons for his chosen boulders to work their way to the top of the San Rafael Range. "Serpentine comes through the Pacific, from the trench out there, and it works its way to this continental shelf. Then it turns, and the Pacific shelf goes under. Tectonics; you know. Serpentine is a granitic rock that comes from the melting of the Pacific Plate, like Half Dome. It came up, pressurized with heat and water and the serpentine minerals, and metamorphosized," he explained.

He started sculpting at about 14. "When I got here in 1967, I was 18, out of high school. I was at Copenhagen Gallery for the first eight years," recalled Cody.

It was on the upstairs loft of the Copenhagen gallery, way back in the Vietnam era, that I was blown away by a Cody serpentine that was half soldier's helmet, half crouching baby. I doubt that anyone who saw it could ever forget it.

Almost from the start of his career, Cody was a phenomenon. Critics compared him to Rodin. Still in his teens, he got a full page in the *LA Times*.

His works are in collections all over the world. He carved a twenty-ton serpentine Triceratops at Knott's Berry Farm. His first big serpentine carving can be seen in the Santa Ynez Historical Society Museum collection.

"In 1976, we came to Los Olivos. There was no other business here. Solvang had no place to park, so I said 'The hell with it, I'll move to Los Olivos," laughed Cody.

His sons Flynt and Quinn, Miguel Ortiz, and Englishman Rupert Gray give him a hand, and carve works of their own. His wife, Felicia, runs the gallery in town.

"I just want to do big pieces from now on," said Cody, gazing at the massive, raw marble columns, huge serpentine boulders, and other stones all around him in his back yard, near Mattei's Tavern. "I'm so tired of doing the small ones; the same old coffee-table size. People would rather spend thirty-forty-fifty thousand on an outdoor piece.

"The clients have changed now. All my great old clients that were used to galleries and museums, all the older folks who know anything about art, they're all 80 or 90 years old. They don't buy anymore," he mused. "People my age would rather come over here and buy something from me, than go to a gallery. They like the hands-on aspect, seeing it done."

The leaping cetacean will be the centerpiece of a learning center, where kids can stroke its glistening skin.

"I'm glad they're incorporating fine art into the whole learning thing," chuckled John Cody. Then he rolled the glistening green sea creature over, and returned to polishing.

## 55. The Nature of Woman

Part of the richness of the valley is the vast array of talent here, in all walks of life. More proof of that is alternative healthcare practitioner Deborah Lee Davis' 2005 book, *The Nature of Woman,* featuring a host of outstanding local ladies.

"I believe that when one is able to appreciate themselves within the primal elements of nature, they are able to discover the beauty of life in its pure essence," writes Ms. Davis. "These women I have chosen for this photographic journal are all open to change, accepting challenges as they come, as well as being open to life and listening to their own personal inner guidance."

"These women never greet a new day the same way...I personally hope they will touch your life, as they have mine," says Ms. Davis.

"I love people, and I love faces," photographer Davis told me. It's a labor of love that was first inspired on the street corner in Los Olivos in 1975. She's worked on it for the last eight years.

Forty-two women contributed personal philosophies, and are portrayed in rich, evocative, black-and-white portraits.

Ailie and Sarah Chamberlin, Dorothy Jardin, Sandy Collier, Joan Spiers, Princess Esra Jah, Susan Gottesman, Lu Dahlan, Ruth Allen Raymond, Lindy Kern, Adelina Alva-Padilla, Dorothy Mari, Barbra Minar, Dorothy Alder, Casey DeFranco, Laura Wilkening, Judy Adams, Carol Lacy, Thekla Sanford, Shenkar Jah, Pat Bell, Margy Houtz, Rose Mari, Rona Barrett, Rachel Cervantes, Bobbie McMorrow, Marcia Rubinstein, Regina Jensen, Ann Grigorian Gravitt, Barbara Nance, Hattie Feazelle, Susan MacDonald, Bev Walter, Cynthia Devine, Seyburn Zorthian, Catherine Clark, Sophie Hershkowitz, Karen Langley, Stephanie Haymes, Joanna Wogulis, Nancy Lippman, and Edona Romney share their thoughts, and grace the pages.

"Life is an adventure, and each woman in this book is a heroine of her own life story," writes Deborah Lee Davis.

These are our neighbors: ranchers, farmers, ballerinas, journalists, teachers, actors, producers, entrepreneurs. A race car driver, artists, poets, mothers, writers, riders, students, sculptors, vintners, cowgirls, travelers and psychotherapists.

Here are a few snippets from the lives within.

"I belong in this simple holy place." (Barbra Minar, author, poet)

"I ride my horse every day and I look down at the earth and know that God's hand is on my heart." (Karen Langley)

"Anything I need to learn about life, I can learn from a cow." (Dorothy Alder, rancher)

"Remember, life is about forgiveness...I knocked myself out for years trying to please others. Especially my mother. I think I was around fifty when I gave that up and it was the most freeing gift I have ever given myself." (Carol Lacy, editor, writer)

"Last year when I rode in the Fiesta Parade, a gentleman asked me if I have lived here all my life. I responded, 'Not yet.' I am going to ride till the end!" (Hattie Feazelle, 90)

"I am a great fence builder and I can build six acres of fence easy." (Bev Walter, rancher, cowboy, commercial actor)

"When I became seriously ill, I felt a rush of love from everywhere. It was sort of like the way the light comes in the morning through the trees...I want to be able to see with no judgment." (Susan MacDonald, student of Satchidananda, teacher, yoga instructor)

"I dance my canvas the same way I dance my soul." (Seyburn Zorthian, artist)

"Life is the most beautiful gift we have. Remember, we are here to find out who we are." (Ailie Chamberlin)

"I always look for unusual rocks and always keep a wheelbarrow near by, just in case I have to haul something home." (Ann Grigorian Gravitt, 93)

"When in doubt, err in favor of spontaneity." (Regina Jensen, psychotherapist, world traveler)

"Find something you love and do it." (Marcia Rubinstein)

"I will never forget the first time I worked in the fields, they sprayed with pesticides. They didn't even warn us. All I remember is that I dove under the first truck I could get to." (Rachel Cervantes)

"I want to grow things of the earth." (Rona Barrett, journalist, organic lavender farmer)

"Walking to get my newspaper every morning is a joyous experience." (Margy Houtz, artist)

"Nature is my teacher." (Pat Bell)

"My mission here on earth is to make people feel comfortable and believe in themselves." (Adelina Alva-Padilla, Chumash Native Healer)

"I wouldn't know what to do if I couldn't work the land." (Rose Mari, rancher, breeder of Arabians)

"My soul is African. I am in the process of creating a Nelson Mandela doll…We need to suffer to grow." (Catherine Clark, artist)

"I dance to music everyday. It heals all your pains." (Sophie Hershowitz, 93, artist, musician, painter, dancer)

"The best part about life for me right now, is having my horses as my closest friends." (Sandy Collier, cutting horse and cow horse trainer, first woman NRCHA snaffle bit futurity champion 1993)

"My family is everything to me. My love for the ranch and the animals makes my life worth living." (Judy Adams, rancher, cowgirl)

"I believe it's about humility, gratitude and faith." (Bobbie McMorrow, writer, teacher, entrepreneur)

"…free my spirit, and let it wander, lift my senses, and watch me fly."

(Joanna Wogulis, writer, poet, marriage/family therapist)

"Have faith in things unseen. Look beyond the visible. Listen to the silence," concludes author Deborah Lee Davis.

# 56. Rancho Days: The Vanishing Vaquero Legacy

What is a vaquero, anyway? "Vaca" is Spanish for "cow." Vaqueros are cowboys.

"When the Spaniards came to California, they brought with them a tradition of cattle ranching and some of the finest horsemanship in the world," says Susan Jensen, who with Paul Singer filmed *Vaquero* here in the Valley. "These early cowboys were called vaqueros."

"The vaqueros ran cows over Santa Ynez's beautiful, but formidable, landscape, steep soaring hills and deep ravines. And needless to say, working cattle in this country is not for the faint of heart. It took brave horses and brave men to ride them," said Ms. Jensen.

Visit the SYV Historical Museum or Jedlicka's Saddlery to get a copy of *Vaquero*, a half hour look at the California cowboy culture that takes the viewer to the great land grant ranches where it all started.

Featured are Bill and Chuck King, Jerry Williams Jr., Rick Layman, Leigh Bollinger, Russ, Janet, and Brandon Westfall, Willy Chamberlin, Jake Copass, Wil Bernhardt and Justin Bogle.

Superb craftsmen emerged who elevated the tools of the cattle trade into artwork. Bits, spurs, saddles, rawhide and chaps were tooled with the skill, precision, and love of the jeweler and sculptor.

Outstanding examples can be seen and bought at the annual benefit Vaquero Show of cowboy and western antiques, hosted by the Santa Ynez Valley Historical Society Museum and Parks-Janeway Carriage House. The show commemorates the history and traditions of early California and the American West.

Noted artisans and collectors displaying their works in 2003 included Chuck Irwin, Ed Field, Chuck Willcox, Bill Reynolds, Ernie Morris, Phil Tognazzini, Texas antique dealer Larry Peck and Montana saddle maker Chad Wells. There were rare books and fine art, and a raffle for silver spurs by Gary Field, silver bit and conchos by Ed Field, and a Howard Jensen headstall.

Famed trainer Sheila Varian gave a hackamore and spade bit presentation. Those who have watched this legendary horsewoman in action are awed by her talents. Ms. Varian was inducted into the National Cowgirl Museum and Hall of Fame at the Will Rogers Complex in Fort Worth, Texas on November 14, 2003, for distinguished accomplishments "exemplifying the pioneer spirit of the American West."

## Part 2. Ailie Chamberlin's 99th Birthday

Surrounded by families and friends, Helen Adele Elizabeth van Loben Sels Chamberlin celebrated her 99th birthday in April of 2005 with a stream-side barbeque under towering oaks, amidst the rolling hills and lush grasslands of the family's sprawling, 8,000 acre Rancho Los Potreros.

The illustrious matriarch of the Chamberlin dynasty, known as Ailie to her many friends, played a leading role in local life, from the day she arrived to teach at the high school in 1933.

The San Francisco earthquake started her mother's labor, and Ailie was born April 19, 1906 in Oakland, California. She was known by her initials, H.A.E., to differentiate her from her mother. A younger sibling, unable to pronounce H.A.E., called her Ailie. It stuck.

The oldest of seven children, only her youngest brother, William van Loben Sels, is still alive. He and his wife, Vanessa, drove up from La Jolla for the event.

Ailie van Loben Sels was raised on a ranch in Courtland, near Sacramento. Her grandfather, Peter Justus van Loben Sels, the Dutch consul in San Francisco, was the first person to successfully build levees that could withstand the annual flooding of the Sacramento River. Great-grandfather James de Fremery was a San Francisco banker.

Before World War I, the family raised Percheron horses, herding them 100 miles into the Sierras every summer. The family's long involvement with the high country in the Ebbots' Pass area prompted Ailie's mother to write a book, *Blue Jays in the Sierras*, about their adventures.

One of Ailie van Loben Sels' more remarkable adventures was a horseback ride up the Big Sur coastline in the early 1930's. Her brothers all attended Thatcher School in Ojai, and her brother Peter sustained a rather serious rattlesnake bite while there. He was deemed too ill to finish the school year.

She was given fifty dollars by her father to take the train to Ojai, buy a horse, and ride home to Sacramento with Peter. They rode over the Sespe into the Cuyama Valley, and on up to San Luis Obispo, then to the Big Sur coastline, where convict labor had just begun to carve out the oceanfront highway.

They camped, or stayed with local ranchers. At the Hearst Ranch, in the rain, they asked permission to camp, and light a fire near the creek. The drenched duo were offered a little cottage with hot water and a bath tub.

They were awakened by a plague of fleas in their sleeping bags. They'd been lodged in the temporarily vacant doghouse.

The future Mrs. Chamberlin attended Castilleja, a private high school for girls in Palo Alto. She graduated from Stanford University in 1929, with a degree in botany. She received her Masters in Entomology from Cornell. Coincidentally, her parents had met there, while judging the merits of a bull.

She worked as a governess for a plantation family on Maui, then came to the Santa Ynez Valley in 1933, to teach biology and girls' P.E. at the old high school in Santa Ynez. She taught in a tent her second year, while the new school was under construction, and met her husband, Ted Chamberlin, a local cattle rancher. They were married March 7, 1935.

Ted and Ailie Chamberlin's surviving children are Fred, Willy, Debi, and Sarah. The couple had seven children; two died in infancy. Their oldest daughter, Helen Heyden, passed away in 2003, at age 64.

Grandchildren are Adel Browning, Ann Chamberlin, Cinna Chamberlin Schilling, Mary Heyden, Eden O'Brien Brenner, Russell Chamberlin and Aaron O'Brien. Beth Chamberlin passed away in May 2004.

Great grandchildren are Amanda Browning, Jamie and Dante Brenner, Raleigh and Callen O'Brien, and Olivia and Lauren Chamberlin.

Mrs. Chamberlin has lived on Rancho Los Potreros since 1935. Active in running the ranch, she especially loved riding horseback. She rode with the Sage Hens until her mid-eighties.

She was active with the Republican Women's group, and attended the Presbyterian Church in Ballard. She taught Sunday school there, and was also an elder of the church. She was an early member of the Cowbelles, known today as the Cattlewomen's Association.

Now in a wheelchair, she visited with a crowd of friends. The guest list was a roster of ranching royalty, including Vi Hansen, Wolcott, Teona, and Jessica Schley, Marion Etling, Chuck King, Jake Copass, Joe and AnaLina Alegria, Harlan and Betty Burchardi, Anna Mahler, Paul McEnroe, Mike and Neta Fitzgerald, John and Felicia Cody, Hattie Feazelle, Pat Murphy, Steve Lyons, Joe and Maggie Foss, Penelope Hartnell, Tessie Valeriano, Bill and Barbara Luton, Howard and Ruth Sahm, Claire Bettencourt, Brandy Branquinho, Jeff and Carol Bridgeman, Barbara and Gordon Brown, Joy Chamberlain, Chris and Georgia Colombo, Rosalie Cornelius, Jean and Janine Dewett, Gates and MaryAnn Foss, Cammie and Sherman Herrick, Kathleen Hourihan, Arla and Kurt Jacobsen Hoj, Rod and Jody Jacobsen, Ana Jalas, B.G. and Joann Kresse, Bill and Betty

Phelps, Sandy and Rod Sousa, Gail and Russell Tomasini, Sarah and Ken Twigg, Linda King, and Barbara Wilson.

Family present included John and Betsy Tryon, Adel and Amanda Browning, Johanna and Fred Chamberlin, Sarah Chamberlin and Ben Bottoms, Willy Chamberlin, Maria Alway, Lisa Francesca, Gail and Harry Gelles, Mary Heyden and David Anderson, Max, Dorothy, Anthony, Peter, and Jennifer Maluta, and Aaron and Kelley O'Brien.

Ted Chamberlin died in 1978, at age 75. He was the grandson of Lewellyn Bixby, who came California around 1851, and transformed a flock of sheep into a real estate empire.

## Part 3. Rancho San Julian

It was among the first ranchos, granted in the early 1800's to Captain Jose Antonio De La Guerra y Noriega, fifth Commandante of the Santa Barbara Presidio, in lieu of back pay. It consisted of 48,200 acres along present day Highway One, between Gaviota and Lompoc. 15,000 acres are still in the family.

*Rancho San Julian—Then and Now*, a fine show of historical archived photographs and contemporary photos by W. Dibblee Hoyt and paintings by Vicki Andersen, was displayed at the SYV Historical Society's Parks-Janeway Carriage House in 2003.

W. Dibblee Hoyt is a sixth generation De La Guerra descendent, a photojournalist who has lived on Rancho San Julian for the past 13 years. He teaches digital photography for Allan Hancock College.

Andersen is the current chair of the Lompoc Mural Society and past President of the Lompoc Valley Art Association. She painted the giant 12' x 48' Mission Vieja de la Purisima mural on the grounds of the Lompoc museum, depicting Lompoc's "Lost Mission," destroyed in the 1812 earthquake.

"I like to work big," said Ms. Anderson, who has been painting for 30 years. She majored in art at Cal State Long Beach, and works mainly in acrylic and oils, often with palette knife as her major tool. "I like color. I start out with a crazy orange under-painting. Somehow the colors that go over it are that much more vibrant."

There is a classic beauty of form and function in the simple lines of the ranch outbuildings, vividly portrayed in Andersen's oils. You could almost reach out and touch the hay rake and the little cottages in *Creekside House*.

50 photos and 18 paintings graced the Parks-Janeway Carriage House, set amidst a jaw-dropping collection of coaches, carriages and equestrian equipment.

"Bev Walter, Jake Copass, Ed Fields, Dutch Wilson; there's all kinds of people over here that are connected with the ranch and its history, so it was real nice to pull all of them into the show," said Mr. Hoyt. His mother, Virginia Dibblee Hoyt, appeared in some vintage shots. "Peter Stackpole took a lot of photographs of the ranch in 1941 for *Life* magazine. Then the war started, and they killed the article," said Mr. Hoyt. "He gave my mother the prints, and I've been able to digitize them. They're beautiful, and they've got her branding, riding, being the total cowgirl, which she was."

There was a lot to love. The honest faces. Horses, history, ranch architecture, women in chaps. Close-ups of hands, ropes and rowels, the shadow of the hat on the cowboy's face, girls hanging onto a roped calf for dear life. The concentration and intensity of the riders, and the simple utility of what they're wearing. The whole family at dinner, ten laughing members, three generations. *The Liberty Horse*, a black stallion high on his hind legs, pawing defiantly at the full moon. A picnic under the oaks is a timeless moment of sun speckled, gauzy beauty, with the herd just feet away, a rider coming up on the left, piles of food and equipment at hand.

Famed geologist Thomas W. Dibblee Jr., who still lives on the ranch, appeared at age four in a 1915 snapshot, riding in a Peerless auto.

Innocence and experience jumped out of the frames, as young vaqueros absorb every move. Did they know this way of life was slipping away forever? The physical, visceral action of chasing heifers fills the frame, and you are there in the corral. With Hoyt's mastery of the medium, when that calf gets the iron, you get it too.

"Neighboring ranches had to assist each other on brandings, because that way they could keep poachers away," said Mr. Hoyt. "Everybody came over and helped at your branding, then you went over and helped at the next ranch." He hopes the development that has overtaken the world around his San Julian paradise can be fought off forever. "We don't want to see it sold, we don't want to see it developed and turned into anything, strip malls or whatever," said Mr. Hoyt.

## Part 4. Cattle Upon A Thousand Hills

The epic ranch photo collection *Cattle Upon A Thousand Hills—Ranch Life in Santa Barbara County in the Twentieth Century As Recorded in Family Albums*, was the publishing event of 2004 for ranchers.

"For every beast of the forest is mine, and the cattle upon a thousand hills," reads Psalm 50. Editors Robert Isaacson and Tom Moore dedicate the book to local ranchers Helen Chamberlin Heyden, Bill Sudden, Joe Cabral, Dick Deegen and Lawrence Dutra.

Robert Isaacson's rich, evocative, bittersweet introduction, chronicling the end of an era, is worth the price of the book all by itself.

An excerpt:

"In the mid 60's my family and I went to the last Hollister Estate Company branding held on the Las Cruces Ranch near Gaviota. The Hollister family members had recently voted to sell their four ranches comprising some 32,000 acres...it seemed like everyone that I knew or had heard about in Santa Barbara ranching circles was there watching or taking part in the final branding: Bill and Nancy Luton, Frank Pacheco, Pida and Helen Pedotti, Alice and Duke Sedgwick, Vincente, Ortega, Dibblee Poett, Bill and Margaret Cooper, Clinton and Cynthia Hollister, and Charlie Sudden are just a handful that I can recall now...

"Near the end, the cows were mooing loudly for their calves and busily mothering up. Everyone was eating steak, salad, and frijoles, and the sun was lowering toward the whitecaps of the Santa Barbara Channel. The old ranchers and cowboys in Levi jackets were talking about the good old days, and things were going along as they had for nearly a hundred and fifty years in the Las Cruces Canyon, when something happened that I will never forget.

"A huge, surreal snow-white column silently rose directly up from the western horizon and soared high into the atmosphere, disappearing into a tiny point hundreds of miles above the earth. It was an Atlas missile from Vandenberg Air Force Base, blasting through the thin air into the southern orbit. In those days, seeing a missile launch was likely to remind many cattle people of the bitter ongoing legal battle between the Air force and the Sudden family. The military was then in the process of seizing, through condemnation proceedings, the Suddens' 17,000 acre Rancho La Espada, which had been in their family since the 1860's. Located between Jalama Beach and Point Arguello, the huge ranch fronted the Pacific Ocean for nearly 15 miles and ran over 1,400 head of Hereford cows. It was one of the most respected cattle operations in the county.

"The two hundred or so people at the barbeque fell silent, staring upward at the huge, white column that was collapsing and spiraling into a strange, undecipherable design in the high altitude winds. Suddenly, someone stood up on a bench and booed loudly at the missile. We all burst out laughing. She then turned and raised her glass to all of us. We knew the meaning of that gesture.

"We knew things would never be the same."

# 57. The Vandenberg Air Force Base Odyssey

Gravity Probe B arced high over Los Olivos, a fluffy white tail trailing the searing flame scarring the sky. It's always a sight to see the big missiles fly out of Vandenberg Air Force Base (VAFB), and feel the thumping, disconnected thunder of launch rolling along behind.

I was in Ensenada once when a Vandenberg rocket went up, and saw almost the same lofty arc. Ground distances don't mean much relative to the planetary picture.

Physicists will tell you VAFB is perfect for putting satellites into polar orbit, whether for spy eyes, weather, defense, cell phones, Star Wars, or Einsteinian inquiries. Since the first Air Force Thor went up on December 16, 1958, around 1,900 birds have flown: Minuteman, Atlas, Peacekeeper, Agena, Nike, Titan, Taurus, Scout, Pegasus, Delta. That's almost a rocket a week on average.

I came to California in 1966 with my father. An AT&T engineer, he shot missiles at Kwajalein Atoll for the next twenty years. I don't know why. Far as I could tell, the Kwajaleinos had never done anything to him.

Dad wouldn't explain. He said such info was only available on a "need to know" basis.

After graduating from the University of California at Santa Barbara in 1975, I briefly joined him at Vandenberg. I worked in a immense, drafty hangar filled with gigantic missiles under construction. Owls nested in the rafters, swooping about silently high above.

I once ate my bag lunch in the rear driver's cockpit of a missile carrier, a little glassed-in box, just inches off the ground, tucked behind the wheels of a rig so long you needed a driver for the hind end. It was sort of like a massive fire truck, only with a rocket on top.

One engineer had a charred chunk of crud about the size of a baseball on his desk, part of a guidance package that had survived a fiery re-entry as a disintegrating satellite slipped from space, finishing up in a farmer's field in Montana. They tracked its origin by serial numbers on the transistors. "One of ours!" he grinned proudly.

I had a modest security clearance. I suppose this breaches it. Sorry.

Spywise, every Ivan on the Amtrak that runs for miles through this top secret space station could pop Polaroids of poised projectiles while sipping wine in a velour armchair in the Coast Starlight observation car.

Some launch complexes—in the early days, a fancy name for a concrete slab—are only a few hundred yards from the tracks. Trains have to wait when the rocketmen play with fire.

Cold, windy, foggy Vandenberg has seen boom and bust ever since it was created in the rush towards World War II. The Army originally bought 86,000 acres in March 1941, and dubbed it Camp Cooke.

Five armored divisions clanked about in the sandy soil. In June of 1946 it was largely shut down, only to fire up again in August, 1950, for the Korean War.

In February of 1953 the Army mothballed it. In November of 1956, the Air Force took over.

In 1957, Sputnik and Muttnik (on their second flight, the Soviets sacrificed a puppy named Laika) scared up a robust American missile program. The base was renamed in honor of Gen. Hoyt S. Vandenberg, the Air Force's second Chief of Staff, on October 4, 1958.

In October of 1959, Vandenberg became the site of the first nuclear warhead tipped Inter-Continental Ballistic Missile (ICBM) to be placed on alert in the United States.

Surrounding communities waxed and waned like the moon. World War II P-51 Mustang pilot Jack Adams, later an engineer with GTE in Santa Maria, once told me of entire streets of Orcutt homes left vacant as the base busted.

"I could have bought them each for $75 down," he sighed.

In 1985, I was back on the base to design communications for President Reagan and the press, to be used at the first West Coast launch of the space shuttle. For miles, the hills lining the coastal road through the base were bulldozed so the shuttle wings would clear the ground as it was towed down the tarmac to towering Space Launch Complex 6 (SLC 6) near Point Arguello.

"Slick Six," insiders called it. It's eerily located a stone's throw from the Chumash's revered Solstice Cave, an ancient Native American site some say is a stone age solar observatory.

A poster child for recycling, SLC 6 was originally begun in 1966 for the Manned Orbiting Laboratory (MOL) project. 15,000 acres of the Sudden ranch was annexed to VAFB for the new site by an eminent domain purchase costing $9,842,700.

Like its namesake, the MOL went permanently underground in 1969, after interminable cost overruns and design squabbles, taking ten thousand aerospace jobs nationwide with it.

Old Coast Guard cottages perched on the bluffs, overlooking the wild breakers tearing at the rocky coastline, were renovated to house the shuttle astronauts and their spouses the night before launch.

The President, and the press corps, would watch from the scrubby dunes nearby.

It was all for naught.

After Challenger's heart-wrenching, tragic loss 73 seconds after takeoff on January 28, 1986, shuttle launches here were scrubbed.

The four billion dollars spent on SLC 6 were written off, and it stood derelict again. Laid-off engineers drifted back to the Cape, or Houston.

With no shuttle to put satellites into orbit, the "throwaway" rocket program got an unexpected boost. In 1995, Lockheed dusted off SLC 6 once more, this time for commercial launches.

Launches coming up when I wrote this included three Minuteman III, two Delta II, a Peacekeeper, a Falcon I and a Pegasus. They'll test ICBMs, orbit a Naval Research Lab bird, hoist an environmental satellite, and place NASA's AURA ozone tester in space.

Mission permitting, VAFB tours are available the second and fourth Wednesday of each month at 9:45 am. Call Base Public Affairs, (805) 606-3595, at least two weeks in advance.

## 58. Farewell to a Latter Day Dr. Livingstone—October, 2003

Over 100 friends and relatives of Dr. Louis Netzer gathered at UCSB's Sedgwick Reserve to celebrate the life of the visionary physician, who succumbed to cancer October 10, 2003, at the age of 62.

Born to immigrant parents in Washington, DC, in 1940, the compassionate latter day Livingstone began his practice among the Quinault Indians in the rain forests of the Olympic peninsula, continued it in Borneo and Mexico, and ended it in the Bolivian jungle on a remote tributary of the Amazon called the Rio Beni.

Joseph Conrad's novels, read as a boy, sparked a lifetime fascination with life in the jungle that was to change many lives. Starting with a hand built hut, Netzer treated some 50,000 patients in the Rio Beni project alone, many of them among the poorest people on earth.

Founded in 1997 when Netzer traveled upriver into the trackless Bolivian jungle in a dugout canoe, the Rio Beni Health Project now covers some 200 square miles and reaches 42 villages.

The Valley was blessed to have him practice here from 1971-1997. While carrying on a full time medical practice of his own, he founded the Family School, an elder care facility known as Friendship House, an Alzheimer's facility, and a successful coffeehouse known as Side Street Café.

He raised a family, moderated discussion forums, was a storyteller in schools, took dance classes.

He gave me my pre-college physical, delivered our beautiful daughter, put six stitches in my thumb, and encouraged me to write for his *Coffeehouse Press*.

This book would not exist if it weren't for Lou's support at that critical hour.

He was the last doctor in the area to do house calls, pulling up in his "Mellow Mobile Medical Clinic," a converted Land Rover.

He was larger than life, yet the kindest, most open, approachable soul on the planet. Countless talented young people found an audience at his Side Street Café in Arts Outreach events.

Always in motion, Netzer was a dervish of humanitarian ideas, many of which he brought to fruition. He once bought a Chinese junk, with plans to sail it around the world as a floating medical clinic.

"My problem isn't that I can't make my dreams come true," he said, "My problem is that I have so many dreams."

As friends gathered outdoors beneath tall pines, stark afternoon sunshine gave the scene an eerie clarity, and an impish wind tossed Lou's biography in the air.

"Dad is in the air," said Netzer's daughter, Dr. Dine Castel.

Netzer brought her into the world—"a very difficult delivery," he said—in the remote jungles of Borneo.

"The thing that shines through is compassion," said comedian Jim Farnum. "He was a teacher about gentleness."

Kay Fuller, who is herself courageously fighting a rare disease, played a solo evocative of the jungles Lou loved on a native Navajo flute.

Dr. Randy Hermann worked with Netzer for eight years.

"He would certainly wish us to hug and dance and share, rather than eulogize him," said Dr. Hermann. "Lou, far away, up a jungle tributary, in a small village, a laughing child echoes your spirit."

"Lou's medical practice," said Dr. Reuben Weininger, "was a practice of applied love."

"He had a dream streak, a passion as wide as the Amazon," sang Jim Brady.

Christopher Brady, Netzer's colleague for the past five years and co-worker on the Rio Beni Project, said "He truly believed in caring—every patient mattered."

Project pharmacist Antonio Mendia called, in tears, from Bolivia.

Son-in-law Fabian Castel remembered him in the jungle, "asking thousands of questions and starting hundreds of debates."

"Now," Castel said, "you are part of the river of consciousness, we debated so often about."

Netzer was diagnosed with pancreatic cancer.

In a goodbye read by his ecologist son Michael, he wrote, "My final message is to remind all of you, we are all miracles."

"As we live out our lives on this glorious planet, I implore you to live, repeat, LIVE your lives every day."

Dr. Netzer's daughter, Dine, said that towards the end, as he was in and out of consciousness, Lou scribbled something on a piece of paper.

He wrote these words: "For Love."

Dr. Netzer's legacy of love lives on in the Rio Beni Health Project, now in the good hands of Christopher Brady, Project Director.

## 59. On the Set of *Seabiscuit* With Tobey Maguire (January, 2003)

How to get a free haircut at Santa Anita Race Track: get cast in a 30's movie. "People in the 30's had short hair," said Bill Dance, casting director. "There was a lice problem."

About 150 locals cast in an upcoming film had their hair trimmed and costumes fitted at a drafty makeshift Universal Studios wardrobe center at the mammoth track in Arcadia after landing parts locally.

SY High grad Bryce Youngman sacrificed his shoulder length locks to cinematic verisimilitude.

"It grows back," he philosophized, amid racks of vintage clothes and piles of hats and shoes beside endless rows of betting windows.

Hundreds of would be film stars attended casting calls for the new Universal Studios production *Seabiscuit*, starring *Spiderman's* Tobey Maguire, and Jeff Bridges.

Extras will act as carnival race fans, horse trainers and grooms. The film is directed by Gary Ross, who wrote the scripts for *Pleasantville, Dave,* and *Big*.

*Seabiscuit* tells the true—mostly—story of an unlikely horse dubbed "The Biscuit," ridden by Red Pollard (Tobey Maguire), a half blind jockey plucked from the county fair circuit, trained by "Silent" Tom Smith, an enigmatic, quirky, near mute Texas mustang breaker, and owned by a former bicycle repairman turned Buick mogul named Charles Howard (Jeff Bridges).

Seabiscuit came out of nowhere in the late 1930's to capture the public's imagination and take "The Greatest Match Race of the Century" against War Admiral in 1938.

The script is derived from Laura Hillenbrand's great read *Seabiscuit—An American Legend*. Voted Horse of the Year for 1938, Seabiscuit and War Admiral were both inducted into the National Museum Of Racing's Hall of Fame in 1958.

The "carnie race scene" will be filmed at a secret location in north county. The film is expected to be released in fall of 2004.

Shooting started in October, 2002, in other locations, including Calumet Farms and Keeneland Race Course in Kentucky, New York's Saratoga Race Course and at Santa Anita. A track in Hemet doubled for Tijuana's Agua Caliente.

Some 5,000 blow up dolls from Japan are working long hours filling in for fans at the tracks, adorned with hats and other dashing touches.

Local thoroughbred breeder and owner John Turner, at Keeneland for the fall sale, saw the transformation.

"They filled the grandstand with blow up people, then they put hats and suit look t-shirts on them. They changed the race track at Keeneland into Pimlico, changed the signs and everything," Turner said.

Bill Dance of Bill Dance Casting rode up from Hollywood to pick out the talent in Buellton, adding to the sixteen thousand—that's no typo—characters he said he'll pick for the production.

Dance has cast dozens of films and TV shows, including Oscar winner *A Beautiful Mind*, local producer Ray Stark's *Steel Magnolias*, *The Grinch*, *The Truman Show*, *Jerry Maguire*, and *X-Files*, among others.

Clad all in Hollywood black—there must be an ordinance against wearing colors down there—Dance, who looks a little like former Genesis drummer Phil Collins, ran a surprisingly informative casting session.

I expected all the warmth of a Army induction center, but Dance, who's got to be a frustrated actor, spent a lot of time explaining the movie and the characters, even—I am not kidding—choking up a bit as he describes the part where Seabiscuit determines to be the eyes for the half blind jockey he loves, played by Maguire.

Maguire takes home over $12 million for his work. Extras, chosen for their "depression look," can expect minimum wage plus overtime for three twelve hour days—about $103 a day by Dance's estimate.

I was only there to cover the story, but bizarrely enough, perhaps because I'm a dead ringer for a long shot Louie from Hialeah who would play baby's milk money on the ponies, Dance asked me to be in the film.

Racing historian Ron Hale says that in the 20$^{th}$ century, only three "great" horses—Man O'War, Tom Fool, and Bold Ruler—have gone on to sire "great" horses. John Turner says there's not much Seabiscuit blood at the tracks today. "Pretty much, I think, as a sire he was a failure."

But boy, could he run.

## Part 2. Props That Eat

A bloody Tobey Maguire sparred with numerous opponents, including film director Gary Ross, in a makeshift ring in a freezing cold barn in Los Alamos. Feverish fight fans screamed themselves hoarse, drank moonshine from mason jars, and bet on the action as the young star swung at his opponents and hit the ropes and the mat again and again, his right eye almost swollen shut with a horrific wound.

It was all part of Universal Pictures' upcoming film *Seabiscuit*, on location at a vintage dairy known locally as the Price Ranch. Real life racehorse Seabiscuit was a sensation in 1938, shipped more than 50,000 miles by rail to smash speed records from coast to coast. Maguire was filming a scene in which his character, jockey Red Pollard, sustains a crucial injury.

It was a marathon day for the cast, which included locals hired as background actors. From a "call time" at 4:30 am, they worked an 18 hour day, the longest in the production to date, wrapping up at 10:30 pm.

Ranch owner Cathy Duncan, CEO of Seymour Duncan, put in an appearance as a carnival race fan, as did ranch manager Jim Davis. Davis's work actually began back in October when he planted a field of special grass and laid out a huge racetrack for the project, carving a sweeping oval in the dark sandy loam.

The location scout gets an "A" for this one—all the filmmakers had to do was add a prop windmill and some antique farm equipment and the place was perfect. The makeshift track fronted sagging vintage barns, sheds, silos and a cottage nestled in a hollow of oak covered grassy hills so green they hurt your eyes, under skies filled with low, scuttling, cotton candy clouds.

About a hundred actors swarmed about in vintage clothes amid so much gear it looked like a staging ground for an invasion of Iraq. End to end, the unmarked white semis and house trailers, antique cars and trucks, buses, Kawasaki Mules, golf carts, caterers, costumers, satellite dishes, California Highway Patrol cars, medics, and porta-pottys probably would have stretched a full mile.

Hip young guys in shorts with FBI style earpieces shouted and waved, electricians threw bulky boxes and cable around, and grips struggled with lights, "inky globes", "zip stingers," "flicker boxes," and camera equipment as controlled chaos reigned.

In one scene, extras, known to industry wags as "props that eat," waved and shouted at a horse race as a very young Red Pollard, seen in a flashback, says goodbye to his parents to become a traveling jockey in the rough and tumble county fair horse race circuit.

Pigs spook horses, so a 200 pound, not-yet-honey-baked ham in a pen beside the track had to be locked up. Seven highly paid union crew members chased him for some time before the canny pig took over as director and dislocated one man's shoulder. Eventually Babe followed a dozen Krispy Kreme donuts into the lockup.

Other injuries: A big Panavision camera, weighing about 100 pounds fully loaded, was so close to the track that as the six horses flew by, a jockey's knee knocked the lens hood flying. No harm was done, other than giving the jockey, cameraman, director and insurance carrier near heart attacks.

After the fluke of being cast, I found that my first instinct was to get on camera somehow. Not long after that, my second was to portray someone sitting down. After some hours, reclining seemed very attractive. I suppose that's why so many films feature bedroom scenes. The actors are tired.

It took about 20 minutes to set up for each cut of the same scene, and it was done over and over with slight variations from dawn to dusk, when the action moved into the fight barn. We cheered, waved racing forms, pretended to swig rye whiskey from half-pint bottles, and propped up fence posts for interminable hours.

When it began to rain, the horses disappeared and an extra had to run around the near end of the track to provide "eyeline" for the crowd. Wits quickly dubbed him "A Man Called Horse" after the 1970 film.

The studio does try to lighten the load of all this hard work. After getting into costume and a grueling 15 minute ride from the staging area in Buellton to the catering tent in Los Alamos by chartered bus, everyone knocked off for a hearty breakfast, a decadent array of food reminiscent of a Biltmore brunch.

Carnival horse racing was not an equal opportunity event. Sybil Cline of Los Olivos, Linda Selvidge and Michelle Moreno of Lompoc, and Gerry Hansen of Santa Ynez were among just 11 women on the set, all wearing mid-calf dresses, heavy nylons, pin curls and bell-like "cloche" hats. Hansen, a veteran of 20 plays working her third film, did a star turn in a number of scenes.

Local extras had one thing in common: flexible schedules. They included Bob Hubel of Los Olivos, retired from Big Dog, Janet and Ruben Caballero, who produce Circle Bar B's delightful dinner theatre, Bo Rice of Los Alamos, SY High grad Bryce Youngman, and many more.

While Santa Barbara county residents were in the majority, some extras came all the way from LA. Gossip, half-truths and outright lies about film projects and pay were favored topics while killing time and arcane knowledge about film overtime benefits was much prized. Filming turned out to be like flying: hours of boredom punctuated by moments of sheer terror.

Despite the obvious tensions, overall everyone was largely professional and pleasant and esprit de corps ran high, with the possible exception of the cook who begrudged me an extra taquito. After almost 3 hours of air-boxing in bone-chilling cold in just his trunks, Maguire was still mugging loopy grins as he hung on the rough manila ropes ringing the fight set after the "Cut!" call. Crew hi-jinks included salted peanut wars and tying Director Gary Ross's shoelaces together while he wasn't looking.

As one assistant director remarked, "You can say actors are overpaid—they are—but to have the ability to convincingly convey the entire range of human emotions on demand, and do it again and again and again, all day long, before all those people, and get it right—that's a hard job."

## Part 3. A Drive-by Shouting

Revered management theorist Peter Drucker says an open door policy is the key to success. So I was sitting in my street-side office with the big Dutch door open, when a mustard colored Mercedes slowed to a crawl and actor/artist/agrarian Ben Bottoms yelled "Hey Etling, I saw you in *Seabiscuit*! In the scene with my brother!" and sped off.

Ben's brother Sam rocketed to stardom in 1979 playing stoned surfer-soldier Lance B. Johnson in *Apocalypse No*w. In *Seabiscuit* he portrays Mr. Blodget, the horse trainer to whom budding jockey Red Pollard is apprenticed early in the film.

When I found a showing that wasn't sold out, sure enough, there I was in soft focus, as young Red's dad tearfully tells him, "You got a gift!," hands over a tattered pillowcase heavy with books and symbolism, then abandons him forever.

To have a REAL actor saying he saw ME in the movies was very cool, well worth the ignominious haircut, two long days of tedium and humiliation as "a prop that eats" on the Price Ranch set, and a day shot going to Santa Anita racetrack to be fitted for vintage clothes. I've forgiven the costume police for crying about the reporter's notebook in my back pocket, and gotten over being cut from the fight scene.

Days of shooting in and around the Valley add up to just a few minutes of this fine film, but they are lush minutes indeed. Gainey Ranch glows a glorious green as Seabiscuit's future trainer Tom Smith is introduced during the Wild West show scene. La Purisima Mission was put to work as backdrop in the Tijuana scene where Buick mogul Charles Howard meets his wife to be.

The crucial fight scene, shot for two and a half hours in a chilly Price Ranch barn, lasts under a minute, but is bloodily vivid. Watch for my evocative knees. A number of Los Alamos locals had their faces on the big screen in a major way as young Red bids his folks adieu, including a great shot of garrulous Bo Rice. Bryce Youngman saunters by as well.

*Lost In Translation: My *Seabiscuit* adventures turned up on a Tobey Maguire website in Spain, in Spanish. I hit the auto-translate button.

Original sentence: "Feverish fight fans screamed themselves hoarse, drank moonshine from mason jars, and bet on the action as the young star swung at his opponents and hit the ropes and the mat again and again, his right eye almost swollen shut with a horrific wound."

Translated version: "Febris admirers had fought and cried out until being roucos, they had drunk whiskey caretaker of jars and they had made appositive in the races while the young star competed with its opponents and struck of meeting to the ropes of ringue of boxe and fell on the carpet interminable times, the almost closed right eye of so swelled which had a horrible wound."

## 60. It's A Small World, But It Has Big Tornados

It was a hard way to get a free glass of wine. The tornado had destroyed five C-130 cargo planes, thrown a car and driver fifty feet in the air, blown out windows, and devastated United Electric Supply, sending dozens of workers diving under desks, before it headed my way.

"There's a lot of stuff flying through the air over there," pointed out my wife glumly, as we sat stuck in gridlock on Interstate 95 in Delaware, taking a little vacation. Moments before, torrential rain had brought visibility to zero and flooded the freeway, turning it into a parking lot. We were sitting smack in the middle of the eye of what was left of Hurricane Jeanne.

It was a *Wizard of Oz* moment. Through a break in the terrifyingly majestic, swirling black clouds, riven with lightning, there was nothing to do but watch in awe as Mr. Twister headed straight towards us.

Thankfully, it was fading. Now merely a healthy whirlwind, it dropped a sodden rain of fiberglass insulation batts from the destroyed building as it passed overhead. One landed on our hood.

All in all, it seemed like a good time to stop for the night. I had resisted this suggestion for about two hours, sailing down the sodden freeway buffeted by waves of white water thrown up by passing trucks like combers crashing over the bow of a sinking ship. I managed to creep, chastened, to an exit, and went anywhere the traffic was moving for an hour or so, trying without success to dodge swollen streams blocking the roads and chaos on the highways, looking for lodging.

Thirty roads were closed. People were abandoning their cars and walking home. It seemed we faced a night in a very small rental car.

Through sheer dumb luck, we stumbled across the plush Inn at Montchanin Village. You know the saying: any four-star resort in a storm.

When the power failed there, the maitre d', who had no idea where we were from, handed us—what else?—a complimentary glass of LinCourt chardonnay, made in Solvang by Bill Foley, and named in honor of his daughters, Lindsey and Courtney.

More small world moments: At the Inn at Thorn Hill in Jackson, New Hampshire, executive chef Richard Schmitt, and pastry chef McKaella Cooper Schmitt, both boasted extensive Santa Barbara resumes, having worked at El Encanto and the Four Seasons, among others. McKaella's parents own the inn.

At the 1830's vintage Ashby Inn in Paris, Virginia, a Sanford Pinot Noir was on the wine list. This tiny town of about fifteen homes is so old that when George Washington slept—under a tree—here, he was still a surveyor.

I hope he rested better than I did on the old mountain pass to the muddy Shenandoah (I waded in up to my ankles and sang "I was born by the river…") sixty miles west of Washington, where the red clay of the Piedmont rises to meet the rounded, haze-shrouded Blue Ridge.

Ghosts woke me up all night: Stonewall Jackson's men, Mosby's raiders, all bone-tired and weary, riding by to die in forgotten battles, or make it home broken in health like my great-great grandfather. Changed, haggard souls, marching through the warm humid night, from a bivouac in the oak grove below the village, to an uncertain destiny.

Come morning, only wisps of fog hung low on the rolling green hills.

At the new National Museum of the American Indian in Washington, the Chumash are represented with a remarkable circa 1820 basketry tray woven by Juana Basilva (1780-1838). It's roughly 24" by 18" in size, and may be found in the glass case just outside the resource center on the second floor, sponsored by Virginia Ortega and family members Nicolasa, Carmen, Rebecca, Veronica, Jordan, Sophia, and Sandoval.

What were the odds? There in the foyer of Janet and Gary Robison's tiny, beautiful, seven room Maple Leaf Inn near Woodstock, Vermont, stood Candy and Ron Mente. They asked how the town cat, Maya, was doing.

The Mentes sold their Los Olivos home in 2003 and moved to Jacksonville, Oregon, where Ron rides with the local search and rescue team, called out 44 times last year, including facing down a cougar. They were enjoying a fall foliage tour.

*Top cat: For years, the mayor of Los Olivos, black and white Mayacat, has made the rounds of businesses here, meowing for choice morsels, turning up her little nose at ordinary fare. Frequently found at the post office, she has dodged cars, dogs and tourists, surviving with a wary personality. A kitty coquette, Maya draws the line at being picked up.

One female visitor foolishly lofted Maya, and suffered her slashing escape. The damaged tourist's benighted knight errant then chased the cat onto the roof of the video store. Hunter and quarry disappeared over the gables to the sound of cracking roof tiles, as the agile kitten led Mr. One Too Many Wineries on a merry chase.

# 61. I Whacked Rudolph—Carnage on San Marcos Pass

I hope Santa can make his rounds safely this year. I think I ran over Rudolph on San Marcos Pass.

"You're not the only one," said CHP Accident Investigation Review Officer Jeanne Malone. "Lots of people hit deer. And cows."

And horses, turkeys, a bear, two mountain lions, coyotes, skunks, possums, raccoons, pigs, dogs, cats, buzzards, etc. It's enough to make you crawl under the covers and stay there.

The Buellton CHP office has gathered partial statistics on the carnage, starting in 2000. Those figures are startling. In the last three years in the area they serve there have been at least 126 collisions with deer, 18 with cows, 8 with horses. Add the bear, and that's 153 really bad days for everyone concerned. Many hits go unreported.

"They hit them on the Pass,' said John Peterson of Precision Auto Body. He mends myriad mishaps.

At one time I drove the Pass every day. I hit two deer then. This was number three, all within a quarter-mile of each other, along the alfalfa fields by San Lucas Ranch, just south of the river. My daughter hit one at the same spot.

The worst danger is at dawn, when the deer move up the hills for safety, and dusk, when they head to the river for water. Frequent fog off the riverbed adds to the danger.

All of my animals jumped out of the dark into the front grill of the car. A sickening thud, a screech of brakes, assorted ugly noises from the radiator which has just met the fan blade, and I'm parked by the side of the road waiting for the tow truck, thanking God it didn't turn into a multi-car melee, or finish up with the deer in the back seat.

Missing the deer was never an option. There wasn't time to swerve, and perhaps roll the car into the ditch or oncoming traffic.

After Bambi Two, I seriously considered installing a bumper mounted ultrasound device said to make a sound deer don't like. I had my doubts. A deer who takes on a four thousand pound projectile traveling 55 miles an hour probably wouldn't be put off by an annoying whistle. But John Peterson has a friend who installed the whistle after four Pass accidents. He says it works.

"You really ought to talk to her about this road," said the CHP officer who wrote up my daughter's deer. He considers the Pass to be blood alley.

Avoiding Highway 154, a road with no margins for error, is a good idea if you can, especially for teenagers, who have less driving experience and more to live for than the rest of us. Unfortunately, there's plenty of danger everywhere. Thirty two collisions with animals were on Highway 101, 29 were on Highway 246, 34 were on Highway 1, and 31 happened on the Pass. Four deer were hit on Alamo Pintado Road, in the heart of the Valley.

It could have been worse.

"You didn't hit the white one, did you?" asked my son.

"I hope it wasn't the albino," said the secretary at the CHP office.

God help whoever smacks Ghost Bambi, the white deer known to hang out on San Lucas Ranch's lush fields. If you survive the crash, you'll be shredded by an angry mob.

For decades San Lucas Ranch has banned hunting and busted poachers, and deer by the dozen can be seen there at twilight, munching alfalfa just off the busy road. I like deer, too. I just hope no one gets killed.

The Swedes build tall fences along the road in dangerous areas. In Canada's Banff National Park, there are overpasses for moose, landscaped with natural vegetation. Good ideas, but expensive. It costs nothing to drive slower in the dark by the fields the deer love. You also may get rear-ended. Not by me, though. I'll be on 101.

Driving is a dangerous business. We take it on faith that the road will be there, unobstructed, as we sail through the darkness. Sometimes it isn't.

One rainy night about thirty years ago, several hundred feet of Hwy 154 just west of Paradise Road slipped away down a canyon in a muddy landslide. At least one car flew into the resulting chasm. By a miracle, no one was killed.

Freud said, "Life is too hard for us. It is full of pain, suffering, and despair."

Looking down from heaven, Rudolph would call that whining.

# 62. If I Could Turn Back Time—An Orphan's Christmas

> *"Cast thy bread upon the waters, for thou shalt find it after many days."*
>
> —Ecclesiastes 11.1

For most of my life, what I knew about the Etling family line stopped with my father's father. He was Benjamin Werner Etling, and he was orphaned in St. Louis at the turn of the century.

He knew next to nothing about his parents. All we had was their names, Christian and Elizabeth. The family line came to a screeching halt, a dead end, a black hole.

After 49 years of not worrying too much about all this, it began to bother me. Psychologists, have at it. There's a paper here.

I did some research. You would think his parents would show up in birth or burial records. No such luck. And their church is long gone.

I cast some bread on the virtual waters. I fired off e-mails to message boards, wrote the St. Louis Public Library, home of voluminous records, searched old copies of the *Post-Dispatch*, wrote the County and the City of Saint Louis. I got into it, but got nowhere.

Oh, a few crumbs came floating back. Hans-Georg Etling of Germany, a total stranger, e-mailed to say the origin of the Etling name was really obscure, but might refer to a person in a remote wasteland, or perhaps a noble person. The thought of being a remotely wasted noble perked me up.

I paid $79.95 to join Ancestry.com. They informed me they did indeed have census information on Etlings, but I had to upgrade to get it. This little hostage crisis was promptly solved. I paid $39.95 more, and learned that a man named Christian Etling emigrated to St. Louis in 1846 from Alsfeld, Germany, with his sons Benjamin Werner and August.

This was too early to be the Christian I was looking for. Probably, I thought, it was his grandfather. There aren't that many Etlings around.

I e-mailed a present day descendant of my new Uncle August's branch of the family tree. He expressed polite skepticism before he disappeared altogether, probably off to bury the family fortune in a safer place.

Hey, I had my own doubts. I still had no real proof.

People were saying snide, "why bother" things to me, like "I can't stand my live relatives. What do you want to dig up your dead ones for?"

I didn't really know why myself, but I was seriously on assignment. A cyberspace Sherlock Holmes, I would unravel this hundred year old puzzle or go over the falls, locked in mortal combat with a mysterious Moriarty.

The search had became an obsession. People in the office were begging to use the computer. I shooed them away. I made more coffee, and searched old cursive census forms, day after day.

Finally, in the 1880 Federal Census for St. Louis, Enumeration District 65, image 9 of 63: Jackpot. Bingo. Eureka. A chill came over me as the image pixilated into focus. There it was, the missing link. My bread was back. The whole soggy loaf had just sailed into port.

The entire family appeared before my eyes, as if I had walked in while they were sitting down to dinner on June 3, 1880. There was my missing great-grandfather Christian, plus five brothers and sisters, with Great-Great-Grandfather Benjamin Werner I at the head of the table. Generations of crabby Germans suddenly lined up like bowling pins.

When the jubilation wore off, a sobering reality set in. There were relatives rolling around St. Louis when my Grandfather Benjamin and his brothers Harry and Heinrich went into the orphanage. They let those children go, instead of reaching out to help. That hurt.

The biggest revelation, though, was about my obsession. I realized one day (and I have to tell you it shook me up, cause I am a really grounded, no-nonsense, unimaginative, very dull kind of guy—ask anyone!) that unconsciously I must have thought if I just tried hard enough, I could somehow even now get my grandfather out of that orphanage.

I think I wanted to find some key in those endless archives that would set him free, and save his little brothers from dying there.

That didn't work. I'm sorry, Grandpa.

## Part 2. Oh, Holy Night—The Ghosts of Christmas Past

When I was a little kid growing up in Winston-Salem, North Carolina, my parents had me convinced that Santa did everything himself.

Of course, I knew my engineer dad had made the big tinfoil wrapped letters spelling out "Merry Christmas" that adorned our roof, put up the colored lights on the eaves, and risked his health at night repeatedly hosing down the sidewalk in the freezing cold so we four boys could joyously slide on it in the morning.

But when I went to bed Christmas eve, the hearth was empty. The next morning the living room had magically filled up with a handsome tree, stuffed stockings, and piles of presents. It was awesome. Good job, Santa.

There was no attempt to reconcile this magic with any religious beliefs, though we went to church and Sunday School, as everyone I knew did. Little Tommy Pearson down the street grew up and wrote a hilarious send-up of the omnipresent nativity pageants in our town in his fine first novel, *A Short History of A Small Place*.

There came a Christmas eve when I didn't go to bed like a good little boy, but stayed in the living room to watch the magic. I wanted to know what really happened in the wee hours in that cozy knotty pine paneled room, before the glowing embers of the cheery fire.

Holy cow, what a mistake that was. By the time the tree was dragged in, set up, draped with lights, sparkly ribbons of lead tinsel, and the heirloom glass ornaments, tempers had flared, and chaos reigned. My parents and oldest brother were Santa's helpers, working as smoothly together as a bag full of cats.

After the tree stand disaster, light bulb failures, and some broken ornament crises, pine needles and tinsel and empty boxes were strewn everywhere. When most of the mess was cleaned up, my dad looked over and asked wryly, "Sorry you stayed up?"

Well, yeah, I was, to be honest with you. Of course, I wouldn't admit it, then. And I really did love hanging the heavy lead tinsel. When lead tinsel was outlawed by the EPA, I knew my youth was over.

But that was a ghost of Christmas future. Late on that first eve of revelation, a tired, sadder and wiser lad, I trudged upstairs to the big attic bedroom I shared with my brothers, somberly contemplating the messy backstage flurry required to produce the sublime.

Downstairs, I imagine there were gift assembly disasters that lasted long after I was fast asleep. "Tab A goes in slot B..." Still, the next morning was magical, anyway. And everybody was happy again. Good job, mom and dad.

Most years dad's parents, Ben and Selma Etling, came down from Hendersonville, N.C, where they'd retired after grandpa's career with Ford in Detroit. Some years mom's parents, Ben and Helen Prellwitz, drove their blue and white '56

Olds 88 all the way from Brokaw, Wisconsin, where he ran the big yellow log crane at the paper mill.

One sad year, the newly purchased presents were stolen out of the car in the Thruway Shopping Center parking lot. One happy year, it snowed Christmas eve and we got to try out our new sleds Christmas day. Win some, lose some.

We dragged the sleds about a mile through the woods to a little lake about half the size of a football field. After throwing the biggest rocks we could find out on the ice to test it, we sledded down the snowy slopes, flew off the bank, four feet in the air, and landed on the slick ice with a resounding thump, sliding effortlessly out into the center, where we later played hockey, with sticks and a shoe polish can filled with BB's for a puck.

On the first jump my face smacked the sled, and I got a fat lip. I pressed it to the ice to keep it from swelling, where it promptly stuck fast.

Down at the shallow end of the lake, where the stream came in, I loved to lie on the frozen surface and look through the clear, icy window into the spooky, murky underworld of weeds and gloom below.

For a few years, this was an annual routine. Then one of my classmates at Sherwood Forest School lost his brother and two friends on a similar pond.

The boys fell through the ice and drowned.

As if it were a big bathtub, our lake was drained.

I hiked over to see. In the mud was a flashlight I had lost night sledding. A river of putrid fish skeletons spread for a hundred feet away from the outlet at the base of the dam. One carcass was almost two feet long. I had no idea there were fish in there. I respectfully rolled a big stone over the lunker's remains.

My classmate was a dead ringer for a very young Harry Potter. As we sat at a table in the cafeteria, he tried to explain what had happened, but he didn't understand it himself.

He looked straight into my eyes. Behind his horn-rimmed glasses was a swirling well of sadness and confusion as deep, dark and cold as outer space.

Enjoy this holiday, and every day beyond. As Ecclesiastes, 11:7, says, "truly the light is sweet, and a pleasant thing it is for the eyes to behold the sun."

## 63. The Best Gift Of All

This is a Christmas story. It's about friendship, faith, resurrection, and coming home.

The Valley received a fine Christmas present in 2003. Goodwill ambassador Tom McCord, a former resident who now lives in Socorro, New Mexico, was here visiting his great parents, Jack and Mary K. McCord.

Tom was my best friend at SY High, class of 1971. He was a good student. He surfed, was on the wrestling and football teams, was funny, good looking, and well liked by all. Upon graduation he headed off to Humboldt State, where one terrible night in 1973 a fall from a beachside bluff left him in a coma. He was 19 years old.

I was standing by the dining table in my mother's kitchen, facing the front door, when I was told. Time stood still.

"He can't die, can he?" I asked my mother in disbelief.

After several months passed, Tom's mother called me with good news. He had begun to move his eyes.

I went to see him at a hospital in Oakland. I talked to him for an hour. He stared at the ceiling. He didn't move a muscle. There was not a flicker of recognition.

Years of slow recovery followed. His family moved to Virginia, and for a long time he was at Bethesda Naval Hospital.

Slowly, he awoke. Little by little, Tom returned to us.

Through it all, this gregarious, kind, open-hearted guy, who always had a bevy of friends from all walks of life, honed his stellar sense of humor and a fearless, ebullient charm that melts the heart.

Today he works in the library at New Mexico Tech in Socorro, a tiny town kept alive by the engineering school. A state program for the disabled has helped him buy a home.

"The state of New Mexico has been good to Tom," his mother once told me.

When I visited him there, and we went out for breakfast, he greeted everyone he met. If they weren't friends before that moment, they were after. Making his way down the street with the swinging gait his injuries left him, he had a trail of smiling people in his wake.

He still suffers from retrograde amnesia, a short term memory loss that can lead him to ask the same question several times in a conversation. But ask about any music figure of the last fifty years, and you'll find an encyclopedic knowledge of their myriad career twists.

I walked through the picturesque plaza in Santa Fe with Tom one day. After a 20 minute conversation with a girl he'd never met before in the corner bookstore, he got a big hoorah from some rowdies who thought he was drunk like them, due to his walk.

"A lot of people think I'm drunk," he shrugged. Then he greeted a woman whose face looked like an imminent thunderstorm. Her whole persona screamed "Don't bother me!" I was frankly scared.

There is nothing complex about Tom's greeting, which is along the lines of "Hi! I'm Tom McCord. How are you today?" His sincerity and openness breaks through people's defenses.

The scary woman beamed. Her entire countenance became radiant. They chatted amiably for some minutes before we continued around the tree lined square, bathed in a golden glow of good will.

That was in 1982. I have not seen such a remarkable transformation before or since.

Yet that's a typical day with Tom. He has brightened many thousands of lives. When I chauffeur him about on his visits here, it's the same scene. He's always mobbed at the Mission Santa Inés by friends trying to catch up on things since his last visit. I have to make an appointment to see him.

The greatest gift of all we take for granted. It's lost in the day-to-day round of petty annoyances. Just being here, alive, drawing breath, and looking on in wonder at the mystery and majesty of it all, is the ultimate miracle.

A few special people like Tom McCord, risen from the dead, hold that truth in their hearts.

If only we all did. What a truly merry Christmas that would be.

## 64. A New Torah Scroll

Seventy-five members of the Santa Ynez Valley Jewish Community enjoyed a special Shabbat Service to formally induct SYVJC as a member congregation of the Union of American Hebrew Congregations and to dedicate a new Torah Scroll on November 22, 2002, at the Royal Scandinavian Inn's Meadows Restaurant in Solvang. Rabbi Linda Bertenthal of UAHC officiated.

Rabbi Bertenthal's infectious sense of joy and fine voice energized an emotionally charged 90 minute service largely sung a cappella by her and the congregation.

She said, "Tradition relates that when Israel gathered at Mount Sinai, truth was revealed to us amidst much lightning and great claps of thunder, and God seemed to speak...When Torah came into the world, freedom came into the world. The more Torah, the more peace. The world stands upon three things: on Torah, on service, and on deeds of loving-kindness. It is up to us to see that the world still stands."

Esther Saritsky, President of the Pacific Southwest Council of UAHC, said "You're in a place where being Jewish is much more effort than in a Jewish milieu., yet you have chosen to keep this faith, and for that I wish you such mazel tov that I can barely say it."

The Union of American Hebrew Congregations provides support to congregations, plus leadership and vision on Reform Judaism's spiritual, ethical and political issues. It is the single largest Jewish organization in the US, representing more than 900 different congregations with over 1.5 million members.

As part of the induction ceremony, a new Torah Scroll presented to the congregation was dedicated. The Torah, by tradition received by Moses from God on Mt. Sinai and containing the first five books of the Bible (Genesis, Exodus, Leviticus, Numbers, Deuteronomy) is the holiest and most revered cornerstone of Judaism. It represents a covenant between God and the Jewish people.

The new Torah, covered in red felt with a chased silver plaque, consists of two large scrolls measuring about three feet long and half a foot wide each.

A certificate of recognition from State Assemblywoman Hannah-Beth Jackson was also presented.

The SYV Jewish Community was devastated by the passing of spiritual leader Michael Weinstein. Abe Gottesman said, "Michael not only taught many youngsters their bar or bat mitzvah prayers, but he was also the leader of our religious services in which he extended to us his erudite wisdom, as well as the spirit which emanated from him."

President Nelson Schneider said, "The great outpouring of support for the Weinstein family in their time of need gave us all a sense of purpose at the same time we were suffering such an untimely loss."

SYVJC maintains regular Shabbat Services and have a rabbi and Cantor officiating at a full complement of High Holy Day services. They are dedicated to increasing religious activities, Jewish education opportunities, community interaction and philanthropy.

President Schneider said, "We are now implementing a plan to hire a rabbi, to lead the religious activities throughout the year."

About 100 member families make up the Community, which has grown rapidly in recent years. They sponsor many activities, including a community Seder during Passover, a Hanukkah festival and a Sukkoth event, plus significant local community charitable work and social events.

Officers of SYVJC were President Nelson Schneider, VP Colin Cooper, Treasurer Janet Rogers, Secretary Karen Goldstein, Membership chair Aggie Margolis, Adult Education Chair Ron Green, Events Chair MaryBeth Lepowsky, Finance Chair Michael Balaban, and Social Action Chair and newsletter editor, Connie Schneider.

Alex Taylor and Tammy Cravit co-chaired religious activities, Carole Tacher handled publicity, and David and Sid Goldstein and Mel Dreyfuss were at-large board members.

Services are generally held on the 2$^{nd}$ Friday and 4$^{th}$ Saturday of each month at different members' homes. Friday night services are held at 7 pm, with a potluck dinner afterwards. Saturday morning services are held at 10 am.

You might think that after 9/11, compassion for all who suffer from terrorism would have increased dramatically. Yet George F. Will wrote recently that "anti-Semitism is a stronger force in world affairs than it had been since it went into a remarkably brief eclipse after the liberation of the Nazi extermination camps in 1945. The United Nations, supposedly an embodiment of lessons learned from the war that ended in 1945, is now the instrument for lending spurious legitimacy to the anti-Semites' war against the Jewish state founded by survivors of that war."

Mr. Gottesman said, "Judaism has a rich heritage of thousands of years of teaching the highest moral and ethical values, as well as experiencing a way of life with God. It offers sacred wisdom for the benefit of all mankind."

## 65. An Old Fashioned Christmas

There's no need to fly to Vermont to get that Currier & Ives feeling this holiday season. Try Christmas in the country, in Los Olivos. The town's having a party, and you're invited.

It's called Olde Fashioned Christmas, and it feels like Dickens' Christmas Carol without snow or Scrooge. There's an entire Victorian village full of friendly folks. Good will is rampant.

Shops and even offices open their doors for an annual open house that warms the heart. Free food abounds. Luminarias line the charming streets, the little Christmas angel lights the tree, carolers stroll, and infectious good cheer fills the air.

More than a social event, it's a time machine, taking you back to a Rip Van Winkle America lost for generations. After all, this is a town with an active Grange. Tireless Judy Hale, a host of dedicated volunteers, and the Los Olivos Business Organization make it happen.

Los Olivos is a fun trip on any day, but this will be magical. The official festivities are the first Saturday in December, from four to seven. Come early. Have lunch at Ron and Julie Benson's cozy sidewalk café, *Panino*, or at *"R" Country Store*. Find calm with the day spa delights at *Spa Vigne*.

Go wine tasting. *Richard Longoria, Andrew Murray, Daniel Gehrs, Arthur Earl, Los Olivos Vintners* and *Kahn* wineries all have their own tasting rooms in town. *Los Olivos Tasting Room* and the *Los Olivos Wine Merchant* host multiple vintners.

There's a thriving art scene. *John Cody Gallery* showcases Dave De Matteo, Eyvind Earle, and other great artists plus his own world famous serpentine work at Cody Gallery. *Ralph Young's Gallery* hosts Merv Corning and much more. *Gallery Los Olivos* is a co-op featuring 42 regional artists. Don't miss Greg and Teresa Duer's *Grand Tales*.

Visit the *B.C. Davis Sculpture Studio*, and Tatiana Maria's truly eclectic collection. Wander through the *Judith Hale Gallery* sculpture garden.

Explore. There's more to town than Grand Avenue. Treasure hunt up dusty Jonata Avenue to see Joel Sansone's stunning enamel on copper work at Sansone

Studio. Original woodblock prints by Patti Jacquemain may be found at *Mission Creek Studios*, on Nojoqui Avenue, across from St. Mark's Church.

Antique lovers will want to visit Christian Rheinschild's *Farmhouse Antiques*. Christmas shoppers will strike gold at *J. Woeste, Wine Country Home*, or *Details*. You don't have to be a cowboy to love *Jedlicka's Saddlery*. Look at all those hats!

Grab a copy of Jim Norris's *Historic District Walkabout* at Ranchland Real Estate and amuse yourself picking out historic structures. Be sure to wander over to Mattei's Tavern, now the home of Brother's Restaurant, where travelers once waited for the stagecoach to SB or the steam train to Los Alamos. Hotelier Felix Mattei knew a captive market when he saw one, establishing this local landmark in 1887.

Seek out the *Wildling Art Museum*, located just behind Mattei's. Dynamic Director Penny Knowles, formerly of Mystic Seaport Museum and the SB Museum of Art, has made it a must-see. A wildling is a wild plant or animal. The museum's focus is the American wilderness. There's a bonus: Wildling is inside the oldest home in Los Olivos, the historic Keenan/Hartley house, built of redwood about 1882. Admission is free.

Pay special attention to the Victorian at the corner of Nojoqui and Alamo Pintado Avenue. The town is named after this historic Rancho De Los Olivos homestead. Former owner Alden March Boyd was 22 in 1885 when he left Albany, New York, bought 157 acres near Ballard and got to work planting 5,000 olive trees. The Pacific Coast Railway borrowed the name of his ranch for their new town in 1887; his house was moved to town in 1991.

Twilight is when locals fill the streets for music in the park, cider, snacks, and the tree lighting ceremony. Bring a coat. When the sun goes down in the Valley, so does the thermometer, and you'll want to bundle up. If you're staying over, you might meet genial star Fess Parker at his deluxe Wine Country Inn and Vintage Room, smack in the center of town.

Sam and Shawnda Marmonstein's busy *Los Olivos Café* is always a good bet for dinner. Matt and Jeff Nichol's atmospheric *Brother's Restaurant at Mattei's* is a favorite of the Hollywood set. Rich and Lauren Cundiff have made the *Los Olivos Grocery* on Hwy. 154 a showplace if you want to raid a great deli.

Every day is a gift. That's why it's called the present. If the simple joy of a day in Los Olivos is not gift enough for you, take it up with Santa Claus. He'll be in town, too.

## Part 2. Notes from Americanaville

*We be rockin': The fine new rock in Lavinia Campbell Park now bears a brass plaque, commemorating the newly acquired park parcel smack dab in the center of Americanaville, also know as Los Olivos.

Like the massive meteorite it resembles, the craggy, charismatic sandstone boulder really tumbled here from space! A space on the bed of Vince Torres' flatbed, to be exact. The generous Giorgi family donated the instant icon, already a favorite of the under-four-year-old rock climbing set.

How many towns of 1,000 pony up $264,000 for a town park? Way to go, LO. Preservation of Los Olivos (POLO) spearheaded the effort, and a committee consisting of members of POLO, LOBO (Los Olivos Business Organization), the Rotary and the Grange will manage the acquisition.

Lavinia Cambell, 98, gets a big round of applause for selling below market value for a good cause. The land has been "borrowed" from her for years as an unofficial park. It's sporting several fine new picnic tables, too.

*Rock, paper, lawsuit: The Los Olivos Business Organization (LOBO) incorporated and filed for non-profit status, partly to avoid personal liability for the directors in case someone trips over or falls off the new rock, or drowns in the porta-potties they pay $525 a month for.

That precaution triggered 30 pages of IRS forms and Franchise Tax Board paperwork and some $500 in fees. LOBO President Richard Crutchfield and VP Dave Gledhill are wading through the morass. Is it too late to vote for Steve Forbes?

*Pole position: After many years of faithful service, Bob Whitmore officially resigned his position as Flag Chairperson, passing the torch to Dan Joyce and Warren Anderson. One of the few towns anywhere to have a flagpole smack in the middle of the main drag, this town takes flag duty seriously, only lowering Old Glory to half staff for deceased Los Olivians and the odd President.

*Stop that hearse!: That policy has caused some flaming funeral fracases, too. A few years ago, sheriffs were called to hunt for a mourner who lowered the flag without permission to honor a beloved friend with the temerity to live and die in Santa Ynez. Maybe it was the padlock keeping the banner mid-mast that provoked such dire ire. The bereaved made good his escape.

*Five or six wars later: A poignant bronze plaque on the flagpole's burly base notes it was raised and dedicated in April of 1918 in memory of the veterans of World War I, and includes this wish: "THAT WORLD PEACE WAS NOT MERELY A DREAM."

*Liberal left: You can spot locals here by their left turns. They cut the corner in front of the flag pole.
Radical right: Out-of-towners awkwardly circle around it, to the right.
Middle of the road: She's smart, funny and cute, and she just ran over my feet. Former *AM Los Angeles* and *USA Today, The Television Show* host Ann Abernethy-Gursey drove past the pole as I scribbled notes mid-street. "Looks like a column to me," laughed the TV veteran.

*Gopher it: It seemed for a while the old Los Olivos gas station was going to have a moat around it. It was just a trench connecting the many monitoring wells. I know gophers with fewer holes than the century-old former filling station. New addition: Carina Cellars has a tasting room there now. Consilience (it means "unity of knowledge") just opened up the street, founded by Brett and Monica Escalera and Tom and Jodie Daughters.

*New York to Paris, via Los Olivos: The Auto Club of SoCal has a photo showing the Italian car *Zust* parked in front of Mattei's Tavern, during the epic 1908 New York-to-Paris race.
Julio Sirtori was trying to catch George Schuster and the American team, who were in a Thomas Flyer. He didn't. The Americans won, tooling down the Champs-Elysees after a scant 170 days en route. Three of the six cars in the race made it to Paris, a trip of 12,427 miles, according to the Auto Club. A centennial race is in the works for 2008.

*Pottymouths: My desk by an open Dutch door sometimes makes me the unofficial town greeter. Red-faced, the lady was screaming at me at the top of her lungs. "I'm never coming here again!" she screeched furiously, and stalked off. People were staring.
She was just the latest vocal tourist in a long line of them, stretching back to Los Olivos' founding well over a century ago, to discover there are no upscale public restrooms here, only humble porta-potties.
A rash of lawsuits filed by a disabled man didn't help. Private loos were permanently padlocked faster than you can say "vexatious litigant."

The glimmering promise of a public potty brought abundant praise to the Saarloos family and John Peckham's proposed Stage Stop Plaza project, as a conceptual overview of the three-acre, 50,000-square-foot commercial-residential complex at Grand Ave. and Hwy 154, the gateway to Los Olivos, was presented at the Valley Planning Advisory Committee meeting.

"We think it's a project with a lot of promise, and a handful of glitches to be hammered out," summed up county planner Stephen Peterson.

Concerns aired at the voluntary first look by committee members and the public included sewage, parking, traffic patterns, building size, and affordable housing. Potential public benefits cited included restrooms, a park, more parking for the town, and a museum.

Sandra Wright wanted to screen potential tenants. Jon Bowen suggested the project provide sewer service and parking for adjacent properties, preferably underground. A memorial to the Pacific Coast Railway was mentioned by Lansing Duncan. Alex Rossi didn't think private property owners should bear the burden for public restrooms.

The rush to flush was the hottest issue. Los Olivos has no sewer, plus a high water table.

"We went to the moon. We had to learn to handle our (sewage)," said Gary Petersen, in charge of engineering waste disposal for the project. His firm has greened up the White House and the United Nations. His grandfather was one of the first park rangers at Cachuma Lake, in 1952.

"If we can't satisfy the county on these issues, the project will not be built," architect Barry Berkus assured 30 attendees. The project may use a digester system similar to that currently in operation at Dunn School.

Barry Berkus is a director of the Wildling Museum, and tackled the project in part as a labor of love, to help the Wildling find a home there. Negotiations are on-going. Renowned world-wide for his talents, Mr. Berkus took the helpful amateur advice with his usual aplomb.

"This is my life," he smiled serenely.

*The strawberry man cometh: For many years, Larry Moog has sold baskets of luscious strawberries door-to-door in downtown Los Olivos, Solvang, and Santa Ynez. He distributes beautiful berries and unfailing good cheer from under a white straw cowboy hat, working out of his mobile world headquarters, a parked pick-up.

Mr. Moog mostly lives in Lompoc. He bought a small rugged ranch in Nevada recently, after prices here went out of sight, and he spends the off-season there, fencing and fixing. Robert Moog, inventor of the Moog synthesizer, invited him to a family reunion, but Larry says they're not related.

*Antique, she's not: *Playboy* magazine did a shoot at Christian Rheinschild's Farmhouse Antiques in Los Olivos, posing September 2004 playmate Scarlet Keegan, a local, amidst the toys and kitschy curios of the past.

"Some young people came in and said 'This is perfect! We're from *Playboy*, and need to take some photos,'" said Mr. Rheinschild. "There were about eight people, a big truck full of equipment."

"Is everybody going to keep their clothes on?" Mr. Rheinschild asked. Indeed they were, he was assured.

"I didn't want our town image to go downhill," confided Chris, "We're in enough trouble already."

The crew introduced Mr. Rheinschild to Scarlet Keegan.

"She lives here, and the photos were to provide background on her,' says Mr. Rheinschild. "They took the little black car off the porch and put it out in the front yard, and I have a giant rabbit inside, so they set up a shot with that. Everyone was very nice," he said. "Plus, I got a hundred bucks."

*Greetings from Graceland: Suppose you hailed from the land down under, an entire continent chock-a-block with wallabies, billabongs, large red rocks and the dulcet tones of lilting didgeridoos. What's your must-see vacation spot?

I have an ornamental Danish mailbox outside my office door in Los Olivos, for midnight messages and the odd beer can. Some Australian tourists deposited their vacation mail in it by mistake. Six postcards, all picturing and extolling the wonders of—what else—Graceland, Elvis' be-pillared Memphis manse.

I forwarded them to 'roo land.

*The last glass: An era officially ended on Saturday, June 25, 2005, when friends at Bob Senn's tasting room, the Los Olivos Wine and Spirits Emporium, poured the final glass, and shut the doors for the last time. Mr. Senn died of lung cancer on May 8, 2005.

Locals once knew the white, hip-roofed cottage sitting out in a field, a half-mile south of town, as the Montanaro Market. Many remember making a chilly summertime foray inside the spacious walk-in cooler, to pick out a cold drink, or a half-frozen candy bar.

Mr. Senn's memorial service there, on June 18, 2005, filled the surrounding field with parked cars and trucks, as friends came out in force to salute a wine aficionado who was involved with the local industry for 30 years, and befriended many vintners when they were just starting out, offering bountiful encouragement and advice.

The co-operative tasting room Senn started in 1993 in the century-old store gave small wineries a vital public presence.

The Herthel family, who own the property, hope to make the Montanaro Farm a living Los Olivos museum. Many of Bob Senn's artifacts will be maintained at the site.

*A pat on the back: It was a night for music, dinner and pats on the back, as about a hundred persons gathered at St. Marks' Episcopal Church in Los Olivos for the first annual Pat On The Back dinner. A show of hands indicated the majority of crowd were not members of the church.

Ever-inventive Rev. Chuck Stacy designed the evening, as a way to give Man and Woman of the Year honors to a host of deserving souls.

"Tonight, we celebrate people who do little things, all the time, which turn out to be big things, which make this such a great place to live," he said.

"For years I was involved with the Man and Woman of the Year award, frequently giving the invocation. Then I got into nominating people, but nobody I ever nominated won," Rev. Stacy explained.

"And I thought that was too bad, because any preacher in this valley gets around, and you see things. When the valley really perks right, people don't care who you are, in terms of your denomination, or your gender, or anything like that."

"When we first moved here, I was told by somebody, 'You know, Stacy, you're not going to be judged by what you have, but by who you are.' I felt really good about that, because I didn't have anything."

"That's always been the richness of the valley, people being people to each other. It doesn't matter what you have, it's who you are."

*A good party is when you're not buried alive: The holiday season is here. We wish for peace on earth, and good will toward others, even real estate agents.

At this time of year, the annual slings and arrows of outrageous fortune suffered by weary realtors are assuaged by the munificence of ever-generous title companies, who throw bash after sumptuous bash. When Lennon & McCartney penned *Can't Buy Me Love*, they obviously hadn't been to a title company party.

LandAmerica Lawyers Title held their gala at the atmospheric Sunstone winery on South Refugio Road, where a 5,000 square foot "cave" barrel room includes an iron-gated cache of fine vintages.

I expected Edgar Allen Poe to stalk in with a raven on his shoulder, whispering "Amontillado? I have my doubts."

Really well done fake cracks and $30,000 paintings adorn the walls. Or, you could get a logo baseball cap. The tasting room is complemented by a kitchen with wood-burning oven worthy of a gourmet magazine, and it was in full swing, thanks to Jeff and Janet Olsson of New West Catering.

Soaking up the ambiance were many of the valley's real estate professionals, including Mike and Micah Brady, Ruth and Del Hoover, Carolyn Garth, Carey Kendall, Mary Jo McNamara, Terry Roper, Julie Morell, Joe and Alice Olla, Eric and Debbie Christianson, Michael Bagshaw, Bill Grove, Patty Armour, Patty Fitzgerald, David and Marlene Macbeth, Robert Etling (yo bro!), Jonee Hanson, Lisa Boyland, Laura Drammer, Sylvia Stallings, Rich Condit, Allan Jones, Petie Kern, Randy Stone, Scott Foss, Jenae Roha, Doreen Thompson, Marty Greenman, Irene Bierig, Janice and Larry Edwards, Pete Robertson, and Meryl Bernard.

LandAmerica staffers on board included the ever-affable Joe Wolfard, Lucy Padilla, Jessica Overall, Lara Woodward, John Hebda, and Pam Martin.

Near as I could tell, no one was actually bricked up alive in the Rice family's honest-to-goodness, built into the hillside catacomb, as in Edgar Allan Poe's creepy story, *The Cask of Amontillado*.

Too bad.

Ha! Just kidding. The Valley needs its 140-some active agents desperately, and we can't spare a single one.

Fred, Linda, Ashley, Bion, and Brittany Rice established their organic vineyard estate in 1989, specializing in Rhone and Bordeaux varietals. Consulting winemaker is Daniel Gehrs. The architecture resembles wineries in the Provencal countryside.

Chicago Title booked the elegant Nuuva Restaurant in bustling Ballard, where Chef Sylvia dished up delights. Inez Alston, Nancy Byrum, Jim Gray, and Lynette Pollorena hosted that fete.

Versatile, talented singer/guitarist Jonathan Wilde, a one man band on his big Gretsch guitar, sailed effortlessly from *Rawhide* to Willie Nelson to Van Morrison to *Music of the Night* from *Phantom*, complete with cape.

It was a special treat to see beautiful, ebullient Diane Clark Martin, my wife's best friend since first grade at Solvang School, down from Emmett, Idaho, and her dad, long time local building department stalwart Charlie Clark, now happily retired, at the party.

Most of the agents already mentioned were there, plus Sharon Pike, Trevor Pacheco, Christina Forsythe, David Sutton, Lynn Moore, Wayne Natale, Bob and Donna Crowe, Jackie and Greg Pensa, Bob and Donna Tucker, Joy Forbes, John Fredericks, Jerry Long, and David and Marlene Macbeth.

All hail Macbeth! Dave and Marlene do a bang-up Mr. and Mrs. Santa Claus act for charity, kids' organizations, and the disabled.

## 66. Annual Review

People ask if it's hard to write a weekly column. The tough part is to write something interesting enough to bother reading, without getting everyone mad at you. Lawsuits I can live without.

I first applied to work at the *Santa Barbara News-Press* in 1975, when I graduated from UCSB with my newly minted English degree. Sadly, they were not impressed. Discouraged grads take heart: undaunted, I persevered, and sure enough, a scant 27 years later, I got the call.

When I had a real job, I had a formal annual review. It asked questions like: Makes decisions? Quality of? I hear this little mantra in my head when I do something suspect. If you never do anything, you never do anything wrong.

Smart bosses had me write my annual review myself. After all, who knew me better?

Looking back over the year, I find my work is sometimes Presidential, as in the immortal words of Ulysses S. Grant, Ronald Reagan and Bill Clinton, who all said "mistakes were made." Alert reader Bonnie Raskin, for example, pointed out that the cabinet containing Torah scrolls is known as the "Ark," not the "Ark of the Covenant." Chided Ms. Raskin: "The Ark of the Covenant was by tradition the repository of the tablets received by Moses on Mount Sinai, and has been lost for millennia."

So maybe that wasn't Indiana Jones I saw lurking in the bushes outside the event after all. My personal apologies. Ask George Tenet: even the CIA has bad days.

Waking up in the middle of the night thinking "I should have said THAT," is a job hazard, as is reading my e-mail and thinking "I should NOT have said THAT."

I have been flattered by exaggerated ideas of my powers. After writing about one movie star's ranch, I was asked if I could help get a reader a job managing it. Sorry!

When I suggested drivers should not run over Lance Armstrong on his training visit here, one aggrieved cyclist let me know his life was worth as much as Lance's any day. Well, sure. Just ask your mom. But let's face it. It wouldn't make the front page of every paper in the world if Mr. Grumpy was, God forbid, abruptly flattened.

The unkindliest cut of all: "I don't get the *News-Press*." So live in darkness. You're missing out on a funny, erudite, good-looking, award-winning columnist. That would be Starshine Roshell. Other feedback: One of my colleagues said "I can't read all that!" And, "For an opinionated guy, you're pretty good at not saying anything." Ouch! But my admittedly feeble attempt to be invisible is not accidental. This is a community column. I'm just the moderator.

Editorially, I've been a very lucky writer. Most of my work escapes notice. Writers view editors roughly the same way a Ferrari owner views a derelict waving a claw hammer approaching his car.

In his 1935 poem *The Years*, Maynard Dixon said "Now as the years pass more quickly...ever more do I know that to win some happiness here, I must hold myself up, above petty disputes and distinctions, keeping some largeness of heart, alike for those who trust me and those who distrust me..."

That's my goal. If I can clear up some misconceptions about the Valley, all the better. For example: A gracious lady who has lived very happily here for five years now was initially told by her Santa Barbara friends, "You won't last a week up there. They live like animals!"

I want to set the record straight, but I need to know: Which animals are we talking about, exactly?

# 67. Skiing the Santa Ynez Valley

The falling snow muffles all sound. The limbs of the pine trees droop low under gravity defying drifts. Moving fog makes mysterious apparitions of figures in the mist.

I am skiing cross-country on Figueroa Mountain, a 4,528 peak in the Los Padres Forest northeast of Los Olivos. The tips of my skis emerge like periscopes from beneath the powder with every kick up the steep trail.

Tracks of wild animals leading off into the forest are still filling up with new fallen snow. Suddenly, a shadowy figure about the size, shape and speed of an attacking timber wolf materializes, heading straight towards me with lightning speed and an unearthly howl!

I dive off the path into a drift. My chortling son streaks by, howling with glee, on the world's fastest sled, my father's venerable sixty year old Flexible Flyer.

Dusting myself off, I continue through this powdered sugar world, a silly grin stuck on my face and snow melting down my back.

The Santa Ynez Valley has some great cross-country ski areas. The only problem is that there's rarely any snow on them. To ski here, patience and determination are as important as athletic ability, for just about anyone who can stand up can cross-country ski on mild terrain.

The road to Figueroa Mountain from Los Olivos is glorious on a snowy day. When the morning dawns white, It's a favorite with adventurers ditching work and school to go to the snow. Cross-country skiing is one exhilarating way to enjoy the brisk, fresh air and dazzling brilliance of a day in the snow. Sleds, saucers and inner tubes are also wildly popular. The National Forest has numerous roads which double as beautiful trails. Take a picnic lunch; there are no commercial facilities.

The secret spot for sledding is the sweeping meadow to the north of the road about a mile past Figueroa Mountain Campground. Park by the cattleguard just short of Ranger Peak. A quarter mile ride is assured even in light snow. In the best of conditions, the intrepid sledder can double that.

In March of 1999's epic snowfall, you could have skied down the street in Los Olivos, but it may be another fifty years before that happens again. That's when the last snow fell in town.

# 68. Eternal Vigilance—New Year's In Baghdad

You get to know other people's kids in a small town. You take on the pride of a parent. You see kids toddle, hear about their school days, watch them grow to be scholars, athletes, cheerleaders, artists. Before you know it, some of these young men and women are nobly serving their country in the armed forces.

As the new year dawns, soldiers around the world dream of home.

Valley native Morgon Johnston, age 21, wasn't home for Christmas in 2004. He had to fly back to Baghdad. He'll spend New Year's day driving the perimeter of his post, watching for bombs and snipers.

It takes a few days to make the trip. He flew to Boston, then Germany, then Kuwait, then Baghdad. It's a total of about twenty hours flight time. He's in the Army Military Police there, stationed about three minutes away from Baghdad International Airport.

Morgon Johnston's family moved to Solvang when he was in second grade. He went to Solvang School, and Santa Ynez High. On March 13, 2002, he joined the Army. Basic training was at Fort Leonard Woods, Missouri. He's been in Iraq for eight months now.

Back home for two weeks furlough, he said, "It's going all right."

He's down-to-earth, quiet, businesslike. When I pressed him for his story, he was modest.

"There's nothing I can tell you that you don't see on the news," he said at first.

The Third Infantry Division was mopping up when he arrived.

"We got there right at the end of all the big stuff," said Morgon.

His work day is an endless round of eternal vigilance.

"On a typical day, I do security around our little installation, just drive around and make sure there's no breach in the walls, no bombs on the side of the road, look for any kind of suspicious activity."

Off duty, he's inside those same walls.

"After I do that for about eight hours, I do whatever. We stay on post. We really don't go downtown, or mix with the nationals much, unless we need to escort our supply, to go get needed items."

Things have calmed down somewhat, since his arrival.

"When we first got there, we received a lot of sniper fire, so we'd have to respond to that. We found a couple bombs on the side of the road. One detonated and knocked me off my feet," he noted matter-of-factly.

That kind of dangerous duty is all in a day's work for the young soldier.

"For about a month we had a sub-mission where we'd escort EOD (Explosive Ordnance Disposal) around Baghdad, the whole area, and find unexploded ordinance, and provide security for them while they picked off all the ignitions."

He hasn't run into any other Valley natives over there. He'll be back in Baghdad until April, and in Europe after that. His long term plans include writing and literature.

"I have to be in the military until 2007. I don't particularly enjoy being an MP. I was thinking of going into Special Forces Airborne Selection until my time is up, and if I enjoy that I might stay in," he said.

"Otherwise, I want to get out and go to college, and get a degree in writing. English literature, something like that," said Morgan.

He's working on a novel. Three chapters are already on disk. Chapters 4-7 are handwritten, because he's been deployed.

He seemed rightfully dubious that we can fully grasp the cultural and emotional shock the solders go through.

"It's really different being over here, than it is being over there," he said thoughtfully, clearly seeing some vivid images in his mind.

After some arm-twisting, Morgon admitted there might be something the folks at home could do.

"Keep praying for everybody over there. We all appreciate everyone's support," he said. It would be nice, too, if people put together some care packages.

"Food, snacks," he suggested. "Tobacco products are popular."

May they all come home safely.

# 69. Love & Spare Tires—Bringing It All Back Home

*"We live to honor the memory of those who have gone before, and to prepare the way for those to come."*

—Pearl S. Buck

Following are a few snippets from my life. This is not a narrative; more like a walk past someone's lighted windows. We catch a glimpse, and must imagine the rest.

I met Debra Lee Doll Mitchell in eighth grade, in 1966.

Her grandmother's brother, C.V. Nielsen, came over from Hjorring, Denmark, and started Nielsen's Lumber Yard in Solvang, still run by the cousins and flourishing today.

A year and a half out of high school, on December 17, 1972, we married.

Leah was born in 1979; William in 1982.

D. is singing a lullaby. In her arms, Leah, 11 months, is trilling low harmony. They circle the white couch.

Lee drops her head on D's shoulder, still talking softly, D. humming sweetly.

D's murmur.

Lee's occasional growl.

Lee's bedtime, 8 pm, Monday, February 4, 1980.

New Year's Day, evening: D. is kneeling by William's bed. He is finally shutting his eyes, under his truck and car sheets and race car quilt (actually a "Hot Wheels" sleeping bag). She is serene in a red robe, so timelessly beautiful. William is cherubic; tousled blond hair frames his perfect sweet face in the darkened room.

"Momma, come sit by me," is his plea at bedtime, and Debra may sit by his bedside for an hour before he closes his bright eyes, still clutching a tiny truck in each hand.

"William, tell me about your life. What do you like?" she asks.

"I like trucks and spare tires, and truck pillows and truck sheets and my mommy and my daddy and my Leah and myself. I like bulldozers, and usually I don't like HeMan."

He is four and a half. He says to his cousin Anna: "Don't you want to just fool around with my trucks a little bit?"

Anna: "No!"

When I play guitar, Leah says: "Please don't sing! I hate it when you sing! You're too singative!"

(Leah, years later: "Actually, hearing you sing *Hey, Mr. Spaceman,* is one of my fondest memories. I heard it at a street fair in Berkeley, and I cried.")

A six and a half, Leah calls William "Honey" and "Darling" and takes him on make-believe shopping tours.

William coos "I love 'oo, Leah!" as they ride in the car.

William runs in to the house with his baseball cap on backwards.

Bill: "Hi, William! Are you a pirate?"

William: "No, I am not a pirate. I am a nice boy with my hat on backwards."

Later: "I'm not your best friend in the whole wide world, Daddy. I don't like you. I'm going to kick you off the potty chair."

Driving home in the darkness through the foothills, we are watching for deer on the road. William says, almost to himself, "I like deer. Deer are happy. I like deer—and I like spare tires."

"William, what do you want to be when you grow up?"

"A spare tire man."

Business trip. Each night I was gone, William snuggled up with D. As he settled down, cozy and warm, he said, "I'm going to say good night to Papa."

"Goodnight Papa," he murmured, in a sweet happy little boy voice.

After a moment of listening for a reply from across the miles, he added musically: "I can't hear you!"

William and Leah run from one end of the house to another, joyously playing games. They wrestle and argue and fight like two kittens, having a wonderful time. William runs down the hall and throws himself on the bed on his tummy like a seal, with such speed that his feet flip up almost over his head. He is ready for his bedtime story, Laura Ingall Wilder's *Little House in the Big Woods.*

Leah plays piano marvelously, hammering out songs she has never heard. She complains incessantly about practicing, but she's doing well nevertheless.

William is excited about getting a chest from Grandma E, a treasure chest, he calls it. It is a chest that my great grandfather used to bring his belongings to America from Germany. He proudly fills it with toys.

Another day, he insists on searching the garage for hours to find an old telephone. He talks on it for a day, then consigns it to the closet. His will power is extremely strong, and his powers of persuasion irresistible.

They play in the tree house. Leah wants a new shelf, high on a limb. William is exploring the hillside nearby. He whacks at the dirt with his golf club, digging some steps. Then he pretends he's mining for gold. Leah grinds acorns for a pretend stew. The cat stretches languorously in the sunshine.

Christmas: Zooming through the aisles full of items the kids marked in the catalog, D. says with glee, "Don't you love this!"

Picking out trucks and Barbies and stocking stuffers, books and markers, Play-doh. Carrying the big boxes out to the car in the florescent-lit parking lot. The traffic flows through the colors of the shining city.

Like at Sears in Winston-Salem years ago—the shiny new bikes, the big store; curving stairs and the candy counter and gumball machines. Grandma Selma gave me a penny. Out came two flat Chiclets, with a Lion's Club emblem on them.

From Somerset Maugham's *A Summing Up*: "When would-be philosophers carry on endlessly about solipsism and the meaning of life, it becomes readily apparent they have no children."

Parents know the meaning of life. It is to nurture and protect and educate their children, to perpetuate the race with better people, who enjoy a higher standard of living than their predecessors. We are here to use the knowledge of those who have gone before us, to smooth the path for those to come. No one who comforts their crying child after an injury has any doubts about their existence. A small child's sweet reality is so vivid, it overwhelms sense and emotion, and sweeps you like big surf into the roiling cascade of life's mad ocean currents.

It's still dark. William swings open the bedroom door, races over and climbs into bed. "You have such a nice warm bed. My bed is always so cold. MMMMMM." He snuggles up to D.

I say "Snuggle up, snuggle bug."

"I don't want to snuggle with you, because you don't always wear your jammies."

We play Lego, building a complex helicopter. William wants to listen to Bruce Springsteen. Leah works on a fine, thin walled house. William sticks my tie in his shirt: "Look! I'm a fat businessman!"

A Wednesday evening in August: William shows me his special hideout, behind the water tank and the silk oak tree. The late sun is lighting the oats with golden rays.

"William, there's so much to do here. Look at all the places for us to explore."

William: "Well, what are we waiting for? Let's go!"

We set off down the west canyon through the stickery oats and the fragrant sage. The day's heat is fading. We follow a deer trail along the perimeter of the sage, between the meadow and the brush. We head under the massive oaks.

"Dad, say we see some wild animals and I shoot them with my sleeping gun, like over there—there's a red headed badger. Bang! Bang! And—what are these called?"

"Canadian thistles."

"These thistles are skunks."

"Ya!"

"Bang! And they have some poison they spit on you. Look Dad, that bull with horns is out of the fence, charging us! Bang!"

Blissfully unaware of his ferocity or sudden demise, the bull quietly chews oats on the hillside.

We gather moss for the clubhouse kerosene lantern at the big oak.

"Say we're lost, and there are no houses or people here, and we'll never get home again." I do.

We crest the hill and find the road.

William: "We must be dreaming —there's a road and houses and everything."

At the clubhouse, William arranges the moss on the blue lantern and we hang the Wisconsin license plate he got from Grandma E on the door.

A William and Leah exchange: Something about turning off the TV:

William: "Leah, that can be solved, but right now it is mis-solved."

Leah: "William, I am tired of your explanations."

William: "Oh, am I catching Dad's fever?"

William is in bed with D. and me.

"Mommy, what is love made of?"

"Love is a feeling, honey."
"What are feelings made of?"
"Love is when you like someone very, very, very, very, much. Who do you love?"
William hugs her. "I love you, Mommy. And I love Leah and Papa and Kitty. And I love myself."

In the car on the way to get groceries, Bruce Springsteen sings "I wanna know if love is real."
William: "Of course love is real."
Leah: "I'm wasting away in the shadow of William."

Out in the driveway, D. has just returned from her two mile run. The sun just disappeared. The wind is slightly chilly. I hug her; she is warm and sweaty and beautiful in her shiny silky electric metallic phosphorous green shorts and white cotton tank top.
Leah: "Do I exist?"
"What?"
"Do I exist? Nobody pays any attention to me."
She gets a big hug.
"Of course you don't exist. You're only dreaming this."

At Kings Canyon: William, apropos of nothing, in the darkness of the tent: "The world is the biggest thing in the world."
Friday: Hike to Roaring River Falls; Zumalt Meadows trail and pictures. Hike south of camp. Visit old cabin and Roaring River Falls in the evening.
Saturday: Hike to store. Pine needle trail along river. Lying in the sun on a rock. Leah the fish, swimming in the freezing glacier fed water like a rainbow trout, with a big smile on her angelic face, platinum hair shining in the sun. Noon: bear in the camp. Cooking: Breakfast: fire, coffee, pancakes, bacon. Dinner: chicken, hot dogs.
Hug a kid. Leah so moody. William: such wisdom from a five year old.
Quiet D., in the sun by the rushing water.
"What do you believe in? I don't believe in anything."
"I believe in you."
A Heineken in the river, wine at night. Touring Grant Grove, Leah won't talk. Trees are so tall; people so small. Israel and Thomas' old cabin in the grove.
Ask for nothing + expect nothing = Peace.

He dreamt of the Wisconsin cabin. He vowed to remember those empty rooms, that foggy lake, with the loon cry echoing like an anguished goodbye.

Waking up next to her once was more joy than most people experience in a lifetime.

So again they were there. With his hand locked snug around her, in the 34 degree dawn. Fog drifted off the lake outside, slipping through the birch forests. Warm and cozy and at peace with his family around him, as the loon calls echoed through the mists.

This elusive peace that haunted his life was like the mysterious island of children's fables. It seemed to land from time to time to intrigue for a while, and then vanish, to return again when the world needs warmth and courage and bravery.

Leah: "I caught nine fish; three bass, and six sunfish. Grandma Prellwitz cooked them, and I ate one bite. It was very good!"

At Glenbrook, on Lake Tahoe, Nevada: Walking up the snow covered hillside holding Leah's hand, (she'll be six in March) the prismed snowflakes beam bright shards of color across the white, sunlit slope. Lee's rosy cheeks betray the cold.

She carries her saucer sled, on which she has just flown down the 300 foot long slope at terrifying speeds, shouting with joy and excitement, as I follow on the bouncing Flexible Flyer sled that was my father's. Worn wood suggests its age, but fifty years of sledding have not yet removed all trace of the colorful emblem on the dark oak slats.

Walking with Lee I fade away to twenty years ago, when with my three brothers and our neighborhood friends, Wilson and Don Crawford and others, coasted and crashed in a farmer's field near our home.

Now, framed by tall mountains, by the cold, deep blue waters of majestic Lake Tahoe instead of the farm pond, the feeling is revived; the cold bright excitement of speed on ice. The powder underfoot is still fresh after days of freezing sunny weather.

This is Leah's first sledding.

"Four more days to do this, Dad!"

The tall, sharp crags of Shakespeare Rock cast long shadows across the field. The afternoon sun disappears too soon behind the mountains that ring the reflecting lake. This old logging camp looks like a New England village, with Cape Cod styled homes clustered on a town square. The sense of history is strong.

Fading tombstones of the pioneers who lived out their challenging lives here are neatly tended in the family burial plot on a sunny hillside, watched over by singing Ponderosa pines, swept by the soft winds.

Along the lakeshore, the sand is filled with round pebbles worn from the surrounding peaks. A tiny piece of rusted iron appears, a reminder of the life of the sawmill town that flourished here over a hundred years ago. Weathered pilings above the surface of the wide lake bespeak old docks, days of frenzied logging, the clamor of saws, trains, wagons, and ambitions long disappeared.

The quiet lake changes with every minute of every day, week, year, decade, century; always different, always the same, so real, so formidable, and hauntingly beautiful.

Seagulls from the California coast soar in the blue skies and fleecy, fast moving clouds above the snow covered ranges. Canadian geese cluster near the tree lined shore. A fat crawfish walks just offshore, inches underneath the glass clear water.

Home again. I am waiting for William Ryder to wake up, so we can play trucks. He has about 40 cars and trucks he carries in either a nylon pouch with LIFE emblazoned on it, or a plain brown sandwich bag. Too full, it spills when he sets it down.

William prefers to drive the trucks about in a modest race-like way, with a friend if possible. Driving trucks with William Ryder is the best.

William jumps into our bed once or twice every night, usually finding some strange position like sideways atop the covers to lie in, and insists on it by kicking anyone foolish enough to argue. Waking up with William Ryder, like a cherub out of a Reubens painting, tousled and angelic on the pillow in the early sunlight, is a benediction.

Nine pm: William is in our bed, on the far side of D. by the door, lying on his back in his yellow pullover pajamas with feet, humming in lilting tones GA ga ga GA ga GA in ascending and descending tones, and REAL MEAN GROWLS (then he laughs).

This after an evening of running his motorcycle over the floor of the China Palace in Buellton.

D.: "William! Get up!"
Response: motorcycle noises.
He hums us all to sleep.

Leah sits on the desk by the computer.
"What'd you say about me?"

We are going camping with her kindergarten class for graduation, at Sage Hill Campground, on the river beyond Paradise.
 William: "A whale is a pretty big thing to put in a refrigerator."

A Saturday in October. William is 5. He peppers me with questions.
 "Dad, why does the earth have to turn?"
 "How many planets are there?"
 "What are stars?"
 "What planet would you like to go to?"
 "What planet is red hot on one side?'
 "Why does the moon shine at night?"
 His mother comes in.
 "Dad and I were having a very interesting conversation."
 Bedtime.
 "Let's continue our interesting conversation, Dad."

Walking in the quiet evening twilight. William has an oat straw in his mouth.
 "William, do you have a tractor?"
 "No. I have two horses. I used to have three, but I sold one."
 "What'd you do with the money?"
 "I don't sell 'em for money."
 "What about your other horse?"
 "He won't get up. He doesn't have any legs."
 Later—William has put on his cowboy boots. He adds a kerchief and a plaid shirt. He has put a peacock feather in his straw hat.
 Leah: "What happened to the other horse?"
 "Him? Oh, he's out in the pasture. I put a brand on him that says 'For Sale.'"

Business trip. William: "Dad might bring me a Ghostbusters shirt."
 Leah: "Don't get your hopes up."
 William: "Why not? Because if he doesn't, my hopes might go down, down, down to China?"

We moved to a new house.
 Leah: "It's too sad we're leaving so soon after we got our new garage door opener."

To my children: Trying to capture your spontaneity, your beauty, your energy and creativity, is like trying to capture light in a jar. The photographs show how quickly you've changed. So suddenly, you are no longer babies, but a little girl and boy. And then the lines of your body lengthen and you're youngsters, fast moving and hilariously funny, or shatteringly sad, or marvelously inquisitive.

Leah at seven on William at four: "William is so outlandish."

And clever beyond belief. We worry so about you, and love you so much, and hate to scold and corral you.

There are so many moments I want to remember and tell you about, special hugs and kisses and funny sayings and happy times. Popcorn and apple cider evenings, days when at dawn as I leave for work I find Leah reading her new book (*Ramona At 8*) in her warm, bright, sunlit room, looking so comfy and happy, while William snuggles up to D. in our bed, so handsome and warm in his baseball pajamas. Soon he will get up and play cars and trucks or draw, or go see his friends at playschool, or his beloved grandparents.

You are so strong and healthy and innocent and loving. Leah dances in the evenings, dressed in costumes of her own making, to Tchaikovsky's *Nutcracker* and *Swan Lake*, glowing and enthusiastic. William builds cars and trucks and planes from Lego, in fantastic varieties and combinations, never saving them for more than five minutes.

You both ride so wildly around the driveway on bike, trike, or tractor, zooming in joyous circles after each other, chasing, laughing, skinning hands and knees on the hard pavement, crying for D. to come make it better.

Hiking through the canyon with you on Sunday, you both ran down the path through the green grass under the thick oaks, both so perfectly beautiful and happy. Dashing ahead, you hid in the fallen branches of an oak that had split in two, leaping out and calling as I came upon you, and we continued on, both of you clambering over the big green steel gate so agilely, as if on the school jungle gym.

We looked at acorns and milkweed and the lush green grass peeking out under the brown stalks of last year's growth, then climbed the steep hills of sagebrush and grass and oak trees, back up to the house.

We went to Gaviota beach, and built a sand castle.

Leah: "This is the city of Troy. Dad, you build the Trojan horse."

You are so intelligent and alive. I fashioned the Trojan horse with a seaweed saddle.

We walked along the water and nearly lost William's shell bucket in the surf. We had hot dogs at Gaviota restaurant. The two of you sat across from me in the booth at the window, eating long hot dogs, so sweet and playful and serious in the sun.

At Refugio we walked along the broad sandy beach on a falling tide, and went round the point, past the surfers sliding on three foot glass waves. We explored the tidepools below the crumbling rocky cliffs in the ruddy glow of the afternoon sun. We bought a snack—a drink and a Snickers bar—and you both sat on the beach towel, sharing sips of 7-Up, in the back seat of the car on the way home, Leah dying to see D., working at the store; William thrilled by the unexpected old car convention we stumbled across at Nojoqui Park.

I loved those moments, and a million others like them. They were the best in my life. When you think of me, think of me loving you so, and of those happy times.

# 70. Conclusion—Equal Opportunity Developer Bashers

"Growth versus no growth brings out rage," wrote Mary Murphy, summing up the local mood-in 1976. Slow and no-growth sentiments have been percolating here for a long time.

As more and more refugees from city sprawl arrived, their voices became louder, reaching a crescendo at 2004's tumultuous, standing-room-only General Plan Advisory Committee meetings.

As the Chumash Casino and Resort mushroomed unchecked, and additional tribal developments have been proposed, opponents have been labeled racists by Fess Parker and the tribe. That's not it.

This is a compassionate community. In forty years here, I've heard two racist remarks, and they stunned me so, I could show you where I was standing when I heard them. Everyone locally is glad on some level that the Santa Ynez Band of Chumash Indians has achieved economic self-sufficiency. Not long ago, the reservation was a poor place. Charities gave out presents there at Christmas. Now the Band gives out presents to the less fortunate. That's a nice turnaround, an American success story in the Horatio Alger mode to warm the heart.

Balancing this good will with the reality of the Casino's impacts is the hard part for the community.

A resident since 1966, I'm hard pressed to remember any development plan that wasn't opposed by somebody. Local preservationists are equal opportunity developer bashers.

Solvang's first mayor, Willi Campbell, recently brought by a copy of *New West* magazine, which ran a cover story on the Valley on Dec. 6, 1976, entitled *The Dream Life in California's Shangri-La, And The Fight To Save It*.

"...Protected by a ring of mountains and a history of innocence, it brings to mind the valley of the Blue Moon, from *Lost Horizon*—the place where time stopped, Shangri-La."

Having nicely set the stage, writer Mary Murphy dived into "the controversy that has divided families and lifelong friends," and examined "the threat that could put a Pizza Hut and Orange Julius on every street corner in Shangri-La."

"The values here," said Brooks Firestone, "are family, simplicity, cultural stability, kindness and a lack of evil. Nobody cares who you are or who you know. Nobody is in a frantic search to keep up with their neighbors."

Ms. Murphy wrote, "The same sharks who have been nibbling away at the Santa Barbara coastline are threatening to move inland and turn Shangri-La into the next San Fernando Valley."

Profiles included the Firestones, Peggy and Slick Gardner, Vince Evans, Ted and Willy Chamberlin, Pat and Monty Roberts, John Wiester, and Joe Saitta.

A Malibu resident, Joe Saitta wanted to develop 3,000 acres just north of Jonata Springs Ranch. Almost thirty years later, every development proposal there has been opposed, and it remains a cattle ranch.

I've observed that any development group with designs on anything in the Santa Ynez Valley had better come prepared to suffer. They may suffer slightly less in the incorporated cities.

There was fierce opposition to an Alisal Ranch plan to build 1,000 homes and an Indian park around their man-made lake in 1971.

"Alisal had one and a half years of trouble and uncounted expense before receiving a final denial," reported the *Valley News*.

Residents stopped the zoning busting Ronald McDonald Cancer Camp in Happy Canyon. Solvang fought outlet malls and fast food chains.

A group home for unwed mothers in a residentially zoned area fell by the wayside. Opponents lost the war to stop the Rancho San Marcos Golf Course, but won the battle to deny it a liquor license. The City of Buellton was sued over redevelopment.

Aghast Los Olivians scuttled developer Investec's proposal for the Montanaro property, forming Preservation of Los Olivos in response. A commercial lot was purchased by POLO for a park, to preclude development.

The County Housing Element's proposals for high density cluster homes caused a hubbub in 2003. The General Plan Advisory Committee train wreck saw massive public meetings, shouting matches, impassioned speeches, political upheaval. Last October 29, numerous SY residents turned out to pummel two mixed use commercial/residential projects proposed on Meadowvale Road at Hwy. 246.

The hot button has never been who's doing the developing. It's development itself. There's a heartfelt, sincere, passionate, widespread conviction here that this is a special place, and deserves special care. The quality of life we all enjoy is a direct result.

As Mary Murphy so presciently wrote about growing pains in 1976, "The dilemma—and the struggle for a solution—reaches out across the state."

Local historian Jim Norris stuck his head in the door. "You should read *Napa*," he growled. So I did.

*Napa—The Story of An American Eden*, by James Conaway, published in 1990, chronicles the battle to preserve agriculture and open space in a rural California valley, in the face of an onslaught of development. That sounds familiar.

"The Valley had changed in a basic way," writes Conaway. "The old cattle-and-horse-ranching culture, like the prune and walnut orchards, was gone, and with it the dominance of people who rode western and considered themselves down-to-earth, without interest in social advancement."

It's a remarkable history, and a cautionary tale. Conaway's 2002 follow-up, *The Far Side of Eden—New Money, Old Land, and the Battle for Napa Valley*, continues the saga, slogging through land use battles, court cases, and many a long Board of Supervisor's meeting.

Our local oak slaughter merited a mention. "When the Kendall-Jackson wine conglomerate cut thousands of oaks in the Central Coast region in plain sight of the highway, the Sonoma syndrome had been given quite a boost, adversely affecting the entire (viticulture) industry," wrote Conaway.

Sonoma syndrome, explained Conaway, is shorthand for "entrenched and virulent opposition to vineyards."

"Napa's tragedy, like that of any common ground, derived from the presence of too many human beings and the unending attempt by the individual to maximize his gains," Conaway said. He quoted from former UCSB professor Garrett Hardin's famed 1968 essay, *The Tragedy of the Commons*.

"Ruin is the destination toward which all men rush," wrote Hardin, "each pursuing his own best interest in a society that believes in the freedom of the commons."

I've introduced you to the Valley, just a little. I wish I could have done more, and done it better. But there it is.

Joanne Rife was the editor of the *Santa Ynez Valley News* in the mid-1970's. Mrs. Rife concluded her 1977 history of the Santa Ynez Valley, *Where the Light Turns Gold*, with this:

"And over in the high-ceilinged, gloomy Veteran's Memorial Building across Mission Drive from the mission, the people of the Valley gathered in hot debate about the future."

"To grow large or to grow larger. To retain agriculture or let it go. To make some money or lots of money."

"The arguments waxed and waned, flew back and forth, provoked anger, dismay, disillusionment."

Thirty years later, the debate continues.
The timeless story of this place will continue long after all of us are gone.

# About the Author

"What brought me to this place? My parents. I was 13 years old. My mother was nearly dying from asthma in humid Winston-Salem, North Carolina, so my father found us a new home."

"An AT&T engineer, he got a job at Vandenberg Air Force Base, and shot missiles at Kwajalein Atoll for the next twenty years."

"'I don't know why. Far as I could tell, the Kwajaleinos had never done anything to him."

A resident of the Santa Ynez Valley since 1966, William Etling graduated from Santa Ynez Elementary School, Santa Ynez High, and the University of California at Santa Barbara, majoring in English.

His Master's of Business Administration work at Cal Lutheran University ended when the college cancelled their Santa Barbara program. They swear it had nothing to do with him personally.

He's a surfer, real estate broker, father, son, husband, and writer. His *Santa Ynez Notebook,* a column about life in the Santa Ynez Valley, appears twice weekly in the *Santa Barbara News-Press.*

His wife Debra's Danish grandparents came to Solvang in 1932. His two children were born and grew up here; both graduated from UCSB. His daughter earned a Master's degree in Journalism from UC Berkeley, and writes for the *Santa Barbara News-Press.* His son is in the second year of the Master's in Journalism program at the University of Southern California.

His father-in-law, Renton Mitchell, was one of the most successful real estate agents in the valley. His mother, Marion, is the former Director of Nursing of the Lutheran Home's Recovery Residence, and past president of the Visiting Nurse Association and the Republican Women's Club. His father, Ben, is a retired rocket man; and can be seen playing trumpet with the Solvang Village Band at Danish Days. His wife, Debra, runs Charlie's Playhouse, a toy and children's clothing store; his mother-in-law, Doris Mitchell, owns the Solvang Children's Shop.

William and Debra Etling live near Los Olivos with the troublesome Hucklecat, their good dog, Loki, and Big Guy and Little Gray, two wild (okay! feral!) cats, who have a tree house in the big oak.

# Appendix: A Valley History

I swiped this from my daughter, Leah Etling, who wrote it while still in grade school. It's the best capsule history around. No wonder she later won national recognition from The National Trust for Historical Preservation, the Associated Press Sports Editors, and the National Education Writers, plus multiple California Newspaper Publisher's Association awards for her work.

## A Valley History—February, 1991

Come back to the Valley. It's waiting, just beyond the rolling mountains and the blue waters of Lake Cachuma. Roll down the windows and small the warm, fragrant scent of summer hay. Cows rest under the outreaching oak branches, escaping the hot summer sun.

Santa Ynez is a ghost town at midday in August. Mirages rise off the blacktop, and dust creates ghostly images of a bygone era. Only a few locals venture into town, to enjoy popsicles at the Santa Cota market or a cold beer at the Maverick Saloon.

It all started with the two brightly wrapped packages under the Christmas tree. What were they? I wondered. Books, I knew that much, but what kind? Good or bad? As in turned out, the answer was good. The books, *Beans for Breakfast* and *The Gates of Memory* by Grace L. Davison, started me on a quest for information on Santa Ynez Valley History.

Although I have lived in the Valley all my life, my interest in its history started only a month ago. Before the Christmas of 1991, I took the Valley for granted, with little interest in the people and the events that took place here before I was born. When it was announced in my writing class that we would have to pick a topic to write a paper on, I knew exactly what I wanted to do: Santa Ynez Valley history.

Many of us take the beautiful places we live in for granted. The children growing up in the Santa Ynez Valley are no different. In our Social Science classes, we learn of world history, American history, and many other types, but never of the history of our own towns and how they began. Hopefully, this chapter will help readers begin to understand the land we call home.

Although the Chumash Indians were really the founders of this community, the place most historians begin with is when the Santa Inés Mission was founded.

## The Santa Inés Mission

On September 17, 1804, the Santa Inés Mission was founded by Friar Estevan Tapis. The patriarch of the California Missions, Father Serra, had died twenty years earlier. The spot chosen for the new mission was the site of the village called Alajulapu, and it overlooked the beautiful Santa Inés River. Santa Inés was the last of the southern missions, the third to honor a sainted woman, the nineteenth out of the twenty-one missions, and it completed the chain of missions between San Francisco and San Diego. Alajulapu boasted fertile fields for crops and grazing animals, and the Indians who lived at the mission raised wheat, barley corn, beans, and other crops. They also dressed the hides of animals, extracted tallow for candies, and wove cloth. Before this work began, however, the Indians had to be taught how to built the mission. Beams were brought from the San Rafael Mountains, pine logs were prepared and tiles were made. Even today, some buildings are styled on the Mission's classic architecture.

In the beginning, Jose Calzada and Jose Romualdo Gutierrez were in charge of the Mission. It was designed by Father Javier de Uria. Up until the horrible earthquake of 1812, construction was an ongoing process. But after the quake, building practically had to be started over again. The chapel was destroyed, and all the buildings were damaged, either in pieces or completely beyond repair. The Mission was rebuilt, and the new church was dedicated on July 4, 1817. One-fourth of the original structure remains standing today, with eleven of the original 22 arches. In 1810, the Mexican military forces in California became dependent on the missions, the result of a political problem in Mexico which cut off support to the missions. The Indians were forced to supply the soldiers, causing an unhappy labor arrangement which led to Indian revolt in 1824. In 1836, the Mission had overcome its problems and was clearly a prosperous place. Its inventory consisted of 8,040 cattle, 1,923 sheep, 343 horses, 987 fruit tress, and 45 mules. In 1904, Father Alexander Buckler and his niece, Mamie Goulet, began a twenty year reconstruction of the mission, and the result was the beautiful building that graces Solvang's skyline today.

## Ballard

In 1830, George W. Lewis was born. Little did his parents know that their new son would play an important part in Santa Ynez Valley history. In 1850, Lewis came to the Valley, but soon left for Mexico, leaving his land in the hands of a friend, William Ballard. While Lewis was in Mexico, Ballard started the Ballard Station, a stage coach stop for weary travelers. When Ballard died, Lewis returned from Mexico and started the tiny town of Ballard, named for his friend, in 1880. Ballard was the seventh town in Santa Barbara County, and for two years it was the only town in the Valley. The streets were 60 to 100 feet wide, and were named in honor of Lewis' friends and relations. Ballard featured the only public general store in the Valley for a time, which had groceries, dry goods, and medicines. Ballard also had a post office and a blacksmith. Before the post office became a part of the general store, it was nothing more than a box nailed to a tree!

One of the major features of Ballard was Ballard Schoolhouse, which was not only a school, but a gathering place for all early Valley residents, who flocked to the little schoolhouse (originally railroad yellow) for weddings, funerals, church services, dances, meetings, debates and other social activities. The new school featured white plastered walls, six big windows, a blackboard, and two anterooms (one for the boys, one for the girls). It was clearly a relief from two earlier schools, which had been held in a granary and an abandoned saloon. Today, the schoolhouse is inhabited by the next generation of Valley residents—Ballard School's kindergarten class.

Ballard today is anchored by the Ballard Inn, making the town a peaceful retreat for tourists, as well as a quiet hideaway for residents.

## Santa Ynez

In 1882, the Wild West came to the Valley, with the founding of Santa Ynez. Named after the Mission and the river, this western town quickly became a thriving village with a post office, many saloons, a barber shop, harness shop, millinery shop, a drug store, a Chinese laundry, and many homes. A rivalry was quickly established between the Valley's first town, Ballard, and the new town of Santa Ynez. Signs were put up saying "One and a half miles to Virgin City" (Ballard) and "One and a half miles to Buzzard's Haven." (Santa Ynez)

At one time, Santa Ynez was the social and economic center of the Valley. One of its greatest assets in its heyday was the College Hotel. which had visitors from as far away as Chicago and Los Angeles. It featured some of the Valley's grandest architecture until it burned to the ground in 1935. Unlike the busy hubbub of long ago, today Santa Ynez is an old town with false front buildings and a western sprawl to it. Although it is a quiet town, buildings are still being built in the old style in hope of economic rejuvenation.

Santa Ynez was founded when Bishop Francis Mora received permission to sell the College Ranch, which consisted of thousands of acres of land. Santa Ynez Valley Land and Improvement Company bought it and subdivided it, selling the land for between six to fifteen dollars per acre. Although it was to be named Sagunto, residents took the name of the Mission instead.

A post office was opened on July 2, 1883, with mail coming from Santa Barbara and Los Alamos. The first Valley newspaper, the Santa Ynez Argus, was started in Santa Ynez by King and Merrill in 1888.

## Los Olivos

In 1887, the Valley's third town, Los Olivos, came into being with the coming of the railroad. In 1882, the same year Santa Ynez was founded, the Pacific Coast Railway was completed to Los Alamos from Port Hartford. In 1887, the rails continued to Los Olivos, and the trains came chugging in.

The newest town was named after Rancho de Los Olivos, which raised olives and was owned by Alden March Boyd. Los Olivos had a store, saloons, a livery stable, a station which housed a telegraph office, a hotel, and at one time boasted a second hotel and an engine house, both of which burned to the ground, and were never rebuilt. Today, the railroad has been rerouted along the coast, and Los Olivos is made up of mostly homes. One thing that remains is historic Mattei's Tavern which was a stage station in the 1880's and later a hotel, a tavern, and a restaurant. It was owned by Swiss immigrant Felix Mattei and his wife. Today, many of the downstairs rooms are in their original state, and the tavern is open every night for dinner. Another of the Valley's quiet towns, Los Olivos is a remembrance of days gone by.

## Buellton

In 1867, Rufus T. Buell was struck with gold fever, and on his way to California to seek his fortune. He ended up in the Santa Ynez Valley, where he purchased 26,634 acres of land for his new ranch, San Carlos de Jonata, which means Saint Charles of the Wooded Area. The ranch was complete within itself, with a post office, a public store, and a blacksmith. It had many animals, including cows, sheep, hogs and horses. The residents of the ranch busied themselves with the dairying, farming, stock raising and cheese factory duties which had to be carried out to keep Buell's venture prosperous. As the result of a dry year, Buell lost 10,000 acres to a San Francisco bank, which sold them to the Santa Ynez Valley Land and Improvement Company, and this was the start of Buellton.

Recently, Buellton became a city. It is famous for Pea Soup Andersen's restaurant, which attracts visitors from all over the U.S. Unlike most of the Valley towns, Buellton is not a tourist attraction, and is basically dedicated to serving the public, with many motels, restaurants, and gas stations.

## Solvang

In 1911, there was a meeting in San Francisco. Although the people attending the meeting did not know it, they were about to become an important part of Santa Ynez Valley history. The motive behind the meeting was to find a place for a new Danish colony in California, patterned after a similar project in Grand View, Illinois.

The educators found, in what became Solvang, a land which had the climate, water supply, fertility of soil and beauty that they were looking for. They purchased 9,000 acres from the West Coast Development and Land Company, and thus the town of Solvang was founded. In 1914, Atterdag College came into being. Atterdag means "there shall be another day" in Danish. In the beginning, the college had no textbooks, no exams and no degrees. It was a full time college until 1937, and between 1938 and 1951 it was used during the summer.

Today, Solvang is still primarily a Danish town, but there are people of other nationalities here also. There are four Danish windmills, patterned after Danish mills. Ferdinand Sorensen's (a local architect and designer) windmill was the first. The town of Solvang is now largely Danish architecture of the Old World type. Driving down the streets of Solvang, you will see native thatched and aged copper roofs, with storks on the rooftops, which the Danes believe bring good luck.

The people involved in Solvang's birth were Reverend J.M. Gregersen, Rev. B. Nordentoft, and P. Hornsyld, who headed the committee to start Atterdag College. Early residents of this beautiful Danish town, appropriately named "sunny field," included the Nielsens, Petersens, Iversons, and Christiansens, descendants of whom still live here today. Advertising brought people from Northern California, Oregon, Washington and the Midwest. Buellton gained from Solvang's publicity, and many Danes settled there as well.

## Afterword

My thanks to Wendy McCaw, owner of the *Santa Barbara News-Press*, and Jerry Roberts, Editor and Vice-President News, for the opportunity to write;

and to my parents, Ben and Marion Etling, for everything else.

Your comments are welcome. E-mail, call or write:

William Etling
PO Box 426
Los Olivos, Ca. 93441

(805) 688-0500
e-mail: synotebook@comcast.net
website: www.ranchlandre.com

978-0-595-36190-8
0-595-36190-0

## People in the news

### Jackson's Neverland closes

LOS OLIVOS, Calif. (AP) — Here lies Neverland.

Trains once packed with laughing children no longer roll around the grounds. The arcade that pulsed with rap music, the curse words edited out, has fallen silent.

After years of rumors about its demise, the fantasy playland Michael Jackson created as a celebration of childhood and a retreat from his troubles is going dark.

The pop star, now living half a world away, dismissed many of the remaining employees Thursday after agreeing to pay hundreds of thousands of dollars in back wages to avoid a lawsuit by state labor officials. His spokeswoman characterized the moves as those of someone who will be away for an extended period, not someone abandoning a home for good.

Following his acquittal last year, Jackson moved to the Middle Eastern kingdom of Bahrain.

He left behind troubled finances, a tattered reputation — and Neverland.

The 2,600-acre estate, which Jackson purchased for $14.6 million in 1988, is tucked into the California countryside amid wineries about 100 miles northwest of Los Angeles.